The Fight for Fordhall Farm

The Fight for Fordhall Farm

The battle to save a way of life

Ben & Charlotte Hollins

HODDER

First published in Great Britain in 2007 by Hodder & Stoughton
An Hachette Livre UK company

First published in paperback in 2008

2

A CIP catalogue record for this title is available
from the British Library

ISBN 978-0-340-95125-5

Typeset in Monotype Sabon by
Palimpsest Book Production Limited, Grangemouth, Stirlingshire

Printed and bound by
Clays Ltd, St Ives plc

Hodder & Stoughton policy is to use papers that are natural, renewable
and recyclable products and made from wood grown in sustainable forests.
The logging and manufacturing processes are expected to conform to the
environmental regulations of the country of origin.

Hodder & Stoughton Ltd
A division of Hodder Headline
338 Euston Road
London NW1 3BH

www.hodder.co.uk

Contents

This book is dedicated to our late father, Arthur Hollins.

Foreword by Hugh Fearnley-Whittingstall

I'm a huge fan of Ben and Charlotte's, and a great admirer of all they've done at Fordhall Farm. If you're interested in a sustainable future for British farming, how could you not be? But it's not just what they've achieved at Fordhall – it is the virtuous circle of inspiration that they've sent spiralling out from their remarkable little corner of Shropshire.

Ben and Charlotte's energy, enthusiasm and sheer stubbornness in the face of disaster, has not merely rescued one beleaguered farm from the brink of closure, it has moved and mobilized a vast army of admirers, who have in turn become evangelists for a way of thinking about farmland and food production.

The way in which one family and their supporters have defended and championed Fordhall has preserved it as a vital and vibrant part of the local community. But it's also demonstrated, in a quite unexpected way, the existence of another, wider community – a community of people, up and down the land, and indeed across the world, who care passionately about where their food comes from. These are people who like to eat food grown by other people whose names they know. Among them are the farm's 8000 shareholders, who have each stumped up hard cash in celebration of the idea that small-scale farming connected to the local community can remain a viable way of life. I'm proud to be one of them.

But it doesn't stop with us. I'm also thinking of many others who have read or heard about the farm and found themselves sympathetic to its aims: to produce food organically, with the highest animal-welfare standards, and in harmony with the environment and with the land's history. This book, by turns charming, inspirational, funny and moving, can spread the story even further. And it can challenge others to aspire to these values. In my own life, both as a smallholder and with my various River Cottage hats on, I've tried to show people in an honest way how good food is produced from the land, and what patience and dedication is required of those who produce it. Their reward – our reward – is to see people shopping, cooking and eating with a conscience, and a sense of responsibility and community. And maybe even taking up the challenge of growing some food of their own.

How we feed our families, and the way we share good food with friends, has always been important. But in a modern food culture increasingly dominated by industrial agriculture, multinational retailers and huge global brands, it's more crucial than ever. It's all too easy to surrender one's individuality and succumb to the megacorp approach to food and cooking, to grab something from the supermarket chill cabinet and bung it in the microwave. But it's a suicidal path. It erodes one's own quality of life, and puts huge pressure on the land and those who farm it. It simply isn't sustainable.

What's now happening at Fordhall Farm is the perfect antidote to that. Ben and Charlotte are educating their visitors – inspiring them – so that whoever comes to Fordhall leaves with a new perspective on food. With an emphasis on what is local, organic, seasonal, natural, and even wild, visitors are sure to leave with the desire to cook more often and with better ingredients.

If you think your own approach to shopping and cooking could do with a boost, *The Fight for Fordhall Farm* is sure to provide it. Once you've read it you may well find yourself making a resolution to visit Fordhall for yourself. You should. It's a wonderful place.

Introduction by Tom Oliver

In a country where individual prosperity leaves many people dissatisfied but where some people are still scandalously deprived, the fight for Fordhall Farm is an important story. It matters because it is a story about attaching value to the common good and recognising that satisfying achievements costs a great deal of effort, which it is nonetheless worth expending. And it matters because the crucial relationship between people, landscape and food is one that needs all the help it can get from inspiring examples, such as the one set by Ben and Charlotte Hollins. This brother-and-sister team have turned out to be leaders, possibly to their own surprise. The local countryside and the local community have greatly benefited and so too will countryside and communities further afield in the future.

My first contact with Fordhall Farm occurred just after I had launched a Campaign to Protect Rural England (CPRE) report in September 2005. Our report challenged everyone to recognise the fact that many powerful forces were steadily reducing the superb farmed countryside of England to a fragmented, diminished state. More and more of it would be interrupted by development and what was left polarised between intensive agri-business and the landscape of lifestyle. The document said that unless there was a widespread effort to resist and reverse these pressures, they would go on, remorselessly.

The report was entitled 'Your Countryside, Your Choice'.

Charlotte and Ben had, as it happened, already made their choice not long before, about the countryside they particularly knew and loved. It was the sort of choice that people applaud, but rarely make, for one reason or another.

They chose to try and save the farm that had been managed by their family for generations. They chose to stick where they were, even though they were barely in their twenties. They chose to risk failing after working desperately hard and allowing themselves to believe in what they wanted. And, what was significant for the rest of the country, they chose to fight for traditional farming on a scale that many hardened agricultural commentators had long since written off as unviable. It was their countryside and they made their choice.

It was an inspiring decision for an increasingly large number of other people. When I first visited Fordhall in February 2006, I was struck by the unselfconscious dedication of everyone around the farm, many of them volunteers. Ben, Charlotte and Sophie Hopkins, the campaign's Project Manager, were working seriously hard, each fitting in and holding down several part-time jobs, as well as running their campaign. Visitors dropped in during the weekend, boosting morale but not interrupting the work in hand. Steadily, the Fordhall team spread the word, built up their contacts, engaged the media, raised more money and kept each other going. They succeeded in saving the farm from fragmentation and development.

The effect on those who have been involved with the project has been remarkable. Businesses have acted generously, individuals have made countless magnificent contributions, the local community has recognised how lucky it is and the message that good choices make a difference has travelled far and wide.

Fordhall Farm represents one of the most valuable and most

vulnerable aspects of the countryside: an attractive and productive landscape, full of history and wildlife, run by people who know their land intimately. The English landscape is largely made up of a pattern of farms that respond to the subtle variations in geology, topography, river patterns and climate. Farms are the essence of the character of the countryside, the synthesis of natural processes and human effort. They also provide habitat for a wide array of wildlife and they are our most extensive historical document. Locally developed management techniques and customs add to the varying patina of place. In them rests much of our national identity. There were once countless farms like this. Every year there are fewer. But here is a place where the process has been reversed. Read *The Fight for Fordhall Farm* and be hopeful for the future: of the English countryside, of wise and dedicated farming, and for all of us who stand to benefit from a long-term future for places like Fordhall.

Tom Oliver is head of rural policy at the Campaign to Protect Rural England (CPRE).

Introduction
Charlotte

I t was hard to believe that it was all over. No matter how much I tried to convince myself otherwise, I knew in my heart that the long and beautiful summer of 2003 could be the last we spent at Fordhall Farm. Unless something incredible happened, by next spring we would be gone, leaving behind a dilapidated, neglected family home and the 140 acres of land which, at the end of it all, were the reason we were being forced out in the first place. The land was too economically valuable to the property developers to stay as it was. They had been snapping at the heels of our landlords for over a decade, greedily coveting fields that contained, for us, a different kind of richness – something that no multinational corporation could ever hope to appreciate or understand.

My father, Arthur Hollins, had nurtured the land at Fordhall since the 1920s. He had worked hard in the face of perceived wisdom to create a farm that worked in harmony with nature, not against it. He farmed nature's way, and he was both mocked and admired for it. Previously recognised for his youthful vitality and energy – proved when, in his late sixties, he fathered Ben and me – Dad was now an ill man, sapped of all his strength and in no state to fight. He was in his late eighties and for him to leave Fordhall Farm and the farmhouse he was born in all those years ago was unthinkable. The prospect was slowly destroying him. But there was no doubt it was going to happen.

That summer I had graduated from the University of Central Lancashire and returned home to a mess, both literally and metaphorically. The draining process of fighting eviction notices had left the farm on its knees. The smart cars belonging to people visiting our once-thriving country club and restaurant had long since gone, replaced by a motley collection of rusty old oil drums and smashed-up caravans dumped by travellers. The few cattle remaining on the farm from Dad's once-productive beef suckling herd frequently became lost in the overgrowth of the unmanaged fields, and our garden had gone the same way. The grass grew to waist height and the stinging nettles swamped garden flowers that had once bloomed so fruitfully.

The air of dereliction was no different inside the house. Mum sat on the settee in the blackest of depressions, surrounded by yellowing heaps of paperwork that blocked the route from one end of the room to the other. If I even suggested a tidy-up she would scream at me, and I would run up the broken boards of the staircase to my bedroom, just to get out of her way. I didn't have the energy to fight her; there had been enough fighting at Fordhall Farm over the years, and the landlord had finally won a long battle to evict us.

The state of Fordhall mirrored our feelings at the time. As

a family who have lived in one place for generations, you build a sense of ownership over your home, regardless of whether you legally own it or not. Our father had spent his life building up the fertility of the land after he inherited the tenancy from his father in 1929. When you put your whole life into something, you gradually become part of it, and that was exactly what Dad had done at Fordhall. The landlord had remained in the background, someone never seen or heard from. But the 1990s had brought him into our lives. Land was valuable and in demand and the face of the British countryside was changing for ever. Suddenly, from a quarter we had forgotten existed, the landlord became a force we realised could not be defeated. After generations of farming at Fordhall, in the beauty of the Tern Valley in North Shropshire, our family would be evicted by the end of March 2004.

'Charlotte, just leave it, it's over.' Ben, my nineteen-year-old brother, looked at me in pity. I'd just finished one of the rants for which I was famous in the family. It was a good thirty-minute affair, during which I'd complained about the state of the house and the cruelty of someone who would evict a very old man from the home he loved.

'I know it's over, Ben,' I replied. 'I'm not stupid. I can see that.'

'So what's the point of going on like this then? Who's it helping?'

'I don't know. I'm upset. I can't help it.' The lack of rights for those who worked so attentively on the land infuriated me.

Ben softened a bit. 'We're all upset, Charlotte,' he said. 'It's not doing anyone any good. We've been given notice, and we have to start sorting things out. We've got to find ourselves somewhere to live.

'We have to face facts,' he went on. 'They want us out and we've got to find somewhere to go. We can't leave it to the last minute; Dad's not well enough.'

Dad hardly moved much from his rocking chair by the fireside now, and rarely spoke. When he did, it was with the gentle intelligence that had always marked him out, but the expression of his thoughts, audibly at least, was not as clear as it once was.

'But it's just that there's so much potential here,' I was revisiting my rant. 'I know it could be something really good again. This farm has such an amazing atmosphere and history. If only . . . '

'If only we had a million pounds,' chipped in Ben, finishing off my train of thought. 'No, make that two million. That's what it would take, and even if we had that, would we really have the skills to build the business back up again?'

Of course he was right. Practical, pragmatic Ben, standing there by Dad's old and broken red Nuffield tractor in his dirty checked shirt, looking every inch the farmer's son he soon wouldn't be any more. I could see I was dreaming again. Opportunities for young farmers are few these days and land in Britain has become a commodity rather than a resource. And with no power, no experience and no capital, Fordhall was a commodity far beyond our reach.

'OK, I know. We've got to get on with it. First job is to sort the house. Mr Godsal is coming round in a few days. Let's try to make a good impression.'

'What's the point?' Ben argued. 'We're supposed to be leaving in six months' time. I don't think a quick tidy-up is going to make any difference. Plus, Mum probably wouldn't let you do it anyway.'

I knew Ben was right again. The landlord had spent thousands of pounds trying to evict our family from the farm. He wasn't going to change his mind simply because there was now space to sit on the previously heavily cluttered chair. Moreover, Mum's continual fight to hold on to Fordhall had left her depressed, which meant that she found it very difficult to let anything go, whether it was useless or not. She was only just holding on to her sanity. However, we found the mess and the dust in the house embarrassing, and I wanted Mr Godsal to see that we were at least making an attempt to stay on top of things.

Mr Godsal was the landlord's agent and, over the years, the bearer of consistently bad news for our family. In twenty-five years here, Mum had never met the landlord and Dad had only had occasional meetings with him, so it was up to Mr Godsal to deal with the unpleasantness on his behalf. He was the epitome of an upper-class English countryman. Stern-faced, with an authoritative way of speaking that resisted all arguments, he seemed to embody all the struggles and hard times we'd endured here over the years.

Mr Godsal visited on a warm afternoon in October 2003. Despite the shabbiness, the farm was in its full early autumn glory. Insects hung in huge clouds over the lower meadows and the woods throbbed with birdsong. It was the sort of sky you'd sit out for hours under, thanking your lucky stars that you were here. Yet we were inside, gathered in the old 'club room', named in the days when Fordhall's country-club facilities attracted hundreds of visitors, but now dark from years of dust and fire-soot, while Mr Godsal outlined our fate. Mum and Dad were sitting either side of the old fireplace in the club room, Mr Godsal perched on the settee opposite the fireplace and I sat behind him. Ben was the only one missing, having retreated to the lounge next door. Although Ben and

I had been working on the farm since our stockman left in 1996, we had remained distanced from the long legal battles between the family and the landowners. This was an important meeting but it didn't seem our place to interfere, or become too involved.

Mr Godsal was polite, but firm. He wanted to ensure that the eviction process would run smoothly and asked us what plans we were making to depart. Mum still could not contemplate the idea of leaving Fordhall and vehemently protested the grounds they were using to evict us. But it was no use. We had been through arbitration and the verdict had been given in the landlord's favour. The fight was over and her arguments no longer mattered. However, she could not give up. 'No one knows what we've been through. Arthur has been here all his life – doesn't any of this matter?' Years of anger, hurt and frustration came spilling out across the room. Every time I feebly tried to step in with a 'calm down, Mum' or 'we can't change anything now, it's all over', she ignored me. She needed to have one last go at trying to convince the landowners that what they were doing was wrong and unjust. Mr Godsal sat in silence as she passionately and stubbornly fought for Fordhall Farm.

In a bid to show the agent that we were reasonable people, I tried to explain to Mr Godsal that we were looking into the possibility of finding a council house. He nodded at me with a fleck of sympathy, but Mum simply would not accept the inevitable fate of the Hollins family.

Ben was sitting quietly in the lounge. He couldn't face seeing his fate played out, and had chosen not to be with us. But the club-room door was slightly ajar, and he could hear every word.

On and on Mum went, until she ran out of words or breath, I wasn't sure which. Mr Godsal allowed a moment's silence while Mum's words hung in the air, and then finally spoke.

'I think you should listen to your daughter, Mrs Hollins,' he said in measured tones. 'She's making sense. The past is the past, and you now have to think of the future. You need to make plans. If it helps, I'd be more than happy to write a letter to the council to make sure you get near the top of the housing list.'

'I don't want to live in a bloody council house!' screamed Mum. 'This is our home! Mine and Arthur's and Benny's and Charlotte's. We don't want to leave. You don't understand the history in this place!'

Mr Godsal blanched a bit, and if the situation hadn't been so horrible I would have laughed to see him get a dose of hot-blooded Yorkshire temper.

I'm glad I didn't laugh. Up until now, Dad had been silent. Then, without warning, he suddenly rose up from his chair and pointed his finger, slightly crooked from an old farming accident, at Mr Godsal. His whole body shook with frailty and anger, and he fixed the hapless land agent with a damning stare. In a calm but stern and powerful manner that was clearly driven by deep emotion, he said: 'You know you are killing me by doing this! You've never stopped, and you never will stop until I'm dead. You have completely knotted my body, like a piece of bale twine that has been twisted so much it has doubled back on itself and cannot twist any more.' He paused. 'The funny thing is, you don't seem to care.'

In the ensuing silence, Dad sat back down in his chair. It was obvious he could not quite believe what was happening. And there was no question that losing Fordhall was affecting him physically as well as mentally. Mr Godsal was speechless.

I could hear Ben crying in the lounge next door. Dad hardly ever got angry, so to hear this coming from a sick man of eighty-eight was heartbreaking for my young and sensitive brother. I left the club room and gave Ben a hug as he sat on the settee with his head in his hands. But I knew Dad was right; losing Fordhall *would* kill him. All his life he had put every bit of his energy into making the farm something he could be proud of and now it was being pulled out from under his feet by people who seemed not to see the intrinsic value of the land, just the money they could make from it.

Wisely, Mr Godsal realised it was time to leave. I showed him to the door. He apologised as he left, but reiterated the purpose of his visit – to make sure we were making plans to leave Fordhall by 26 March 2004. I asked him if he would write the letter to the council's housing department, and he said that he would. For that, at least, I was grateful.

I shut the front door and walked through the old bar room, its shelves full of dusty, half-drunk bottles of spirits and liqueurs, a reminder of happier days at Fordhall, and back into the club room. Mum was still raving about the past, she was still fighting. But with no money, no help and not a legal leg to stand on, how could we fight any more? It was time to accept the situation, move on and move out.

When Mr Godsal left the house that day, the reality of our situation hit us all. Any hope that had glimmered inside us was well and truly gone. We realised that we had no more money, barely any livestock left to sell, and certainly no power to affect the landlord's decision.

I thought back to my father's outburst. Full of frustration at the situation and his own physical frailty, he still managed to be articulate, poetic even. Sadly, words weren't going to solve anything now. We were at the lowest point of a long struggle to stay at Fordhall, and it seemed only a miracle, something so utterly bizarre and out of the blue that it would stretch any credibility, could save us now. Not so much a twist of bale twine, but a twist of fate.

1
Ben

The master bedroom at Fordhall Farm, like almost every other room in this traditional farmhouse, is crammed with the weight of the farm's history. While we do try to clear clutter away on a regular basis, we seem to be a family that finds it difficult to let go of its past. The broken tractor at the side of the Dutch barn, the disused swimming pool at the bottom of the farmhouse garden, the old-fashioned drainage pipes in the farm's water meadows – all tell the story of a very special farm and a way of life that flew in the face of conventional thinking, and defied all attempts to bring it into line.

Dominating Fordhall's master bedroom is a four-poster bed made from solid oak that would take four men and a shire horse to move. It must have stood here for fifty years at least, and the room itself has seen the arrival into the world of three generations of Hollinses. If you sit on the bed and look out of the window you can see almost all of the land surrounding the farm, right down to the River Tern, Fordhall's natural, meandering border. This is the land – the tufted, patchy-looking fields lying alongside boggy water meadows to the southeast (Long Meadow and Hall Meadow) and drier, sandy ground to the north (Cottage Field) – that has been the source of so many problems at Fordhall. It is also the land that has proved to be so inspirational, especially when everything else had gone and only hope remained.

My dad, Arthur Hollins, was born in the master bedroom on 20 May 1915. Just under seventy years later, on 20 July 1984, I arrived, but I came into the world at Shrewsbury Hospital, not in a Fordhall bedroom. Arthur was old enough to be my grandfather, and most of my friends thought that's exactly what he was. In fact, his second marriage had been to a woman much younger than himself. Charlotte was born two years before I was, and it tickled him to have two young children at his age. Although he was getting on in years, he was always young at heart.

He was also labelled eccentric by some and, with his fluffy white hair, tweedy suits and his habit of talking in long, seemingly rambling monologues, you could be forgiven for thinking he was slightly odd. But many others saw him differently; to them he was a pioneer of a movement that is only now becoming accepted into mainstream culture: that of organic farming.

Like many new ways of doing things, Dad's route into this type of farming (which he never termed 'organic', to him it was just 'natural') was a reaction against conventional wisdom. People often tell me he was ahead of his time. He was born in the middle of the First World War, and because of an effective blocking of imports to the UK by German U-boats, there was a demand for home-grown food to be produced as quickly as possible. Before the war, the farm was a typical mixed dairy farm, with the lower land set aside for grazing livestock and haymaking, and the higher, drier ground devoted to crop-growing in rotation. The dairy was also used for cheese-making, and by 1914 this was an important source of income at Fordhall.

The war, however, changed everything. The top fields were ploughed for badly needed potatoes, and newly developed chemical fertilisers were spread on the land to make the crop grow rapidly. It worked, and soon Dad's father, Alfred, was doing exceptionally well out of the demands of wartime. He was still a tenant farmer, but now he was a wealthy one, and he aspired to the trappings of the rich. Alfred became a member of the local golf club and bought a new car to travel there in. A loud, monied and hard-drinking set of hangers-on replaced the simple farmers he'd previously associated with, and Fordhall became as much an after-hours men's club as it was a working farm. From bitter experience, I know that late nights, lots of alcohol and an early start to a day's work on a farm just don't mix, and as Dad's father lay in bed trying to fight off constant hangovers, the farm started to become neglected.

The boom period disappeared with the end of the war, and while Dad's father fooled himself that he was part of the smart set of the times, the reality was that his debts were growing and he had no way of paying them back. He applied more and more chemicals to his land to reproduce the level of growth he had seen in the war, but the more chemicals he scattered and the more he ploughed the land, the more he stripped the soil of its vital nutrients. The high ground at Fordhall has a very sandy, free-draining soil and it leached out any fertilisers applied. Down in the meadows the ground is naturally peaty and boggy. So what he did manage to harvest were thin pickings, and could hardly compete against profitable farms on more naturally fertile land. His response to the growing crisis was to drown his fears in alcohol.

Then there was his health. He began to suffer from terrible headaches, which we now know marked the onset of a brain tumour. If his work at the farm had been erratic, now it was almost completely non-existent, and as he lay dying in the master bedroom the creditors started to close in.

This was when Dad and his sisters started to take a more active role in the farm. Even though he was barely a teenager, the main responsibility fell on Dad's shoulders; as the only son he was handed the duties of someone much older than himself. He was charged with 'doing the pigs' before and after he went to school, every day, 365 days a year. Strangely enough, when Dad's health began to decline later in his life, and our stockman was made redundant due to a lack of money, Charlotte and I had to muck in before school. While other children enjoyed their cornflakes over breakfast TV, we were out in all weathers, 'doing the pigs' just as Dad had done when he was our age.

When our grandfather Alfred died in 1929, the true extent of his debts came to light. The farm was almost bankrupt and the then landlord, who lived at Buntingsdale Hall, which can still be seen through the trees just beyond Fordhall's boundaries, was starting to ask some difficult questions. He had been gracious enough to waive various missed payments in the past, but these had mounted up and they couldn't be ignored any longer.

Alfred had two brothers, Tom and John, who were both farmers, and when he died they came to the farm to take a hard look at the situation. What they found was a family in poverty, and a farm that was almost unviable. Tom, the more dominant of the two, and of a harsh and unsympathetic nature, tried to take charge. He demanded that the family be split up, and the four children separated to work on different farms. Dad's mum broke down in tears as Uncle Tom shouted at her to 'face the facts and face reality'. Dad, aged just fourteen, jumped in to defend his mother and threw Uncle Tom out, boldly telling him he would farm it himself. Dad wrote about this incident in his own book, *The Farmer, The Plough and The Devil*. Every time I reread this scene, knowing it took place in the club room, the same room where we had our own reckoning with the landlord's agent who wanted us to leave Fordhall Farm, the hairs stand up on the back of my neck. At that moment, the shadows of seventy years past came to haunt the Hollins family once more.

Dad was true to his word and, after meeting the landlord and persuading him he could make a go of it, he took over the running of the farm. He had to leave school, probably to the relief of the masters who had taunted him for falling asleep during lessons but didn't realise he'd been up early to complete his farm work. For the next five years he struggled to make any kind of living, and the Depression that affected the country economically after the war made matters worse. Only cheese-making and poultry-rearing kept the farm going. The land continued to turn a poor yield, and at first Dad took the advice of local farmers who simply told him to throw more fertiliser at the problem. But he was lucky in that he had a farm foreman, a wise old character called Jack, who was silently disgusted with the way Alfred had managed the land. At first, Jack looked down on this farmboy-turned-boss, but as time passed he developed a grudging respect for him. By putting their heads together they managed to find a solution to the problem of the infertile fields.

'More muck' – animal manure to you and me – was Jack's opinion. 'You'll never do any good until you get more muck on to the land,' was what he told Dad. There was a problem, though. If they brought in more livestock during the summer to manure the land, they'd still have to feed them through the winter, which they couldn't afford to do. And their pastures were poor and could hardly cope with what few cows they had on them, so to buy more would put additional pressure on the thin soil. It was a classic catch-22 situation, but Dad solved it, as he solved a lot of things, by watching how nature did it.

One autumn day he spotted a squirrel gorging itself on fallen acorns in Castle Hill Wood to the north-east of the farm. The ground was carpeted with them, along with Spanish chestnuts and horse chestnuts. He remembered a picture he'd seen in a school history book of a medieval farmer watching his pigs graze a forest floor. He ran back to Fordhall and broke the good news to Jack – that if their pigs were allowed to graze the wood and then released back on to the pasture land, they'd become what he called 'walking dung carts'.

He persuaded Jack to give it a go. The foreman wasn't over-impressed, but he was prepared to try anything. 'It might just work,' he grudgingly admitted, and it did. Within a couple of years the soil structure had improved dramatically. Fordhall's fields were fertile once more and it was all done using manure from the animals on the farm. It was a triumph, and Dad felt encouraged to replant the depleted fields with strains of grass tough enough to withstand the demands that livestock make upon it.

Sadly for Dad, this return to what he saw as a more natural way of farming didn't last long. The Second World War was on its way, and again the country needed feeding. Even though my father was a young man, he was excused from service so that he could continue to farm for the war effort. But his methods weren't always appreciated. Dad's fields had barely recovered from their first blitzing with chemicals when the Agriculture Ministry demanded that he maximise his crop yield with fertilisers. Dad thought his way was the best, if not the quickest, and fought for the chance to be proved right. He was nearly evicted by a committee from the Ministry for what they saw as consistently poor yields, but he escaped by the skin of his teeth. As the war came to a close the man from the 'War Ag' who had made an enemy of Dad was transferred and life at Fordhall became a little bit easier.

After the war, Dad worked on an old method of farming, refining it into what he called the 'foggage' system, named after an old English word for grass that hasn't been grazed or cut. In the spring and summer, his livestock were allowed to graze the lower fields on the farm, manuring and fertilising them as they went along. In autumn and winter the animals were brought back on to the higher pastures, feeding on the hardy species of grasses that Dad had introduced, such as coxfoot, which many conventional farmers will try to eradicate. Dad also planted white and red clover, which fixes nitrogen from the air and encourages grass growth. The foggage method meant the animals could stay out all year round, dramatically reducing the costs of keeping them indoors, and needed very little extra feed to keep them going. The system required no fertilisers, no tractors or machinery, and while the animals grew more slowly, providing little yield in the short-term, the meat tasted better and the animals had a healthier and more natural life outdoors.

Predictably, it was a system totally dismissed by almost all the farming community, who thought Dad was a crank. In the 1960s and 1970s the subsidy system was starting, and the vast majority of farmers produced as much as they could as intensively as possible to collect the largest amount in subsidy. Intensive farming, whether it was beef, dairy or arable, was the way forward, but Dad stubbornly clung on to the foggage system, claiming that the benefits for the health of humans and animals, plus the way it used nature gently, far outweighed the financial gain of farming intensively.

But not everyone thought he was mad. Although he modestly never took much credit for it and was loathe to even use the word 'organic', he became something of a hero among those who were 'going back to the land' and farming the organic way. His research into soil structure, and how constant ploughing broke down vital components in the soil, stripping it of its fertility, was picked up on and he was invited to talk at a wide variety of meetings. There is no doubt that his words of wisdom had an effect on those who heard them and went off to start their own organic farms, or at least went away with a new respect and understanding for this more holistic way of working the land.

Nowadays I meet many people who remember hearing Dad speak, or who have read articles on his research. It's great to hear their stories and how they were inspired by his words. They always comment on how his passion for the land was infectious and how they have tried to eat healthily and organically ever since. A visitor to the farm once said to me, while we walked through the wetland meadows, that 'Fordhall is a small oasis surrounded by intensive agriculture'. For me, that sums up this place perfectly. From the A53, the road that passes the farm, you can only see one field through the big hawthorn hedge, so when people visit the nature trail they are amazed at what lies behind it. The wetland meadows are a gorgeous place in the summer when small wild flowers flourish, and in spring they are full of life with wetland birds nesting and feeding. The higher ground is at its very best in July, when the grass comes to seed and you can truly appreciate the wide variety of species, all with different coloured flowers.

Fordhall Farm was chemical free for over sixty-five years, and a perfect example of how man can utilise nature without abusing or losing respect for it. Unfortunately for Dad, though, and for the farm, intensive agriculture and the demand for mass-produced fast food would, for the second time in a century, threaten Fordhall's unique place in British farming history.

2
Charlotte

While Dad was busy with his foggage system of farming and his tireless research into soil structure and drainage, Fordhall Farm was becoming as famous for its newly developing commercial aspects as it was infamous for its organic methods of farming.

Since the beginning of the twentieth century, Fordhall had garnered a reputation for the quality of its cheeses, though it has to be said that cheese-making was a commonplace activity then. And no doubt many farms in the area had an equally well-deserved reputation for the cheeses they sold locally. In those days, locally produced cheese wasn't the novelty it is today. In the era before mass production and industrialisation of traditional farming activities, cheese-making was simply a means to an end. What else were farmers to do with the waste milk? There was no thought given to the idea that such activities could be part of a farm's attraction. The difference was that Fordhall dairy was driven by an inspired and determined force: May Hollins.

It is fair to assume that if, during the Second World War, Dad hadn't bumped – quite literally – into the woman who was to become his first wife, Fordhall Farm would be a very different place today indeed. Dad met May at a dance when he clumsily backed into her by accident. Although she was a city girl from Birmingham she had, through her work in the local land army, developed a very deep understanding of the countryside and wholeheartedly believed in working with nature, not against it. She was based at Shavington Hall, within cycling distance of Fordhall and Arthur's charms. Every day, young Arthur Hollins would get on his bike and ride over to his uncle's farm in Shavington as an excuse to visit May. After a short, wartime-style courtship he asked her to marry him.

On their honeymoon in Lytham St Anne's, near Blackpool, May noticed that the bad stomach Dad was always complaining about had disappeared. She realised that his consumption of fats – milk, butter and cream – had dropped while he was away from Fordhall, and while he was eating vegetables and soup he had no complaints. May's passion for healthy living and the dramatic effects different foods have on the body stayed with her throughout the rest of her life, and would open up a new and exciting chapter in the farm's history.

Dad and May threw themselves into the work of the dairy and started to enhance the flavours of the cheeses with fresh herbs, fruit and nuts. May also introduced Dad to yoghurt, almost unheard of in England back then. She eased him in gently, using a small culture of the yoghurt bacteria to produce a few pots. It was an instant hit with Dad, who found it to be easy on his stomach. It was a natural product that tasted fantastic.

May was a fashionable and charming lady and an innovator

through and through; it was she who persuaded Dad to create a swimming pool at the end of the garden. Friends and neighbours flocked to the farm, and for the first time Fordhall became a local visitor attraction. The officers from the army camp located just across the River Tern were frequent visitors and formed the basis for the Tern Valley Country Club, run from Fordhall during the Second World War. It was the perfect way of making the most of the beautiful gardens. With both May and Dad cooking and hosting various activities for the guests, Fordhall Farm was talked about far and wide. There were tennis courts on the lawn, croquet, archery and picnic areas, as well as the pool that looked out over the Tern Valley.

While Fordhall provided a relaxing and sociable place to go for local people who became members, in a wider context Dad and May were breaking new ground. Today, many farmers open up their land to the public for recreation and leisure, but in the early 1950s it was extremely rare. In many ways, this was as radical a step as farming organically. Having people down to the farm, in one form or another, has been a mark of Fordhall ever since.

Gradually, the demands of the country club became too great to sustain, so Dad and May decided to focus on the farmhouse restaurant. In the face of increasing mass production of food, May was determined to reintroduce good, old-fashioned, healthy home cooking. Just as before, her innovative ideas and forward thinking, together with Dad's enthusiasm and business sense, paved the way for another era at Fordhall Farm. One of the items very much in demand on the menu was yoghurt. Still a novelty, those who were prepared to sacrifice the more traditional English desserts found it to be delicious, and soon the word spread about this strange new product being made on a farm in Shropshire. A visit to the

Channel Islands had encouraged Arthur and May to invest in a herd of Jersey cows, noted for the rich creaminess of their milk, and they were an instant success.

It was the late 1950s, rationing had ended and May saw that products like yoghurt would appeal to a new generation of housewives keen to shake off the financial constraints of the war years.

She was a naturally gifted businesswoman whose skills complemented Arthur's excitement for new ideas, and she felt that if she wanted to know about a new product and how it was produced, others would too. No longer was food restricted to what you could buy in your local area. Transport connections across the country were improving rapidly, and there was an opportunity to promote Fordhall's products, particularly yoghurt, across a wide area. May was determined to make the most of that opportunity.

In Dad's book, *The Farmer, The Plough and The Devil*, there is a funny and insightful passage where he describes how May and a handful of helpers turn up to an exclusive food shop in London to promote their wares. The staff that accompanied May were all conscious of looking and speaking like country people, and none of them wanted to get involved in the 'hard sell'. But to their amazement, they found that shoppers responded well to seeing them in their tweed suits and dairy aprons. Escorted by May, a well-dressed and well-mannered lady, the Fordhall image was fresh, clean and natural. At a time when corner shops were just about to give way to supermarkets, and a whole new way of mass shopping was being encouraged, it is interesting to see from this how some people still looked for authenticity in the food they consumed. This scene is striking, not only for its comedy value but because the message about natural, honest, locally produced and healthy food is one which is once again striking a chord with British consumers. Even then customers seemed to have developed what would be termed today a 'brand loyalty' to Fordhall's products. The staff couldn't understand why this was, but May knew. 'It's because we are an all-organic unit,' she said. 'Everything we grow is the product of a natural process. That's why our products are better. We produce them as nature intended.'

Getting out on the road and delivering the message resulted in Fordhall's dairy expanding, and at the height of production it employed forty staff and turned out two and a half million pots of yoghurt a year, and all this on a modest 150-acre farm. Fordhall's produce was sold to large department stores and to smaller suppliers and markets from John O'Groats to Land's End. During the 1950s and 1960s, given that this was a new food product being sold to British consumers with tastes that didn't go much beyond Spotted Dick and cold custard, Fordhall yoghurt was a very good business indeed. Ironically, and it is almost unbelievably ironic, given everything that's happened since, there was another little yoghurt-making business starting up on a farm in Bavaria, southern Germany, right about the same time. This was the Müller family operation, very similar to the Hollins family's in Shropshire, except with even more ambition. One day, they would come to play a big part in the life of our family.

Meanwhile, back at Fordhall the dairy business went from strength to strength. New lines were introduced, including 'Yogice', a yoghurt- and ice-cream-based delight, and 'Yogtails', curious pots of yoghurt and alcohol. There were other things occupying Dad's mind, though. He had been working on and off in one of the farm's sheds on a machine he believed would change the face of agriculture for ever. After much theorising and examination of the soil, Dad considered that deep ploughing of farmland disturbed the natural cycle of decomposition that went on below the soil surface. He longed for a machine that would somehow break up a mixture of top soil, live vegetation, organic residues and manure, and distribute it more finely across the land, without inverting it and without destroying the soil life. Over time, he developed a machine he called the 'CulturSeeder', which turned the top layer of soil and planted seeds without disturbing the rich lower layers. It is Fordhall legend that he developed this idea with the use of a domestic blender normally employed to crush fruit and yoghurt into smoothies. You can imagine how well that went down with May when she found out what he was up to with all that soil and animal muck in a dark corner of the farmhouse kitchen! She was dedicated to keeping a spotless household and apparently Dad was not in her good books that day.

Early trials of this machine seemed to be successful, and Dad hoped that by patenting it and supplying it to farmers, particularly those struggling against adverse soils, as in developing countries, he would be helping the world's soils maintain their natural vitality. The machine, however, suffered mixed fortunes. A few enlightened individuals showed interest and one company put him on a retainer for a few years, with first option of developing it, but sadly interest petered out and it appeared that Dad was once again a few paces ahead of his time. The prototype remains at Fordhall and, although it is in a bad state of repair, the idea is still very much alive.

While Dad was welding and hammering his machine together, May renewed her interest in promoting Fordhall as a byword for healthy living. In the 1970s she finally persuaded Dad to expand out of the farm, and they put down a deposit on Pell Wall Court, a Victorian house a few miles away. Originally bought as a home for their eventual retirement, because they knew they could not afford to buy the farm, this house became the embodiment of May's dream; it was a place with fresh air, exercise and an organic diet at its heart. Appropriately, it was christened 'Fordhall Way' and, like every idea they had, it caught on and became successful. Visitors came from across the country, inspired by the near-idyllic lifestyle Fordhall Way promoted.

Dad and May had three children together: Robert, Barbara and Marianne. All worked on the farm in the early parts of their lives: Robert with the animals, Barbara in the laboratory with the yoghurt cultures and Marianne on sales and receipts. But Dad always encouraged them to follow their own careers, as he knew without the ability to purchase the farm their future there would never be secure. They all later left the farm but always retained a keen interest in life and activities at Fordhall.

This could have been the end of the story. Dad and May might have gone on to enjoy a happy and comfortable retirement on the proceeds of two successful businesses, and neither Ben nor I would be writing this book. In fact, it was far from the end. A new and turbulent chapter was about to begin in Dad's life; one which threatened to destroy everything he had ever worked for.

In August 1975, as Dad was finalising plans for a nature trail around Fordhall, he received a phone call. There had been a car crash. May was injured, and Dad was summoned to the hospital in Shrewsbury. At first, it was thought May had escaped with just minor cuts and bruises, but on arrival in hospital it was discovered that she had in fact suffered major trauma. Not long after Dad arrived at the hospital, and before he had a chance to see her, she died.

Dad was utterly devastated, and could hardly imagine a life without her. Theirs had been a terrific partnership; his innate knowledge of and love for the land and her drive and foresight had taken Fordhall to places he'd never dreamed of. Now, it all seemed lost. Without May at his side, Dad felt he couldn't keep the dairy going. Things began to wind down. There was a fire in the dairy and new competition in the marketplace and, within a few short years, the yoghurt business had closed down completely. Dad was forced to sell Fordhall Way too, but he was reluctant to completely end the hospitality he had shared with others, so the restaurant side of it moved back to Fordhall Farm to be based in the farmhouse.

At the time of May's death, a young woman living in Bradford picked up a magazine for vegetarians and spotted an advert for Fordhall Way. The organic food and yoga classes appealed to her, and so she decided to book a holiday there. Her name was Connie Trojanski, the daughter of Polish and Czechoslovakian parents who had left their native countries after the Second World War to begin a new life in Britain. Connie was interested in alternative healing and health foods and she thought that two weeks away from the city would do her the world of good. She must have been disappointed when, after booking, she was told that Fordhall Way had closed down. But there was hope: Dad was taking in a few guests at Fordhall Farm, and so Connie re-booked to come to Fordhall at a later date.

What she found when she arrived was good food and excellent company. There were other people staying at Fordhall at the same time, and she remembers thoroughly enjoying the warm atmosphere.

Over the following few years, she came back for weekends to work and have a break from the city. She was also seeing more of Dad too; apparently he used to find all sorts of excuses to go up to Bradford to see her, and she jokes that 'he was really chasing me, and I didn't want him to catch me!'

He must have worked hard on her, though, because she eventually moved to the farm to work on it full time and to see if she loved him. Something clicked, and they got married in May 1981. She was twenty-seven and he was sixty-six; a considerable age gap by any standards, but Mum says Dad had the energy of someone half his age, and she soon settled into the Fordhall way of life. Dad was keen to start a family with Connie, and within a few years of their marriage they had two children: Ben and me.

3

Ben

Dad's natural liveliness and resilience got him through the eighties, and the passion and good humour with which he seemed to tackle everything rubbed off on to Charlotte and me. I'll bet that as a young man he never imagined that on his seventieth birthday he would be the father of two children under the age of five, but he threw himself into second-parenthood with gusto. Although he was still busy with the farm when we were growing up, he was a good father and an inspirational man to be around.

Plenty of people naturally assumed he was our grandfather, and while the 'granddad' references might have bothered a lot of children our age, it never seemed to worry us. Dad just didn't seem to be an old man. He had energy far beyond his years, and a mind that crackled with new ideas. We have a precious video tape of him from the early 1990s, running through our fields after the cows, full of lean vitality and life. He was almost eighty by that time, but he still had plenty of go in him.

It's as well he had the energy he did, because life was starting to get tough at Fordhall Farm then. From the late 1980s onwards, various individuals had spied over Fordhall's hedges, and instead of seeing the lush acres Dad had spent so many years carefully cultivating in his own way, saw only prime development land.

Maybe if Dad had farmed intensively, his returns each year would have been healthy enough to convince the landlord that Fordhall was a viable concern worth protecting. But like anyone who decides to father two children when he really should be settling down in front of the TV with his shepherd's pie and slippers, Dad was always that little bit different. Actually, he was a lot different, but apart from the fact that he liked his tweed jackets and wellington boots at all times, we didn't realise how out of the ordinary he was until much later on. He did things his way and lived life how he wanted to live it – not in a bullying or a preachy, self-righteous sense – but with a quiet respect for the land and the livelihood it brought us. Now, we count ourselves lucky that we had him for a dad, and that we inherited his outlook and the principles he based his life on. Back then, as children, we were just glad to have so many acres of fields, woods, hills and streams as our playground.

Our best friends during our younger years were Adam, Charlene and Leanne, the children of Dad's stockman Terry, who lived in the farm cottage across one of the top fields. Leanne was the same age as Charlotte, Charlene a little older and Adam a year below me, so it was like having other siblings around the place. Summer and winter we'd tear about the farm after school and in the holidays, enjoying the freedom and fresh air that only farm kids know. At the end of the 1980s and into the 1990s all the other children in school were getting into computers, but even if we'd been able to afford one we wouldn't have sat in front of it for too long. I wouldn't say we were hillbillies exactly, but we ran wild and we did what we wanted. We played tig, rounders and cricket, we made rope swings in the trees, we camped out in the wood and cooked bacon and beans on open fires. In the winter we'd wait for a good snow-fall then drag empty corn bags up to the top of the hill, where the Normans had once built a motte and bailey castle. I remember us all shooting down that hill one snowy afternoon, time and time again, until Adam's backside connected with a tree stump, causing that unique pain that comes with a banged tailbone. It was a perfect *You've Been Framed* moment that we could have earned £200 from if we'd had a video camera, but poor Adam was crying his eyes out for an hour.

The cavernous Dutch barn was also a good place to play. It was full of hay bales, so we could make dens and tunnels in there. On hot summer days we'd crawl through the narrowest gaps and climb bales piled higher than the average house, until we heard Terry on the hunt for us.

'Oi! You lot! Where are you? Not on them bloody bales again, I hope!'

We kept quiet just in case he decided to give up and find something else to do. But we knew that while we could do whatever else we liked, the Dutch barn was out of bounds.

'I know you're in there! Come down now! You're gonna knacker those bales by jumping on 'em. Makes 'em sag!'

Reluctantly we'd creep out and face Terry's intimidating glare, usually backed up by Dad giving us a double telling off for being out of bounds and not doing what we were told. By and large, though, Dad was a very mild-mannered man. If he shouted you knew about it and you didn't disobey him again, but it was rare for him to raise his voice. I think he was always consciously pushing us into considering farming as a career for ourselves, as the three children he'd had with his first wife had left Fordhall and followed other paths. But he always said we should make up our own minds. He just wanted us to be successful in whatever we did. He certainly didn't force me or Charlotte to follow in his footsteps. Somehow, we just did.

That said, he might have influenced us more subtly than I realised. We contributed to the running of the farm, albeit in a small way, from an early age. We helped to round up the cows whenever the vet was coming, and at sheep-shearing time we would wrap up the newly cropped fleece and put it into bags. When Terry was on holiday I was allowed to help Dad feed our animals, and I marched proudly across the farm yard in my little green wellingtons, clutching a seaside sandcastle-shaped bucket full of corn. Later Charlotte and I earned our pocket money, a fiver a week, for feeding the pigs and the chickens before we went to school.

Because he didn't use pesticides on his land, Dad had to find some way of keeping weeds, particularly nettles, at bay. The solution came in the shape of two pregnant goats, although I'm not sure Dad knew they were pregnant when they arrived. We picked them up from Shrewsbury in Dad's Rover Vitesse. He liked this car because it was so big and he could fill it up with bags of feed from Rogers Corn Mill in Market Drayton. Dad selected two goats with quiet temperaments, and to my surprise he asked the farmer to help put them in the boot. It was a tight squeeze, even for our sizeable car. I was given the responsibility of sitting behind Dad and ensuring they didn't jump into the back. When we got back to the farm, Dad and Terry unloaded the goats and put them in the Hall Meadow, the field with the most nettles. Unfortunately, it did not have the best fencing, and the goats, being as adventurous as goats are, kept getting out and finding their way to the fields with the best, lush green grass.

For a couple of weeks the goats roamed as they wished, until the day Terry came to tell us that they had both had kids, one of them twins. When the kids were a couple of months old, one of the twins went missing, so Dad asked Charlotte, me, Adam and Leanne to search for it. We spent two whole days searching the farm until Adam and I realised the kids had been jumping into the neighbour's field through the hole-riddled fence from the Long Meadow on the south side of the farm, so we jumped the fence and went to search there too. We scanned the whole field but could not find the missing kid. On the walk back we passed our neighbour's old water well, which had a small part of the cover missing. Adam looked in and shouted, 'It's here, it's here!' I didn't believe him and kept on walking, but he shouted again. I went back to have a look and he was right. The kid was there, in the water. We fished it out, hoping it would still be alive, but it had drowned. We carried it back up to the farm and told Dad and Terry. By this time, Dad had realised the goats were more trouble than they were worth and, in any case, would only eat the weeds if there was no grass left.

One Sunday afternoon in the club room, after a succulent joint of farm-bred pork that he'd spent hours slowly roasting, Dad cleared his throat and prepared to give us some bad news.

'Children,' he began, 'I have something to tell you.' We waited with quiet anticipation. By his tone, it didn't sound good.

'It's about the goats. I'm getting very fed up of them escaping all the time. It's becoming a real distraction when I need to get on with other things. I know you like them, but I'm afraid they're going to have to go.'

He paused, then added: 'But if you're willing to take care of them and pay for the feed you can keep the two kids.' Of course, we said yes. We were at that stage of childhood when all you want is something fun and furry for a pet. Other children got rabbits, kittens or guinea pigs, but Charlotte and I weren't interested in anything so domestic. But making enough money to feed our nanny and our billy goat had us stumped. How could you make money out of goats without selling them? Once upon a time there had been a thriving dairy at Fordhall Farm, but all that had long gone, so the idea of producing goats' milk – to sell or make cheese with – didn't even cross our minds.

It was Charlotte, a couple of years older than me and crucially a tad more worldly wise, who twigged the idea first.

'We could breed from them!' she said. 'Get them to have kids of their own. Then we could take them to market and sell them, and then buy the food for winter. We could do that every year.'

We were nine and eleven, and we were in business together. We called the goats Cuddles (mine) and Greedy (Charlotte's). The breeding programme started on a bizarre note when we found out – contrary to what we'd believed so far – that Cuddles was the male and Greedy the female. As time went on it became more obvious, especially when Cuddles sprouted a fearsome pair of horns and developed a temperament that flew in the face of his cute nickname. In later years Cuddles turned quite nasty, and if you tried to go near him he'd somehow get you in a leg-lock before viciously butting you. We had to get rid of him in the end, but for now he was enthusiastically taking part in the breeding programme, and before long we had some offspring that we could sell.

With Dad overseeing the operation for us, Greedy had her

first kid. She gave birth in spring, which meant she could be outdoors grazing on the new spring grass that provided her with all the nutrients she needed to feed her offspring. We took the first kid up to Chelford Cattle Market in the autumn of that year and, to our delight, we sold it for a decent price. We opened a joint bank account in Market Drayton so that we could save up to buy Cuddles and Greedy the food they needed for the winter, and we looked forward to their next set of kids and another trip to the cattle market.

It might sound strange to city dwellers that we could breed goats and take their kids to market without feeling any pull of sentimentality. We did think the little offspring were cute – of course we did, we were kids ourselves! – but we were also learning that to survive in farming we had to detach ourselves from those feelings and see the process simply as a way of making money so we could keep our little bit of the farm business going.

Growing up, we had no idea that Dad was regarded as a crank by many, but a pioneer by some. He was just Dad. He might have been an eccentric, and I imagine that being labelled in that way would have been something he was quietly proud of. He knew he was always going against the grain but, although his methods had caused him much more trouble and strife than the average farmer, they paid off. Not only did he run a successful series of businesses at Fordhall, his ideas were taken seriously by many forward-thinking people who have now incorporated his pioneering vision into their own farms or smallholdings.

To the untrained eye, Fordhall's fields might look like just another stretch of farmland, but all through my life when I've walked through them, whether in the early morning sun or the pouring rain, I'm always amazed at what Dad did to make this land a carpet of riches. If he'd been younger and I'd been older I could have learned so much from him. But then he learned by trial and error and, sometimes to my cost, but mostly to my benefit, so have I.

4

Charlotte

C ustard and cowpats rarely go together in the same breath,
but both these things remind me of Dad, and they're
both good metaphors for the way he saw life at Fordhall Farm.

The guesthouse side of the farm, which so captivated Mum
when she first arrived, and convinced her to move from the
city permanently, wound down in the mid-1970s when the
restaurant business took over. Dad still enjoyed the buzz of
meeting new people, though, and there seemed to be no better
way to do this than to continue serving meals. This continued
right up until the early 1990s, when Dad's failing health and
the pressures of fighting to save the farm from development
overwhelmed him and Mum, and the restaurant business dried
up for good.

Today, we quite often meet people who remember visiting
Fordhall Farm in its heyday. They always enjoy telling us about
their connections to the farm, but by far the most frequent
comments are from those who enjoyed meals in the farmhouse

restaurant. Looking around now, at the squadron of broken-down old cookers and the sagging hole in the kitchen ceiling, it seems hard to believe that parties of people came here for evening meals and Sunday lunches, but they did, in their carloads, and those visits form one of the strongest memories of my childhood.

Mum and Dad were working hard in the restaurant then, probably to make sure that they were keeping their heads above water, financially speaking. However, I know that a large benefit for them was the enthusiasm and energy that guests brought into the old house. Dad would always have them laughing at his stories and his eccentric manner, although I think that part of the appeal of the farmhouse restaurant was its homely atmosphere. Guests would enter our family home and be looked after in comfort next to a roaring log fire. The meat would be from Fordhall and all fruits and vegetables were locally sourced. The menu was always the same: a roast dinner with all the trimmings. Guests would arrive, sit down for dinner and Dad would walk in with one or two enormous joints of meat and place them on the table in front of them.

'Doesn't it come ready-cut, Mr Hollins?' they would ask.

'Not at Fordhall,' he'd reply, laughing. 'This is a working farm!' And with that, he'd produce a carving set for guests to use on the meat themselves. It never failed to produce a laugh, and it's something anyone who ate here always remembers. This unique dining experience and lack of order appealed to people and made them feel welcome.

While Dad was busy flapping about the kitchen like a trapped magpie, stirring this pot and that, mashing, boiling, baking and roasting all at once, Ben and I fended for ourselves. At such a young age we didn't really like the restaurant meat and three veg anyway – yes, groaning in disgust at platefuls of greenery isn't just the preserve of city children – so we started cooking for ourselves from an early age. We lived on cheese on toast, which we enhanced with crushed garlic.

One of the clearest memories I have is of needing the toilet and being too scared to run past the diners in the bar room. When you're little and around adults, particularly ones who might have enjoyed a few glasses of wine and are relaxing after a hefty home-cooked dinner, you can feel quite small and understandably a little bit intimidated. As I sneaked through in my pyjamas I'd cringe at the hubbub of noise coming from the tables and the cackling voices of people laughing and enjoying themselves. On later occasions, to make the journey less threatening, Ben and I would sometimes accompany each other to the toilet door. We would duck our heads and run through the bar room, hoping that no one would notice us.

But there was one moment that made up for those traumatic trips to the toilet, and it, was one we would wait for all night – the chance to stick our fingers into the custard pot.

I don't know how he did it, as he never seemed to use any recipe books, but Dad made the best custard we have ever tasted. In went maize flour, Fordhall eggs, milk, brown sugar and who knows what else. Out would come this divine, sun-kissed creation that lolled off the spoon and back into the dish. Rubbing our eyes with tiredness, we'd stay up until 10 p.m. or longer just to make sure we got a taste. It was the highlight of my childhood.

'Come on,' Dad would whisper to us, 'there's just a smidgeon left. Form an orderly queue.' Ben and I would be quietly shoving one another in order to get to the bowl first. He always made custard for the guests to accompany his Spotted Dick or fresh fruit salad, and it was so popular that all Ben and I would ever get would be the scrapings from the bowl, but we always shared fairly. We shared everything: our evenings when our parents were working flat out in the restaurant and our play-times on the farm. Mum had always encouraged us to be fair to each other. There was no reason not to share such a gorgeous treat as Dad's custard bowl. In fact, I think that if we had had the freedom to have a full bowl each it would have lost its appeal.

As we sat watching television in the lounge, through the walls we could hear Dad raving enthusiastically to the restaurant guests about soil structure, foggage farming, his cultivating machine and humus, even as they were settling down to their food. He was passionate about Fordhall and its ways, and his willingness to share his opinions with those keen to listen had, over the years, brought him a considerable amount of atten-tion. Many people remember Dad talking about his CulturSeeder. Hundreds of people came to Fordhall to find out more about Dad's system of farming and to drink in his knowl-edge of soil fertility and the importance of respecting the land as a living entity. There were many others who thought he was a crackpot. No one was outright nasty to him, but if you were out with him and he got into conversation with other farmers, you'd hear fairly quickly that they didn't agree with his way of farming. 'It's your way, Arthur, and that's up to you,' they'd say.

The difference between our farm and others around us was most noticeable at the weekly cattle market in Market Drayton. There was a grudging respect for Dad, probably because he'd survived and done well at Fordhall, but his way of farming always got the attention of the auctioneer at the market. 'And now, something special! A treat for you all today, gents. *Orgasmic* animals from Fordhall Farm! Orgasmically reared animals!'

To be fair, and despite the guffaws from around the ring-side, I don't think Dad really minded. If he had he would have given up years ago and farmed intensively, but giving up wasn't in his nature. If you went for a walk with him in the fields you'd get the full story of the soil he had nurtured, complete with dramatic interludes. Without warning he would drop to his knees and gently lift up a cowpat to expose the hidden world beneath. I have never seen anyone give more respect to worms or cow manure than Dad did.

'Look at this, Charlotte,' he'd enthuse, picking up the slimiest, smelliest cowpat he could find, and pointing out the dozen or so worms squirming beneath it.

'I'm looking at it, Dad. It's a cowpat, yeah?'

'Yes, I know what it is, Charlotte, but just look at it.' He'd wave it an inch from my nose and I'd automatically recoil in horror. 'It might look like a cowpat to you, but actually it's a microclimate, teeming with all the good things that give the soil life.'

This life under the soil fascinated him. It was his inspiration in farming. He would explain to me or anyone who was with him about the intricate life beneath the soil and the efficiency of these systems that work tirelessly to sustain life above. Once he had begun speaking about soil, fertility and nutrient cycling he could carry on for hours. He would disappear into an amazing world with complete and utter respect for life within the soil, carefully explaining the vital benefits of earthworms aerating the soil, processing manure into plant-available nutrients and generally holding the whole soil system together. His voice was patient and calm, and his words were descriptive and filled with love. But I'd be sitting next to him as a young girl thinking good, great, can we please finish now, and make sure you wash your hands before you cook dinner? The same went for his lectures.

When Ben and I were young we accompanied him to many

of the talks he gave to Soil Association groups, WI meetings, gatherings of students and Round Table events, and we'd be sitting there, swinging our legs with boredom and wishing he'd finish so we could get home. We'd heard it so many times before, and it wasn't until much later, when I went to university to study Environmental Management, that his message actually sank in and I began to see organic farming in a wider context.

I discovered that I, too, had an innate passion for and desire to look after the earth's soils. I studied conventional farming and organics, and began to see that continual use of chemical fertiliser was inherently bad. It just didn't seem to be sustainable. By putting chemical fertiliser on your land you're bypassing the natural organisms by applying a nutrient direct to the plant. Natural manure will feed worms and millions of microorganisms who will then process the material and release it in plant-available forms. Without this natural addition to the soil, soil organisms are made redundant and die off. The plant still gets its food, but the natural system that has underpinned its existence for millennia has been destroyed. This not only affects the quality of our food, but it leaves behind a system that is completely reliant upon outside resources. Dad's incessant lectures had created in me that same yearning to learn more about the natural world and the millions of organisms that live below the soil surface – suddenly I was enjoying every minute of it, learning for myself what Dad had tried to teach me with that smelly cowpat back at Fordhall all those years ago.

Dad probably illustrated the importance of soil life far more effectively with his crumbly cowpats when on his knees in the field than I ever can. His way of demonstrating soil nutrition certainly attracted attention, evident not least in the number of journalists and broadcasters who visited the farm over the years to meet him and hear about his latest escapades. Although he occasionally wondered why people were interested to read or hear about a system of farming that had been effective for hundreds of years before the twentieth century, Dad always maintained a good relationship with the press, especially in the years when the farm was under threat. It was a lesson not lost on Ben and me when our turn came to take up the cudgels.

5

Ben

Like most farmers, but probably not like many guys my age, I'm up at the crack of dawn almost every day to feed and check my animals. As I trudge, half-asleep, across the House Field, the top field next to the farm, with a bale of hay over my shoulder, a herd of hungry sheep following in my muddy footsteps, I never fail to receive a large wake-up call reminding me why I've chosen this way of life, instead of eating breakfast with my feet up before heading to an office job in Shrewsbury or Stoke. It isn't the main reason by any means, but as it's so much a part of my environment it can't be ignored.

In the distance, just a few hundred yards from where our Gloucester Old Spot pigs are fattening themselves nicely, there is a very big and very dominant factory. It provides a considerable amount of employment around Market Drayton, and it creates products that are sold in every supermarket and corner shop in the country. On the side of the factory, in huge neon-red letters, is one word: Müller.

I don't eat Müller yoghurts. I never have done, and I never will. I've nothing against them as such but to me it's a matter of principle, and I think it's important in life to have a few of those. Over there, where their lorries take cratefuls of Crunch Corner and Müller Rice to all points north, south, east and west of Market Drayton, lie ten acres of our land, concreted over to provide parking space for their delivery vehicles. That used to be ten acres of prime organic pasture land, built up over fifty years by Dad, and sold by the landlord to Herr Müller in the early 1990s so he could park his brightly coloured lorries on top of them.

Ten acres doesn't sound a lot by modern farming standards, but it wasn't just the loss of this land that proved problematic. A multi-million-pound European operation making products that everyone enjoys and providing a hundred or so local jobs, versus a quaint organic farm, with its even quainter organic farmer, that turned out a cow's worth of meat every couple of weeks? There was no contest.

The Müller-Milch company arrived in 1989 and set about establishing its UK base in Market Drayton. It came to this part of the country for two reasons. The first was economic – almost one-third of British milk production came from Shropshire then, and understandably there were plenty of dairy farms willing to sell their products at a premium to a big company like Müller. In fact Müller are one of the few dairies that do seem to pay local farmers a fair price for their milk, a rare thing nowadays with so many supermarkets trying to squeeze every last penny out of the primary producers. The second reason – if it is true, and it was quoted by a planning officer to a national newspaper in the 1990s – was because Market Drayton reminded Herr Müller of Aretsried, the small town in Bavaria where the Müller family yoghurt-making business began. Dad was beginning to make yoghurt at the same time, and I wonder how Herr Müller might have felt if it had been the other way round, and someone had set up a factory next to his small farm in Bavaria with the word 'Hollins' in thirty-foot-high letters on its side?

However, that's where the similarities began and ended. Müller expanded into one of the largest food companies in Europe, and when they came to Britain it was at a time of recession. To bring almost 200 jobs to this part of rural Shropshire was seen as a gift, and North Shropshire Council embraced the Germans eagerly.

So did Fordhall Farm's landlord, who accepted an offer from the Müller company to purchase ten acres of Fordhall Farm. Only one year previously, in 1992, Mum and Dad had successfully fought off an application to move Market Drayton's cattle market from the centre of town and on to Fordhall Farm. I can vividly remember having a small float at the local summer carnival to help drum up support. We roped all our friends in and dressed as farmers and animals, carrying small banners that said 'Save Fordhall Farm'. I say 'float', but actually it was an old pram with a model of the farmhouse perched on top. It must have looked daft, but at least we were trying, and at the end of the day we were awarded a prize for the most original float.

Local opposition and the offer of an alternative site closer to the town centre kept the farm intact, but not for long. It was the start of a long and exhausting decade for Mum and Dad, who now realised they would have to use all their energy to put up a fight to stop the rest of Fordhall from being swallowed up. Mum and Dad didn't have much money even then, but what they did have was support from environmentalists and various local people who'd known Fordhall Farm in its heyday, and didn't agree that building over such rich pasture lands was a great idea.

But that wasn't enough to save the ten acres. The loss of the land to Müller interfered hugely with Dad's foggage farming system, as each field worked in harmony with the others. Losing it forced Dad to reduce his stock levels in the winter in order to maintain enough grass for the rest of the cattle. The loss of any more ground at Fordhall would be crippling, as it is this balance between sandy winter-grazing fields and wetland meadows that makes the farming system viable. The powers-that-be, however, never seemed willing to hear this.

For my whole life, growing up at Fordhall has seemed like one long battle, whether it be the fight against the cattle market, Müller, or the landlord increasing the rent to try to get us out. I would wonder how long we could keep fighting these battles and even whether or not the farm would still exist when I was old enough to take over. Even though they were determined to keep fighting, the pressures took their toll on Mum and Dad. They argued more and more. On one occasion Mum said we should sell animals to pay the bills and the solicitors. Dad refused, as he knew selling more livestock was not the answer. It was a short-term solution and he had faith in a future for Fordhall Farm.

In 2004 we had a big clear out of the Dutch barn. This was no mean task. It's a huge space, and it was literally piled to the rafters with junk of all descriptions. Old furniture from the country-club days, bits of broken farm machinery Dad had tinkered with, paperwork, ledgers, dusty old tables and broken crockery all vied for space with the minimal amount of working machinery and tools that we were using on the farm.

One of the men helping Charlotte and me, an older man from Market Drayton, discovered a box full of old plastic yoghurt pots.

'Blimey,' he said, as he pulled out a pot with a Jersey cow logo on the side that looked as if it was designed in the 1960s, 'I remember this stuff. Fordhall Farm yoghurt. Bloody hell.'

'It was supposed to taste amazing,' I said, seeing if I could prompt his memory a little further.

'Well, everyone loved it. But not at first. No one knew what to make of it. Milk with bacteria in it? It didn't sound that promising, to be honest with you, Ben. When we tasted it, though . . . well that was a different matter. Bloody delicious. He could knock up a good yoghurt, could Arthur.'

I looked at the boxes full of plastic pots, each one brimming with an optimism that had been lost for many years at Fordhall, and I thought of our German neighbours just across the field. It's not that we've ever had *unfriendly* relations with them, but just in case I ever forget what the plans of a multinational corporation did to my parents and their livelihood, I keep those Fordhall yoghurt pots, with their smiling and optimistic Jersey cow logo, safely stored in the Dutch barn, just as a reminder.

FORDHALL

Dairy Products

6

Charlotte

U nlike many of our contemporaries who led carefree lives, Ben and I were learning about the fight to keep Fordhall farming from an early age – it dominated our lives at home.

In 1992, when I was nine, the cattle market wanted to relocate from the centre of Market Drayton to our land. Ben and I wrote letters to the council. I asked them 'not to put a smelly cattle market on my daddy's farm'. Losing Fordhall was understandably too much for me to comprehend, though, and even when Mum dressed me up as a little bumblebee on carnival day, and we walked through the town centre with our 'Save Fordhall Farm' banner, I could not accept that we would ever have to leave. I was a child, and these were the pressures of a grown-up.

We were lucky that a local farmer offered up his land to the council for the relocation of the cattle market, removing for a time the pressure on Fordhall. But when Müller became our neighbour, the pressures returned.

FORDHALL ORGANIC FARM

Market Drayton
Shropshire TF9 3PS

Telephone : Tern Hill (063083) 255
V.A.T. Reg. No. 280 3016 92   18·5·92

Dear Sir or madam

Please do not knock down my dads
Farm because you will Scare all the
wild life away. It is nice and pieace full now But
if the cattle- market etc come it will be noisy
and smelly its will be very horrile. I like the farm
the way it is not like it might be, so please dont
take away the field. I don't wan't the
cattle- market etc to come here because
we will not be able to play in the wood in our
dens. We wont see flowers and grass, it will be
all Lorrys and buildings.

yours faithfully

Ben A. Hollins
Age 7½

Proprietor : A. HOLLINS   50 Years of Organic Farming

Chapter 6: Charlotte

The threat to Fordhall was relentless, but I always tried to leave my thoughts at the farm gate. When at school we could forget and concentrate on being children. Perhaps this was why I enjoyed school so much, and it's certainly why comments from one of my best friends, made when I was about fourteen, hurt so badly.

'Hey Charlotte, guess what I've heard about your farm?' She stood there grinning, bursting with top-drawer information, but eking out the suspense just that bit longer for dramatic effect, and to attract the attention of the other girls standing in the chilly playground.

The spring wind blew my hair into my face, and temporarily covered my embarrassment for what I knew would be a horrible few moments ahead. The other girls became silent. They were afraid of her. She was an expert in verbal bullying and none of us had the guts to stand up to her.

'What have you heard?' I said weakly.

'That by 2010 your farm won't be there any more. My dad said, and he's on the council. It's gonna get built on by loads of factories and houses, or whatever. It's in the local development plan.'

'What plan? I don't know what you're talking about.'

But of course I knew. The local development plan was all Mum and Dad ever talked about, all I ever heard from the time I got home from school to the moment I walked down the drive to get the morning bus. The comments from my friend were hurtful not only because of what they implied, but because it introduced real anxieties into my life as a child. It forced me to take on board the pressures at home when at school. It made long-term development issues at Fordhall real.

This day at school brought to life the harsh realities of the planning system and the disregard it has for the people it affects. We had grown up at Fordhall and we knew Dad had spent his whole life building up the fertility in the pastures. The farm had provided food for thousands and a social experience for many through his guided walks, the country club, the dairy and dining at the farm restaurant. I came to realise this all meant nothing when it came to big business. As a small rural market town, Market Drayton was finding it hard to survive and the council were desperately trying to revive it. A large corporation such as Müller coming to Market Drayton with the number of jobs it would offer was just what the council had been dreaming of, and they hoped it would kick-start the regeneration and expansion of the town.

In my early teens I could not understand how you could live somewhere your whole life and put all your energy into something, for it then to be taken away from you with no regard for its past or future potential. But the planners were guided by the prospects of jobs and money and Fordhall, in its run-down state, was seen as a waste of good building land.

Even so, when my friend told me of the impending development at Fordhall I tried to block it out of my mind. I told her it would never happen. The realist in me knew it was a possibility, but the stubborn optimist part told me that something would come along to stop it. I could not even begin to think about such large pressures at such a young age. All I could do was make the most of our time there. Make the most of playing around the farm; rounders in the fields in summer, sledging down the banks in winter. However, the frustrating feeling of being helpless in a situation that caused so much pain remained with me throughout school and my time at university.

As the pressures of development became a reality, all the energy that had been put into working the farm now went into saving it, and basic housekeeping started to go by the board. Dust accumulated as quickly as the clutter of paperwork, newspapers, invoices, clippings and files that Mum had gathered as evidence in the fight for the right to stay here. If something got broken it stayed broken. If a stair became loose or the corner of a ceiling started to crack, it stayed as it was. Fordhall felt unloved, and I became so embarrassed by it that I never invited my friends back home after school. I'd go round to their houses, take one look at the orderliness of the average family home, and vow not to bring any shame on myself by returning the invite. Some of Ben's friends came, but décor, or the lack of it, doesn't interest pre-teen boys very much and they spent most of their time riding their mountain bikes around the fields.

Terry's children still came to play, as they had done since they were toddlers. But, at the end of 1995, Dad had to make Terry redundant. Mum really didn't want him to do it, because she knew she'd have to take on more work around the farm and she was not, nor did she want to be, a farmer, but the stock levels were dropping and we were struggling to pay the rent. On the day Dad broke the news to Terry, I made a diary entry (see overleaf).

I can remember the week that this happened and the mixed feelings that I had about Terry's redundancy. On the one hand I was already beginning to realise the harsh realities of running a farm as a business and I could see that we could no longer afford to keep paying wages. Letting Terry go was going to put us in a much better position to fight off development. But on the other hand I knew that no matter how much Dad insisted he was able to do the farm work himself, his health was deteriorating, and Ben and I, at only eleven and thirteen, would have no choice but to take a more active role on the farm.

By Charlotte Hollins age 13½
7th December 1995 **12**

This is the day dad gave
Terry the sack and more
or less handed the farm over
to me and Ben. He has got
12 weeks notice (3months). In
that time Terry is going to
learn me how to drive
the tractor and show me
and Ben all the ropes. I
also have to look after
my goats. Dad has got
to write a letter to Terry
about him quiting to
make it official. I am
glad he is quiting it saves
us about £200 a week
which will enable us to
improve the farm alot.

I was conscious that Dad had done this at only fourteen, when his father passed away, and it had not done him any harm. In fact, I think Dad may well have welcomed the opportunity to get Ben and me more involved. A vivid memory of Mum's from this time was of me beckoning Ben into the dining room with my finger. Ben and I walked into the dining room for a short discussion. We emerged shortly after and asked to speak to Mum and Dad.

'You don't have to worry. Ben and I have decided we want to help,' I said. 'We already feed our goats and pigeons before school. It won't take us much longer to feed the pigs too if that will make life easier.'

'Thank you both. That would help a lot,' said Dad, obviously touched by our willingness to pull together, despite our age and inexperience.

We still went to school, of course, but we had extra jobs to do before the school day began. We'd get up early, feed the pigs, put hay out for the sheep and see to the goats, then we'd come back into the farmhouse and make ourselves porridge followed by pink grapefruit and a sprinkling of sugar. We had that every winter's morning; it was a real treat.

It goes without saying that treats were rare. Money had always been short. Thankfully for Mum and Dad, Ben and I were not the types who demanded lots of toys be bought for us. This wasn't because we didn't want new toys and computer games, but we were aware enough of the situation to realise that we would never get them. Instead, we had all this amazing land to play on, we had our goats, and Ben had his fishing and his mountain bike. One of our favourite childhood games was marbles, but instead of using holes in the sand to roll the marble into, we used holes in the bar-room carpet. Years of open log fires had left the carpet with many well-placed holes for our games.

It wasn't a deprived childhood in the conventional sense, for what we didn't have in material goods was more than compensated for by the wealth of our surroundings and the warmth of our family unit. As treats we would go swimming or for a family picnic. Although I did not see the value at the time, I appreciate now the outlook this has given Ben and me on life. It has meant we do not have a burning desire for material possessions, despite how easy it is to fall into that trap. It also taught us to value the support of family and friends.

Christmas was always a bit difficult, though, because kids naturally brag about the presents they got, and we never really had much to brag about. It was a subject I used to dread coming up once the holidays were finished and we came back to school. I created diversions to avoid the typical 'what did you get for Christmas?' conversations and usually I made it through. I just didn't want other children to know we didn't get the same sort of presents they did. In fact, the best Christmas gifts we ever got were cotton sleeping bags. Ben and I spent the whole of Christmas encased head to foot in the bags like giant chrysalises, pretending to be zombies. They were great presents because they were practical and we could also play games in them. It's amazing where your imagination takes you when you only have something simple, like a sleeping bag, to prompt it.

Despite our obvious involvement with farm work, I was keen, when I finished school, to be an accountant. Maths had always been my strongest subject and I liked the fact that there was always a right and a wrong answer. There was no ambiguity. As a result I took maths, business studies and environmental science at A Level.

Chapter 6: Charlotte

As the course progressed, I found to my surprise – but probably to no one else's, particularly not to Dad's – that I was really beginning to enjoy and appreciate environmental science. My maths stayed strong, and I wondered about becoming a farm accountant so that I could satisfy my interests in numbers and agriculture, but even as I passed my exams and earned a place at the University of Central Lancashire (UCLAN) in Preston, I still wasn't completely sure what I was going to do.

My course at UCLAN was a combined honours degree, which included environmental management, economics and maths. After the first year I dropped economics, majored in environmental management and minored in maths. I'd always been a mathematical type of person, but the philosophical and investigative side of environmental management really struck a chord with me and inspired me to know more. Looking back, it's obvious where it was all coming from, but in life you often find that the more distanced you are from something the more you begin to see it objectively. Preston isn't a million miles from Market Drayton, but that short distance helped me to see Fordhall Farm in a wider context.

At UCLAN I concentrated on sustainable agriculture and soil science, and for my dissertation I looked at soil ecology, sustainability, tillage (soil cultivation) and the effects of that on soil biology, and I even used Dad's CulturSeeder machine as a practical example of what could be achieved. The lecturers thought I was overambitious, but they encouraged my studies nonetheless. I could feel the passion for the subject running right through me, just as it had done with Dad, and I was keen to learn all I could. I wanted to know if the talks I had heard Dad give time and time again as a child held water scientifically, or whether all the conventional farmers were right: he was a crackpot.

I conducted the experiments at Fordhall, just behind the Dutch barn. I cultivated three strips of land to measure the effects of mulch cover on plant growth. I didn't have long to do it, but I got some results. They weren't as amazing as they might have been over a longer period of time, but all those hours watching Dad wave cowpats in the air must have paid off. I won a £50 prize. That cash no doubt came in handy somewhere along the line, as I was the only student I knew who was sending money to her parents, rather than the other way round.

I left UCLAN with a first-class honours degree and a desire to learn more about the natural world and its benefits to the farming system. I could not understand why we should bypass such important processes and cycles, such as those in the soil, that had kept the earth fertile for millions of years, for our own systems that were costly and unsustainable. The natural world does a remarkable job and is much more efficient than we could ever hope to be. That was what Dad had built at Fordhall; an understanding and a trust in the natural world. The millions of microorganisms that inhabit the delicate top few inches of the soil surface were feeding his fields. They were free, unlike chemical fertilisers, and stable. All they needed was a little time to develop. I also recognised the importance of the soil as a store of carbon from the atmosphere, and I was amazed to learn that humans to this day only understand one per cent of the microbial population and the role that this group of species plays in life above the surface.

However, looking back, my time at university was not always easy or indeed inspiring. Even at a distance, I felt a responsibility for what was happening at the farm. Money was getting tighter as more went into paying fees for the arbitration battles with the landlord, and more livestock were being sold to cover the rent. Sending money home was the only way I could help. I would sometimes break down when I came off the phone to Mum and she'd given me the latest update of invariably bad news. I even secretly contemplated leaving university to move back to Fordhall and help on the farm. But I knew that, in the long run, it would not solve the problems or make life easier, and I knew my studies at Preston were important and could help improve the value of the farm if the opportunity arose to use what I had learned.

In the summer breaks I had a job like every other student, except mine was at our friendly neighbourhood multinational, ever-expanding yoghurt factory, Müller. I had to earn some money, so I swallowed my pride and went to the place with the most jobs. I didn't see the company as the problem, really. Müller wasn't after our land for personal reasons; it was just business. Eventually, though, it seemed too hypocritical for me to work there, and I left.

I was lucky in that I had good friends at university, who were to become even more significant in my life later on. 'What's that you've got in there?' I would demand, rustling through their supermarket bags. 'What are you having for tea?'

'Oh, I'm out tonight, so I just got something I could bung in the microwave. Could you stick it in for me in ten minutes? I'm going up for a shower.'

I'd look at the ready meal and tut to myself. Two pounds. She had probably bought something just as expensive for lunch, and she might get a takeaway on her way home from the Union. Meanwhile, I'd been in the covered market in Preston town centre, buying bags full of fruit and veg at knock-down prices, which I'd cook myself. A bag of porridge, a big carton of milk and a loaf of bread, plus all this fruit and veg, would easily last me a week, and I'd only have spent ten or fifteen pounds. I couldn't understand why my friends would spend so much extra money on food, especially when it didn't taste nearly as good as fresh produce.

As time went on I learned to be more tolerant of how other people lived, and I came to see that everyone has widely differing expectations. At the end of the day they were some of my best friends. But I did notice that, by the end of my degree course, a fair few of them were starting to buy and cook their own food. Perhaps the smells from my home cooking were tempting them!

Part of my course at UCLAN involved going to Kenya for two weeks and it took my breath away. Our class of eighteen stayed in small huts adjacent to a Maasai village in rural Kenya. The day started at 8 a.m. with an outdoor shower. These were simple mechanisms, nothing more than a shower-head attached to a small bucket. Before each shower you would fill the bucket with water heated in a black sack from the morning sun. After showering, you would refill the black sack to heat water for the next person; a very simple yet very effective solar water-heating system. I was inspired immediately.

My trip to Kenya introduced me to the stark difference between developed and developing countries and the people that inhabit them. The most poignant memory I have of Kenya was the cheerful disposition of the people and their attitude to life. We visited rural villages and small farms in southern Kenya. All relied on the depleting glacier at the peak of Kilimanjaro to provide them with water, and all were struggling. Apart from the rich farmers, who would take more than their fair share, every farmer was doing their best to conserve water and to grow enough food simply to feed their families. Yet, despite their obvious poverty and hard life, they remained positive and enjoyed what they had – their families and each other.

Chapter 6: Charlotte

The Kenyans we met had an enormous respect and understanding of nature. They had to work with it, because they relied upon it so much. They were more connected to the planet than even I was, and I was a farmer. It highlighted to me the huge gap that exists in Britain between people and the natural world. We have so many abundant resources that we take them for granted. It made me angry and embarrassed to know how profligate we are at home with water, energy and land. How we think nothing of spending fifteen minutes in the shower, or turning on the hose to water the garden, or even burying good fertile land under a sea of concrete for ever; and even with all this abundance we still find something to complain about. Yet these people were fighting for the smallest drip of water every day of their lives and they always had a smile on their faces. They had no money, yet they were achieving amazing things against the odds just by working together. There was definitely something to be learned from the African attitude to life.

I decided to stay on and climb Mount Kilimanjaro – 'the roof of Africa'. I was already bitten by the travel bug. Funds were tight but I was determined to have the experience while I was still in the country. I had decided to put the trip on my credit card and to pay it off by working through the summer break. I knew that this opportunity would never arise again and I had already developed a philosophy of 'why do tomorrow what you can do today?' After three days of climbing through rainforest, savannah, moorland, desert and glaciers, my guide and I reached the summit at 6.30 a.m. on the fourth day, just in time to see the African sunrise from the peak. Sitting at 5995 metres above sea level and looking out to the horizon, I felt inspired. This was a continent steeped in deprivation and suffering, yet it had something we didn't.

I returned home with a yearning to travel again. I wanted to see more of Africa and Asia, Australia and North America. But I didn't just want to tick off a list of places I'd visited. I wanted to see how they farmed and work with people on sustainability and land issues. I was hoping that such an adventure would help me to find out what I really wanted to do in life, and I started to make plans to earn money and go travelling after I graduated. I would work and save, work and save, just like I'd always done. The frustrated, helpless feeling I had felt throughout school and university was still there, but it was joined with a new sense of opportunity and a renewed determination to do something that would make a difference. This difference was not necessarily directed at Fordhall, but it would be related to agricultural sustainability and rural communities in England. Above all, what I came home with was a deep appreciation for the place in which I was so fortunate to live.

7
Ben

D espite the difficulties Mum and Dad were having, I didn't have to think too hard when it came to deciding what to do with my life. I loved Fordhall, and I wanted to stay here to farm it. I wasn't bad at school, but I can't say I enjoyed it that much. I couldn't wait for the school day to finish so I could get home and ride across the fields on my bike or see what Dad was doing. I got eight GCSEs and managed to get into Reasheath Agricultural College in Nantwich when I was sixteen, to study for a national diploma.

I guess I didn't need to go to college to learn how to look after the farm. I'd grown up here, and had seen how it worked, day to day, month to month, season to season. But given the battles with the landlord, the decreasing livestock numbers, and the very real possibility that there might not be a farm to look after soon, I decided it was better to go to college and get some qualifications, so if I needed to get a job off the farm

I had something to offer. Despite my enthusiasm for farming and the exciting ideas I was forming about what could be achieved at Fordhall given its enormous potential, I didn't feel it was an option to stay at home and work on the farm. There wasn't enough money and security in its future to make it worth putting my ideas into practice.

I learned a lot at Reasheath. It was a very broad course, taking in animal husbandry, crop production and farm management. It also had a very practical side, and a large part of the course was a year's work placement on a working farm. I chose to do mine at a very intensive dairy farm, for the simple reason that I wanted to see a side of farming that was alien to us at Fordhall. It interested me, seeing animals kept indoors all year round and how high the milk yields were. It was conventional farming in every sense, and it made me glad of my background. That said, I've always thought that forcing the idea of organic farming on people is about the worst way there is to convince them that it's a good thing. You can preach at people, but I think that tends to have the opposite effect. I think it's much better to let people see exactly how you farm organically, to let them go away and make their own minds up.

I had three excellent years at Reasheath, with like-minded people who were passionate about farming and had the natural cheerfulness you need when working on the land. But every weekend when I came home, I was shocked at the terrible state the farm was in.

To make a few extra pounds, Dad had taken to allowing travellers to dump their unwanted goods on our land. They always said they'd come back for them in a week, but they never did, and so we had a smashed-up caravan left in the yard, oil drums full of tar piled up next to the derelict butchery and rusty cars on the side of the drive. The front of the house was covered in a jungle of ivy no one had bothered to keep in check, and inside the house was literally cracking up.

Our house looked like an abandoned building, and it made me wonder if the locals believed people were still living there. Even worse was the state of the fields: overgrown, and infested with nettles and thistles. The years of work Dad had put into his foggage system were lain waste, and yet from his chair by the fire he still talked optimistically about the soil's fertility and how the pastures would sustain the sheep and cattle all year round.

The question was, what sheep and cattle? I didn't need a diploma in agricultural management to know that the few animals left at Fordhall weren't going to keep us going for much longer. The stock had dwindled to minimal levels – just eleven cows, six pigs and six lambs left.

There didn't seem to be any way of turning our fortunes around. The farm was an eyesore and nothing suggested it was going to get any better. Inside, a sick old man and his depressed wife tried to make the best of a bad situation, but it didn't look good at all. And it was about to get a whole lot worse.

8
Charlotte

'Come on Mum, hurry up!' As usual I had to work hard to motivate Mum to do anything. It was the summer of 2002 and she was about to take me back to university. We had planned a day in Preston for her and Dad and I was worried that they wouldn't have any time if we didn't leave soon. Mum moved so slowly these days; everything seemed to be an effort. She would shout every time you spoke to her and she would complain at the smallest of incidents.

Mum had become increasingly depressed over the years. The responsibility of looking after Fordhall following Terry's departure, on top of the demands of two young children and the continual eviction notices, had taken their toll. She had come to Fordhall in her early twenties and had spent her life bringing up children and working in the farmhouse restaurant. As with most farming families, holidays were rare and days were long. But it was the pressure of the last few years coupled with the advancing age and frailty of our father that really affected her. At the time I didn't understand the stress she was under and I reacted badly to her depression. I was angry that she was making my life so difficult and I couldn't see why she looked on everything so negatively.

Each time I returned from university I would be greeted by a dying farm; a Fordhall that was being buried under rubbish and undergrowth. Passing the farm gate, it exasperated me to see the potential that Fordhall had. I didn't know quite yet just what Fordhall could be, but I knew it had something special, something you couldn't put your finger on.

In a desperate bid to regain some of the farm's lost beauty, I would try to clean the house or tidy the garden whenever I was home, but Mum would battle with me all the way. At the time I could not understand why she was so averse to my attempts at improving the house, but I can see now that she was scared of losing yet more control in an impossible situation.

Our trip back to Preston was interrupted by a short visit to the post office, so that Mum could post the rent cheque. Mum and Dad had a somewhat complicated way of paying the rent. They set up a company to tenant the farm, and the rent was paid through this account rather than their joint business account. So twice a year, when it was due, they'd take funds from their account and put them into the company account. Once they were in, they would send the landlord a cheque.

However, because Mum was taking me back to university she didn't want to forget about the rent cheque. So on this occasion she posted it off a few days earlier than normal, and post-dated it because she knew the funds had not yet cleared from one account to the other. The landlord, she assumed, would not cash it until the due date, by which time there would be sufficient funds in the company account. She just wanted to make sure he had it in his hand.

She assumed wrong. The cheque was cashed, and because the funds had not had enough time to enter the account, it bounced. A simple matter, you might think, which could have been cleared up by a phone call and another cheque.

Not so. It was the opportunity the landlord had been waiting for. He sent us a notice to quit, and this time it was an incontestable notice because it followed a notice to pay. The dreaded hysterical phone call I received from Mum a month after I arrived back in Preston confirmed the seriousness of it. We'd had notices to quit before, but they'd followed notices to remedy due to the dilapidation and poor state of the farm. These past notices were being fought through the courts and were draining our money as well as Mum and Dad's health. This was even more serious: a notice to quit following a notice to pay is incontestable.

The landlord, understandably, would not listen to what seemed to be a perfectly valid reason for non-payment. He had been fighting the family for years and this was perfect ammunition for him. Mum and Dad had no money left with which to put up a fight. They were living off Dad's pension and a carer's allowance that Mum had been able to claim. Even more crucially, they did not have the energy. Mum had been fighting for years and she simply could not cope with it any longer. The pressure and the severe lack of finances got to her and she lost the energy to continue the battle. In the spring of 2003 she stopped going to the arbitration cases and the verdict went in favour of the landlord.

Our latest eviction notice was legal and set in stone. We were told that we must leave Fordhall by 26 March 2004. It was something that we had seen coming for years, but when you get so used to fighting you never actually believe it will end – and at the end of it you will have lost.

9

Ben

Both Charlotte and I knew that our chances of a job away from Fordhall would be further improved if we continued our education. So I applied for and got into Harper Adams Agricultural College in the nearby town of Newport, to study part time for a degree course.

My choice of university was an easy one. Harper is only 20 minutes away from Fordhall, and I didn't consider going further afield because I suspected I might be needed at home. There was another reason too – some of my friends from Reasheath were also going to Harper so I knew I would be in good company during my first days and weeks there.

That said, getting to know new people at an agricultural university isn't as tricky as it might be at more conventional establishments. Most students have similar backgrounds, coming from farms themselves, or at least from rural communities, and it's this shared experience that gives Harper students a reputation locally for being a touch high-spirited. Practical jokes and stunts carried out by students were well known around North Shropshire, and I'd heard a lot about the cheap beer and the black-tie balls that usually ended in drunken chaos. Harper students certainly knew how to drink, and I wondered whether I would be able to fit into this lifestyle as well as settle down to some hard academic work.

I was to start the course in autumn 2003. That summer was gorgeous, one of the hottest we'd had for years. Charlotte came back after graduating from Preston, and it was wonderful to see her again. At least together we felt like a bit of a team, even if we didn't exactly know what it was we were joining forces for. The notice to quit was there in black and white. There seemed to be no way around it.

'Crikey, it's a mess, isn't it?' Charlotte had just walked into the garden after months of being away. The grass was waist high and trampled in parts by cattle that had broken through the rotten fencing and escaped. The little statues of Adam and Eve, put up years ago to look out across the valley, had long since fallen down, and there they lay, two broken figures among the nettles.

'I know,' I replied. 'Have you seen all the stuff dumped in the farmyard, too?'

'Not more of it? Why doesn't Mum just tell them to get lost, or put a bloody big lock on the gate?'

Charlotte was frustrated. But I knew Mum couldn't do anything about it. She was too depressed to tackle the fly-tippers who came regularly now. Mum had so much weight to bear on her shoulders and I had a lot of sympathy with the position she found herself in as Dad's health, at eighty-eight, continued to fail. She was trying to keep the farm afloat, doing all of the spadework, feeding the animals every day when Charlotte and I were away at college and university, and ensuring the rent was paid every spring and autumn. She found it almost impossible to cope with, even without the ongoing difficulties with the landlord, Müller, the council and everything else she had to contend with. Never having intended to be a farmer's wife, she felt isolated and unsupported and, in farming, which can be a lonely job, those feelings are very real and can lead to trouble.

'We're going to have to leave, you know,' I said, stating the obvious.

'I know. But it's so unfair. There's so much potential here. If they would just somehow, I don't know, give us some time to get it straight. It can't be that hard, they just need to . . . '

'They don't need to do anything.' I jumped in before the rant began. I'd been on the sharp end of Charlotte's rants before, and I hadn't got a spare two hours that afternoon. 'They want their land back. They want to make money. It's over. Finished. You should get a job, save up, go travelling, and I'll do this degree and sort myself out after that. We'll have to get a council house and just take it from there. It'll be all right.'

I was pulling myself together, making myself aware of the facts. But as the swallows dived on the insects hovering above the Tern and the dwindling band of cows formed a slow procession across our precious meadows, I could hardly believe what I was ordering myself to do. To give up. Was that right? At that moment I didn't know what was right or what was wrong. I just wanted to move forward, and to see an end to the misery that had plagued our family for so long. Besides, a visit from the landlord's agent was imminent and so we had to pull ourselves together to prepare for that. We also had a family day out planned at the Newport Agricultural Show.

This was the nearest such event to Fordhall, and it had always been a Hollins family tradition to take a day off from farm work to enjoy the show. Plus, it always falls around my birthday, 20 July, an extra incentive for a rare family outing.

In years past, Dad and I would rush straight off to see the animals as soon as we arrived. It was a day when pedigree cows, sheep and horses were primped and preened before being paraded round the ring by their owners, most of them local farmers hoping to take home a trophy or rosette for 'best in class'. The farmers also dressed up for the occasion, and I enjoyed watching them, looking smart in their bowler hats and best tweed suits, as they groomed their bulls and fluffed up their fur before walking them round the ring.

But it wasn't just the animals that attracted us to the show. We would stroll round the trade stands, admiring the tractors, farm machinery, arts and crafts, and chatting to the stall holders. Dad met many friends and acquaintances at the show, as it was the perfect occasion for the farming community of North Shropshire to gather, relax and enjoy each other's company. Charlotte and I always wanted to head for the food tent, which was packed with produce from local farmers, and mouth-watering cakes and biscuits courtesy of the various Women's Institute groups in the area.

It was a day we had always looked forward to with relish, but this year none of us particularly felt like going. We didn't have much to celebrate, and the problems at Fordhall seemed to be going from bad to worse. On the other hand, we didn't want to stop a family tradition, and surely we could enjoy this one little bit of pleasure? We would all go, and leave the farm to look after itself. It wasn't as if anyone was going to call on us anyway.

10
Charlotte

The summer of 2003 was horrible. Ben and I mooched around the farm, allowing the realisation that these sun-drenched few months would be the last we'd spend at Fordhall to slowly drip into us. The shabbiness of the whole thing – farm, livestock, rent, eviction – hit us hard, and we both struggled to stay chirpy. Mum's depression had deepened and each day was a battle. She rarely moved from the TV and every time we tried to speak to her, she would shout back with some ridiculous overreaction. Her deteriorating health and her refusal to believe that we would ever have to leave really worried us. I think that she found the idea too painful and wouldn't even contemplate it. She did *talk* about leaving, but would never act or make any arrangements to go. Dad, on the other hand, remained positive and tried to believe that we would remain at Fordhall, despite the reality.

I thought about Kenya, and that exhausting, exhilarating climb up Mount Kilimanjaro. I didn't want to abandon

Fordhall, but if we were being forced out there seemed no point in staying around Market Drayton to see Fordhall's fields disappear under an industrial park or some kind of mixed development. I couldn't bear the thought of it.

But, in the meantime, I needed some order in my life, and it certainly couldn't be found at Fordhall that summer. Cheswardine Hall, a nursing home for the elderly on the outskirts of Market Drayton, was that place. There were routines, procedures and set meal times; it was a welcome change to life at home that had became so chaotic and unpredictable. I was earning money and I was able to make a difference to people. I was away from the clingingly damp atmosphere at Fordhall, something that no matter how much I wanted to, I knew I couldn't alter.

The residents and the staff were lovely, and going there, even when working twelve-hour shifts, was a relief. I quickly became friends with Dagmar, a fellow carer who soon got me chatting and showed me the ropes. Despite the fact that she was about fifteen years older than me, we just clicked – I guess because of the difficulties and responsibilities we'd taken on at Fordhall, I was more mature than other girls my age. Small, blonde, friendly and German, Dagmar had recently moved to Shropshire. She had two children with her husband but the marriage had broken down, and when I met her she was going through a difficult divorce and was hoping to move back to Germany. She had, however, met a Scotsman called Mike and, despite her troubles, new romance was blooming. When we weren't doling out dinners or changing sheets, we had a lot to talk about. Even though our problems were different, we both had tough issues to face.

For anyone involved in agriculture around Market Drayton, July marks the coming of the Newport Show, the big day out for farmers, their families and anyone else connected with the land. We'd always gone as a family, and we were determined to make it this year. Shaking off the black cloud of our problems, if only for one day, seemed a good idea. Dad would also enjoy it, and it might help to bring him out of himself, to break the silence he'd fallen into lately. A gossip, a catch-up and a bit of fun was needed, and so we packed up the car on the Saturday morning and headed for Newport.

While we were gone, something very strange, and indeed ironic, occurred. At the time, Mum was volunteering on a charity stall in Market Drayton on a Saturday, but had taken this particular day off for the Newport Show. That afternoon, a German couple approached Jean and Carol, two of the volunteers and, in good English, asked them if they knew Fordhall Farm and Arthur Hollins.

'Yes,' said Jean, 'of course. Actually, Arthur's wife usually works here, but she's not here today.'

'Then are you able to direct us to Fordhall Farm?' asked the man. 'We would very much like to meet with Herr Hollins.'

'Oh, I'm afraid you wouldn't find anyone there,' Jean replied. 'They've all gone out for the day.'

Her curiosity raised, she pressed home the question she'd wanted to ask when they first mentioned Fordhall, but felt a bit rude doing so. 'Why do you want to see Arthur so much, anyway?'

'Because of this,' replied the woman, and she held up a hardback book. It was in German. Jean looked at it blankly.

'There is a chapter about Herr Hollins,' explained the woman. 'This is a book about British eccentrics, and he has an organic farm, close to Market Drayton?'

Jean nodded her head in agreement.

'Yes, and Herr Hollins has been fighting to stop the Müller company building on his land,' continued the woman. 'We are from Germany, and so is Müller. We are interested to meet Herr Hollins and hear his story.'

Again, Jean explained that the Hollins family was not at home, and wouldn't be back until late. Disappointed, the German couple thanked her and turned to leave. Suddenly, the man stopped, and offered the book to Jean.

'Perhaps Herr Hollins would like to see this,' he said, holding the book in his outstretched hand. 'Don't worry, we have read it. If you could just tell him that we called, and we are sorry to have missed him.'

'I will,' said Jean, and she tucked the book into her bag for safekeeping.

The following Saturday, Mum turned up for work as usual and was told the story of the couple and the book. Dad was no stranger to press interest, but to see something about him in a foreign language and published so recently was exciting. He vaguely remembered a German interviewer coming to Fordhall in the early 1990s when he was first fighting the planned development. The German press liked the irony of a large German organisation moving to England and taking land from one of the first English yoghurt producers. And here was the end result, delivered by two German tourists who had come all this way to see him and had left disappointed. I immediately thought of Dagmar when I received the book. Perhaps she could translate it for me.

'Mmm,' said Dagmar, when I showed her the book during our hasty lunch break at Cheswardine, 'this is interesting. The "gentle prophet of Shropshire", eh? That's some title. He sounds quite a character, your father.'

'He is,' I said. 'What else does it say?'

She scanned it quickly: 'Ermm, "devotion to the land, tenant farmer, crumbles up soil in his hands . . ." It looks an interesting article, but it would take hours to translate it word-for-word. I could do it at home if you like?'

'Oh, would you?' I said. 'It might cheer Dad up, give him something else to think about.'

'Of course,' said Dagmar, 'not a problem. While I'm doing it I'll let Mike look at it to make sure my English isn't all over the place. My apologies if it takes me a while.'

The summer ticked on, but those days of record sunshine failed to penetrate the thick fog of gloom over Fordhall. After the visit in October from Mr Godsal and the melodramatic scene in the club room, we had at least secured a promise from him that he would write to the council on our behalf in the hope that we might get a move further up the housing list.

Applying for council housing was a frightening and horrible task. It felt very unreal to be completing the forms. It just didn't seem to fit, somehow. I couldn't see us moving into a double-glazed house in the town. However, the most important thing was to have a roof over our heads in March, and if a man from the council declaring our house 'uninhabitable' was going to help, then that's what would have to happen.

He arrived one day, a well-dressed young guy clutching a meter that tested for damp. In silence, he looked at the paper peeling off the walls, the creaking and lethal staircase, the broken plastering and the water snaking down the exposed brickwork. Then he loftily announced his judgement.

'I've got no problem recommending that this house is uninhabitable,' he said.

'Good,' I replied as brightly as I could, trying to look for the tiniest spark of something positive about this man's visit. 'Does that mean we'll be pushed higher up the list?'

'Indeed it does,' he answered.

I hated his attitude, and hated the fact that this house, with all its history, had turned into nothing less than a dark, miserable collection of corridors, with its lovely memories buried beneath cobwebs and grime. I didn't want to live in a modern house, even one with a proper bathroom and central heating, which we'd never had at Fordhall. This house was a part of me, and I found it chokingly upsetting to think about going elsewhere. I didn't want my childhood to be wiped clean like an old video tape. But for all that I wanted to stay here, I didn't want to continue living like this.

One October morning, Dagmar collared me as I began to clear Cheswardine's breakfast pots away. 'I've done it,' she said. 'Sorry it's taken so long.'

I'd almost forgotten about the translation. Taking a sneaky break I read it, and giggled. There was something quirky about the English, but it had a lot of passion and it really got to the heart of Dad's love for Fordhall and his 'David and Goliath' fight against a big corporation.

'But that's not all,' announced Dagmar when I eventually put the sheaf of paper down. 'Mike's read it too. I told you that he used to be an engineer, didn't I? He couldn't believe that bit about Arthur's machine. He thinks that could go all over the world, you know. It's an amazing invention.'

'So we've been told,' I replied, 'but nothing has ever come of it. It needs time and money and no one seems to have much of either.' Building a new prototype and researching Dad's design would take more resources than we could ever hope to have.

She pressed on. 'I know, but Mike's really interested. Honestly, Charlotte. It's not just the machine. He loves all the history, and the whole organic thing, and the fight against Müller. He might be able to help, you know.'

I explained that it was probably too late; that we'd had a notice to quit and there was no hope of the landlord going back on it. They'd spent a small fortune trying to evict us, and they certainly weren't going to start feeling sorry for us at this stage.

'Look,' she said, 'I know it seems hopeless, but do you think Mike could come to meet you all? He's very excited about this.'

I groaned inwardly. I didn't want someone else to come to Fordhall, and walk away turning their nose up at the squalor. No one visited us any more. The fight against the landlord had left the farmhouse unloved. This house that had welcomed so many people through its doors and had been the heart of the family for so long was itself struggling to survive. Each room was filled to the brim with files and newspaper cuttings, buried under months of dust and soot from the old fireplaces. We had got used to it, having lived there for so long, but strangers would make an immediate judgement on it. With no feeling for the trauma the family had suffered, they would assume laziness, and so we tried to avoid letting anyone come to the farmhouse.

But Dagmar was having none of it. It was fine, she said, we'll excuse the mess. I knew that it wasn't at all fine, and that she wasn't listening to me telling her how bad it was, but by the time my break was finished she'd persuaded me that we should at least hear what Mike had to say. What harm would it do? I went home and told Ben, and he pulled the same face as I had done just a few hours previously.

But, despite being uncomfortable about the visit, Ben and I realised there was no harm in hearing what Dagmar and Mike had to say. Perhaps the potential of Dad's machine really could be realised. There was nothing to lose by talking to them. They arranged their visit for the following Saturday.

11
Ben

My sister would say that, out of the two of us, I'm the cautious one. If she grabs hold of an idea she likes, no matter how mad it might seem, she'll run with it until it's exhausted. That kind of drive is phenomenal, but sometimes you need a brakeman and, to an extent, I've taken that role.

Maybe I think more rationally. I certainly try to weigh up all the possibilities before I make a decision, and I won't be taken for a fool. Growing up the way we did, aware of the financial pressure our parents were under and conscious that developers were after our land, I don't find it difficult to say no to something I don't want to do. I saw how Dad would be taken advantage of time and again by people who wanted to dump waste on his land, and how he'd accept a few pounds for a piece of scrap metal that we were then burdened with. Perhaps he trusted too much in people's better natures; perhaps he couldn't say no.

So when on that October evening Charlotte came home

after her shift at Cheswardine Hall and talked at length about her German friend's new man being interested in the farm and wanting to meet Dad, I was sceptical, to say the least. I couldn't see a way, short of winning the lottery, that we would ever raise the money to buy the farm, even if it was for sale, which it wasn't. Although I wanted nothing more than to farm Fordhall myself, I also wanted what was best for everyone. At the time, that appeared to be a new house and a new start. We were on course to do that, and I didn't want anything or anyone giving us false hope.

Charlotte has a way, though, of persuading people that her ideas aren't as mad or bad as they might seem, and so together we tidied up the club room in preparation for a rare visit. Dagmar's children, who came with her and Mike to Fordhall, were only little, and they seemed a touch overawed by Dad. Sitting in his favourite rocking chair, he was pleased when the children politely offered their hands for him to shake gently.

Mike eventually steered the subject of conversation round to Dad's machine, and with that story came the whole saga of the previous ten years at Fordhall. We all chipped in, though Mum naturally held the floor as she was the one closest to the drama. It concluded, of course, five months in the future, on 26 March 2004 – the day we'd been given to leave the farm.

'Well,' Mike said, as a silence descended after an hour of talking, 'why don't we do something to try and save the farm? The machine's safe, it's got the patent on it. We can worry about that later. We should save the farm first.'

Mum leaned forward, eager to hear more, and at that point I wanted very gently, but very politely, to place a heavy gag over Mike's mouth. What I thought might happen – someone coming along with a hare-brained idea and then clearing off again, leaving Mum in a state and us having to pick up the pieces – seemed to be happening. Charlotte sensed it too.

'We've been fighting for a long time, Mike,' she explained patiently. 'It's over now. They want us out and we've got five months left.'

Mike was persistent. 'Yes, but have you talked to them, tried to explain why the farm is worth saving?'

We told him about Mr Godsal's visit the previous week, and how it had extinguished all hopes of us staying.

'There's more than one way to skin a cat,' Mike replied, not wanting us to have the last, pessimistic word. 'Look how fate brought us here, with the two German tourists. I think this is an amazing place, you know. Unique. Surely you think it's worth fighting to save?'

Of course we did. But we didn't have much fight – or much time – left. Mike said he'd like to come back soon and have a proper look round. Reluctantly, we agreed. Charlotte and I would take him for a walk around our fields, bedraggled and rain-soaked though they were at this time of year.

He came back a week later. We kitted him out with a pair of Dad's wellingtons and took him across our land, showing him the wood, the site of the old motte and bailey castle, the river and the view across the valley. Before we set off, we stood in front of the refuse tip that was our farmyard as he fired questions at us. Charlotte was being polite, filling her answers with enthusiasm. I couldn't feel that fired up, and was flippant.

'So Ben,' he said, 'what would you like to do?'

'I'd like to be a farmer, please,' I replied with a hint of sarcasm.

'Would you like to have your own farm?'

'Only if it was here. But even if we owned this farm it would cost too much money to get it into working order.'

'Wouldn't you want a farm anywhere else?'

'No. It's bloody hard work, badly paid and lonely. To put in all those hours you need some kind of attachment to a place. So why would I want to do it somewhere else, somewhere I've no connection with?'

'What will you do instead?'

'I don't know. I honestly couldn't tell you. Try to get a farm manager's job. Get a council house. Whatever.'

I wasn't taking any of this seriously, and I was worried that Charlotte was latching on to a plan that would go nowhere. Mike, though, was listening to me, and I suddenly had the feeling that what I'd said about a connection to Fordhall had struck a chord with him.

I was right. There was a plan, and halfway round our walk Mike pulled it out of his pocket. On a scrap of notepaper he'd written a list of things he imagined Fordhall might be in a perfect world: a farm, a visitor resource, a place where people might come to eat and drink, and learn about organic farming. There were ideas about an educational space, which particularly interested Charlotte. To me, it sounded like a theme park. They were grand ideas, and they raised all sorts of questions; not least how much would it all cost, and who would pay for it? I was suspicious. Why would someone we barely knew want to do so much to try and help? But the part of me that was dreading driving past the farm in the future, when it was no longer our home or even a working farm, encouraged me to hear him out. Mike seemed to have the vision and enthusiasm, the energy and positivity that Charlotte and I were running out of.

'Why don't I look at my notes again and draft out something on decent paper?' he said. 'Nothing fancy, just a few ideas about what could be done here, and I'll also do a rough estimate of how much it all might cost.'

There seemed to be no harm in letting him do it. I was still sceptical, but we both liked his enthusiasm, and as long as we didn't raise Mum's hopes by announcing big plans that would almost definitely come to nothing, it would probably be all right.

Mike came back with a folded leaflet that he'd created on his computer. It announced the start of what he christened 'The Fordhall Project'. The project was divided into five areas: work to restore and promote Dad's machine; an educational resource centre; a tearoom; an exhibition area and a working farm. I was glad to see the latter item had made it. I wasn't as cynical as I had been initially and Charlotte's enthusiasm for the project was infectious.

But there was the issue of the money. I knew that restoring livestock and buying farm equipment would not be cheap, especially given the levels of depletion at Fordhall. The purchase of the farm outright would cost close to £1 million. That and everything else we would do over Mike's proposed five phases would cost almost £2 million.

To say that figure represented an insurmountable obstacle would be an understatement, but Mike had faith in the idea that if we really went for the whole resource centre/public attraction/working-farm concept, people would be so inspired to come that we would eventually make this money back. Phase one would see the farm business revitalised and promoted for the study of organic farming. Phase two would be to rebuild the yoghurt factory, phase three would open the Dutch barn as a visitor centre, and phases four and five would be given over to the collection and study of Dad's work, including the manufacture of his machine.

It seemed impossible to believe any of this could come to pass, and yet here was someone who had lifted up the corner of a dark, heavy curtain and showed us the gleam of a possibility beyond it. We had grown up at Fordhall, and to us it was simply our family home. An interesting place, of course, and one presided over by an eccentric old man who had made waves long before his time, but still our family home. We saw no possibilities beyond somehow securing it from the landlord and continuing to farm it. We were intrigued that an outsider could see a much bigger picture.

'Of course it's a huge amount of money,' argued Mike, when I pointed out that even my piggy bank had gone for sausages. 'But you know, if you hit the right person at the right time, you never know what might happen. There are a lot of hugely wealthy people in this country with money to spend, and they might just want to spend it on this. You can only try.'

Fired up, Charlotte obtained a copy of the *Sunday Times* Rich List and started to target the wealthy people listed. Rock stars, industrialists, entrepreneurs, computer tycoons and aristocrats all received letters outlining what we'd like to do, and how we only needed a piffling £2 million to do it with. The underwhelming response was perhaps not surprising.

There was the other issue of the landlord. If he didn't want to sell the land, or thought he could get a better price from Müller, or anyone else, for that matter, why would he be interested in two young people – especially a couple with our surname – who wanted to become farmers and educationalists? It was the biggest hurdle of all, but as usual Mike was hopeful that eventually they would come to the same conclusion as him.

Even the naturally chirpy Charlotte couldn't see how we'd be taken seriously by the landlord in any way. They were just five months away from getting us out for ever. Why would they stop now, and do a complete U-turn?

The answer, as it turned out, lay not in the tribulations of the Hollins family but over the hedge and inside the board-room of our neighbouring yoghurt manufacturer. For some time, Müller had been interested in obtaining more of our land for expansion, particularly the twelve-acre Cottage Field at the top of the farm. But now we heard that they'd changed their minds and wanted to expand on the north side of the A53, effectively across the road from their factory.

It was incredible news and it could not have been more timely. I was ecstatic – for the first time in many years there was a glimmer of hope at Fordhall. First, it meant that if Müller was no longer interested in tearing up Fordhall's fields, the value of the land to the landlord was nowhere near as great as it might have been. Secondly, there was a North Shropshire council plan-ning inquiry into all land around Market Drayton that had been earmarked for industrial development, the twelve-acre field included, due to start in early 2004. If Müller wanted to go somewhere else, the pressure for industrial use was – or could be – taken off this field. We had a chance to persuade the inquiry inspectors that the field should be deleted from the local plan and, if we kept this field, there would be little or no point in big companies eyeing up other bits of Fordhall. Müller already had their slice, and the lower meadows were too wet to build on.

At last, we had something tangible to grasp. If the land was deleted from the local plan, there might be more chance that the landlord would look on us favourably if we wanted to buy it. We needed to gather support for this new campaign and there, among all the paperwork Mum had hoarded over the years, we found the golden egg: a box full of letters sent in support of Fordhall when Müller took their slice of the farm in the early 1990s.

We contacted all those people, and a whole lot of new people who were beginning to hear the first whispers about the Fordhall Project, and liked what they heard. New letters of support came back and we felt encouraged that not only did the writers think we should keep Fordhall's field, they gave us their full backing for the entire project. We canvassed as many people as we could think of for support. We had one opportunity to make a case for the field, and if we blew it we scuppered all our chances of ever getting the project off the ground. But I'm a logical thinker, and I couldn't ignore the fact that Mike could just be building up false hopes and taking our efforts away from looking for a council house or somewhere to stay when we had to leave. I didn't want to struggle on at Fordhall for another year arguing about how to pay for the rent and worrying about more debt.

In the meantime Mike had arranged a meeting with Mr Godsal and returned with an interesting, if mixed, message. 'He didn't say they would sell it to you,' he said, 'but he did say they were keeping all their options open.'

This was a bit more than we'd expected; not much more, but enough to make us think that we wouldn't look totally out of our depth if and when we ever sat down face-to-face with the landlord to discuss the future of Fordhall. After Christmas our family gathered around the open fire in the club room and talked about the year about to end. There had been a lot of disappointments, and plenty of resignation with regard to our future. Dad was not at all well and Mum was very depressed. We still had no money and no generous benefactor had come forward to give us any. The farm was a tip and the notice to quit in March next year was there in black and white.

Chapter 11: Ben

Sometimes, walking around the farm, I would find myself in tears thinking that all the family history and land that Dad had dedicated his life to could be lost and maybe even built over. But we did have the tiniest flicker of hope, ignited by the unlikely combination of three Germans and a jolly, enthusiastic Scot who seemed to see something in Fordhall beyond the collapsing farm buildings and thistle-carpeted fields. We could hardly allow ourselves to hope that 2004 might bring a bit more of this good fortune into our lives. I was cautious, but optimistically so. If Fordhall had been resurrected by Dad once before, maybe it could be resurrected again.

12

Charlotte

E ven beginning to think about saving Fordhall was a daunting task. We had spent so many years fighting against the ghost of a landowner. He had money and Fordhall had development potential. This was a pretty powerful combination and we couldn't see what we could offer instead.

Those early days were spent tirelessly searching for organisations or individuals who might be able to offer help. I cooked porridge mixed with crushed bananas to stave off the intense night-time cold that gripped Fordhall from September to May and I sat, wrapped up to my armpits in a duvet, tapping at the keyboard until I fell asleep. Mike had assured us that the farm was worth saving and that there were many people who would be interested in helping, but to be honest we couldn't quite believe it. Although I was much more positive than Ben, even I had my doubts about the appeal of the farm beyond the Hollins family. It was easy to explain why we wanted to save it, but we found it amazingly hard at the time to see the value it would or could have for other people. As a farmer you are always told how fickle customers are. They shop on price, with no consideration for the farmer or the farm behind it. With this in mind, how could we even contemplate getting the kind of public support we knew was needed to fight our case? Nevertheless, with no money, people power was our only hope.

One of our very early supporters was Danny O'Sullivan from Leaside Wood Recycling Project in London, already a great help to our family in hard times via his regular deliveries of free wood for our fire. Strangely, he had had the same ideas for the farm as Mike, and had written them down years before when Ben and I were still at school. He even stayed at the farm for a while and tried to gather support, but Ben and I were too young and not interested enough at the time to help. Dad was not at his strongest and Mum was struggling to keep the farm afloat, so Danny went home and the ideas got buried.

His help and support when he returned were invaluable. He brought an enthusiasm and energy to Fordhall each time he visited.

'Fordhall Farm is amazing,' he would say. 'It has sustained its vitality through ten years of decay.'

Danny believed that anything was possible, and he had a deep-rooted passion and belief in the importance of Fordhall and Dad's work. At a time when Ben and I were struggling to see a way forward, and through Mum's deepening depression, Danny was a breath of fresh air: a complete inspiration. At the time, both he and Mike were our knights in shining armour.

However, we all knew that large numbers of people would be needed if we were to succeed, and that we had to have the backing of the local press. It was essential that the local paper believe in Fordhall and its future as much as we did. Yet I still had not grasped what it was that made Fordhall different or would enthuse people enough to help save it. I could not understand the desire people might have to be part of a farm again, and this made selling the message to the press very difficult. Nevertheless, one winter's afternoon in 2003 I put on my old walking boots and set off for the office of the town's local paper, just over a mile from Fordhall. As I walked, a sheaf of papers and campaign leaflets under my arm, I mentally rehearsed what I was going to say to the reporter. When nerves didn't render my mind a complete blank, I imagined the reporter dashing upstairs with his shorthand notes, leaving me standing, mouth agape, while he breathlessly told the editor that he had this week's front page splash.

'So . . . tell me again. It's a farm, right? And you want to save it from . . . what?' said the local reporter on my first visit.

She stood in front of me, all made-up and power-suited, in contrast to me in my fleece and knackered hiking boots. Her pen was at the ready on her pad, but she wasn't writing anything. She wasn't getting it.

I struggled on. 'Well, it's been in the family for generations, and my Dad's run it as an organic farm for over sixty-five years. We want to save it from being developed, and we want to run it ourselves, me and my brother, and we want to . . .'

'Hang on,' she cut in. 'So you want to buy this farm, right, and save it from being built on, and you want to find someone to buy it for you?'

'Yes, but it's not just for us,' I stuttered, the implication of what she was saying dawning on me horribly. 'It's been organic for so long and Dad's farming system means that we have lots of different grasses in the pasture.'

'Well, that doesn't mean anything to me, really,' she shot back. 'A field is just a field at the end of the day. It sounds to me like you just want someone to buy your house for you.'

The sad thing was, she had a good point. Why would anyone, apart from us and a clutch of anti-corporate eco-warriors, be remotely interested in helping to save Fordhall? Mike told us that people would be interested if we told them about the project, but here, in the offices of the local paper, was the proof that it wasn't necessarily true. What this meeting did do was force me to look at Fordhall from other people's point of view. The reporter was right in a way. Why would anyone want to save Fordhall Farm when it meant nothing to them? It was not their home, their life, or their business. I felt as though I was too close to the farm and the story to be able to make objective comments. I left the office, feeling completely deflated.

While the journalist might not have empathised with our story, she did actually write a fair account in that week's paper of what we were hoping to achieve at Fordhall, and we were pleased that the message was out around the town. We needed support, written or in person, at the local planning inquiry, to be held at the district council offices in Wem on 6 February 2004.

I was inspired by an email I received from the Shropshire Wildlife Trust, one of the many hundreds of organisations I'd pestered over recent weeks. If they could see what we could see, that this land was unique and important for farming and wildlife conservation, then theirs would be a weighty voice to use. In his email, the Trust's director, Colin Preston, said he was 'most sympathetic' to our position, and he liked the ideas we were putting forward, even if £2 million was 'a little expensive'. But he offered to come and meet us, and we arranged for him and his colleague John Hughes, the Trust's development manager, to visit us at the end of January.

Chapter 12: Charlotte

One night, sitting alone in front of the fire in the bar room, exhausted from the hours at Cheswardine, plus all the project work I was ploughing through, not knowing if I was completely wasting my time with it or not, I took out my diary and made an entry.

I feel in despair about the whole project and I'm feeling very cold. The weather has taken a turn for the worse. The fire is full of logs, but the only areas of activity in terms of the fire are round the sides of it. I sit, cold and confused, watching this fire burning, but not providing me with any heat. After sitting patiently, without me realising and as if from nowhere, the whole fire is burning vigorously, producing an immense amount of heat. I wonder whether this might happen with the farm and the project. At the moment we are getting so much advice from different areas, but we are not generating much heat.

It was a prescient entry. Two days later, Ben and I took Colin Preston and John Hughes on the grand tour of Fordhall Farm. In the little office we'd cleared for ourselves, Colin and John spoke to Dad, and Colin remembered he'd read Dad's auto-biography. It made Dad's day to talk to someone who had not only read his book but was also interested to see what the next generation of Hollinses were doing here. We talked them through the project, then prepared for the real highlight of their visit – the walk across our fields.

It had been raining and we were up to our welly tops in water as we clambered through the water meadows close to the meandering section of the River Tern that forms the farm boundary on the south side. With very few livestock and a lack of management, Dad's old stick drains had blocked and the pastures had become waterlogged. It was a patchwork of wild flowers, reeds and dead grass from the previous summer. But John and Colin were men used to adverse conditions and they waded through mud and water like a couple of snipes. We came up through the lower Long Meadow and were just preparing to climb the hill of the Dutch Barn Field back to the farm, when John suddenly stopped dead. A bright, energetic individual with plenty of character and real knowledge, John's enthusiasm for Fordhall was growing with every soggy step he took.

'This,' he shouted, 'is amazing! It's truly amazing! It's nothing short of an oasis in an agricultural desert!'

We had to laugh. 'It's a bloody mess, more like,' replied Ben, aware of how run-down these fields had become. He had also become conditioned by his agricultural course to look at the fields in a purely commercial light.

'Yes it is,' John agreed, 'but what a beautiful mess! The wildlife here, it's incredible. What an experience, just being here. There's no question it has to be saved. No question at all.' Evidently, John could see the other benefits of Dad's fields and the role they were playing in shaping the natural landscape, even on this dull January afternoon.

Dad had told us many times about the diversity of plants and animals on these meadows, but here was someone else echoing those words, and offering to help in whatever way he could. These were people who knew what they were talking about, and loved what they saw. Granted, they weren't about to throw money at us, but they made it clear that they wanted to form some kind of partnership with us, officially backing us and possibly offering to act, under their charitable status, as a holding mechanism for any money we raised.

I was elated and even Ben, normally reserved, had a smile

on his face. We got a fire going in the club room once they had gone and we watched it burn furiously, protecting us from the creeping chill. This time it burned brightly, with no false starts or hesitations. When an email came from Colin Preston two days later, saying he'd been badgering Mike Scott, the head of planning at North Shropshire district council, about us and the forthcoming public inquiry, I knew we had made a real ally.

The inquiry was looming nearer, and as Colin had made advances to the planners on our behalf, I decided it was only right to follow them up. I plucked up the courage to ring Mike Scott and talked to him about the local plan, the Fordhall Project and the history of planning here. He was more than sympathetic; in fact he seemed very happy that Müller was expressing an interest in developing a site away from Fordhall. He also said that around one hundred letters of support had been sent to the council. They were astounded by the response. So all the door-knocking and catching up on old friends had paid off; we had a groundswell of support under us and tacit approval from a council who presumably didn't want to see more trouble at Fordhall Farm. This could open the way for meaningful dialogue with the landlord. We just had to stand up at the inquiry and speak.

'Ben, please . . . !'

My brother: hard-working, supportive, imaginative, practical, but incredibly stubborn when he wants to be. Not one for making a show of himself unnecessarily, and he was adamant he wasn't going to stand up in a suit, in front of a lot of other suits, to make a case for Fordhall Farm. He was also nervous that continuing to follow Mike's plans was building up false hopes and wasting precious time. Despite backing me up loyally in all my efforts for the Project, he was much more cautious than I was.

'Oh come on, Charlotte,' he groaned, 'you do it. You're good at talking. You're the one with a degree. You know about this type of thing. And you're a . . . '

'A woman?'

'Well, yeah. You are. You're a natural talker. I'm not. Not in front of loads of people, anyway. I'd be too nervous, and muck it all up for us.'

He was only nineteen. He shouldn't have to be doing this. But Dad couldn't do it, his health was not up to it. And it would have been too much for Mum. She had fought for too long and did not feel she could think straight enough to put across a logical argument. Mike was going to speak, but we were the Hollinses and we had to say something. Besides, we were in this together.

'No way,' I said, holding firm. 'You've got to say something, Ben. Why don't you explain why losing the field will ruin the whole farm? You could draw a map or something, and explain it bit by bit. Once you get going you'll be all right. If you start making a mess I'll jump in and help you. Promise.'

'Do you?'

'Of course. I wouldn't leave you hanging out to dry. You know I wouldn't. Come on, Ben. If you don't speak, and the planning goes against us and the field gets built over one day, you'll regret not standing up there. Imagine losing that field, just for the sake of a few minutes' talking.'

He threw me a teenage look from under his dark fringe. 'All right then,' he said to my relief. 'Does this mean I have to wear a suit?'

'You will have to go in something a bit smarter than your jeans and wellies.'

'Of course I will. I'm just not wearing a tie, that's all.'

I could have pressed him on that, but I stopped. He was coming and he was speaking, and that was all that counted.

We went en masse to the council offices in Wem; me, Ben, Mike, Mum and Dad. The meeting was scheduled to start at 10 a.m. We were as relaxed as we could be – Mike Scott had told us it was an informal meeting, just a few people round a table, a presentation and that was it. No need to panic.

But when we arrived the scene was quite different. The council chamber was huge, and it was full. The inquiry inspector was sitting at a high table along one wall, and everyone else perched on long benches like a flock of vultures. The inspector faced a row of chairs for the viewing public and, on either side of him, lined up against the walls, were long tables for us and, opposite, the Müller contingent and their lawyers. It was a daunting scene. I felt sick, my heart was in my stomach and I wanted to go home. I wasn't going to show it, though, not least in front of Ben, who I knew might go to pieces at any moment. Sitting on the benches I recognised various land agents and a smattering of the big boys from Müller. Some of them were here for other bits of the inquiry involving land around Market Drayton, but evidently there had been enough talk generated about our case for them to want to stay. There was also a lot of protesters who didn't want Müller to move north across the A53. Neither did I, really, but I certainly didn't want them to move west on to our land. Again.

With nerves kicking in and without really taking any of it in, we listened to some of the other bits of the inquiry. The men from Müller spoke, followed by the council. As we expected, both made their separate cases for development on the north side of the A53. I was simultaneously trying to calm myself down yet psyche myself up for our turn, but when it came my heart nearly leapt out of my chest.

'So,' said the inspector, shuffling his papers, 'land bordering the A53 tenanted by Fordhall Farm. The proposal is for the deletion of this twelve-acre piece of land from the local plan. We have three speakers representing the Hollins family and the Fordhall Project. Who's first?'

The suited-and-booted waited expectantly. Mike stood up and, as Fordhall Project manager, introduced the project and its aims. My task was to put meat on the bones, to explain the background to the project, why it was important for us and the wider community and how we might implement it. Then, I played my trump card: Agenda 21.

Some weeks earlier, Danny O'Sullivan, our friend from the wood recycling project, had rung to ask how we were doing. I told him about the planning inquiry and how we had the chance to get our bit of land away from development potential.

'Wicked,' he said. 'Why don't you hit them with Agenda 21?'

'How do you mean?' I asked. I'd heard of it, but didn't really know what it was about. So he filled me in, explaining that each local government has their own document, which guides their decisions and moves them towards a more sustainable way of thinking. This document pushes the council to achieve many of the aims that Fordhall also wanted to fulfil. The introduction to our local Agenda 21 read:

The Government's strategy for sustainable development in the UK – 'A Better Quality of Life' – shows us how sustainable thinking needs to be part of everyday life and not something that's switched on for special occasions. It needs to be at the heart of economic, social and environmental decision making, and in everyday behaviour. Sustainable development is about longer-term thinking when making decisions, and what we stand to lose if we persist in going for the short-term expedient, in a world of finite resources.

It was perfect. So, I recited this during the planning inquiry.

'We will show, at Fordhall, that without sustainable thinking and actions, our future is not so rosy, and that thinking and acting in such a way is much simpler than many think. It is not about thinking about how we will live in ten years' time. It is about acting and moulding our way of living today to accommodate the future.

'What about the other headings within the Agenda? "Wildlife and Biodiversity": well, Fordhall is about working alongside nature to achieve healthy and profitable crops and livestock. "Food and Farming": we will continue to promote chemical and additive-free food that is wholesome and sustainable. "Building and Landscape": we will sell locally to reduce food miles and involve as many local enterprises as possible to promote and highlight the quality of Shropshire's environment.

'But, Inspector, to be able to support the local agenda in such a way we need to have the Project, and this is based upon the character, heritage and decades of research at Fordhall. It is exemplified in the year-round grazing system, which simply would not work without the use of the twelve-acre field in question. Let's all work together on this.'

I sat down, and Ben got up, cleared his throat, and began to give his tuppence-worth. He was brilliant. He explained all about the foggage system of farming, and how the loss of this field would make the farm unviable. He had his map, and he pointed out the different fields, describing how the Cottage Field varied from the Mill Meadow and the Long Meadow in texture and summer/winter grazing. I looked at Mum and Dad and they were smiling, really smiling, the first time they'd looked happy in ages.

Ben sat down, and we both kind of flopped forward with relief. By the general tone of the subsequent debate it became obvious what the result would be, even though we knew the official decision wouldn't be announced until much later in the year. Our land would be deleted from the local plan, and while it wouldn't yet go into greenbelt status, we had steered development away from Fordhall until the next development plan in 2011.

The meeting finished in the way all meetings finish, with small huddles of people chewing over the past few hours' events. Our hands were shaken by various people, congratulating us on our presentation and offering their support for the Project. A representative from the Campaign to Protect Rural England (CPRE), who had been objecting to Müller going across the A53, came over and apologised for not helping us with our case. He would be in touch, he said, when we were more firmly established.

Then, a hand appeared out of nowhere and held on to mine.

'That was a remarkable presentation from you all, Miss Hollins, very impressive indeed. I just thought I'd come over to say that.'

I looked up, and almost fell over. The hand belonged to Ken Wood, the managing director of Müller. After all this time; all the hassle, the loss of the ten-acre field in the early 1990s, the effect on the family, here he was congratulating me. I returned the handshake but I hardly knew what to say. He seemed completely genuine with his compliments.

'Hello, Mr Hollins, it's good to see you're still fighting.' He turned and shook Dad's hand respectfully. In a friendly fashion, he said to me: 'Some of his cows once came over on to our land, and I knocked on the farm door to let him know. We got talking, and he told me everything about Fordhall. He showed me the grass and the soil.' He turned to Dad again, smiling. 'You are the only person to get me climbing over a barbed-wire fence in my suit, Mr Hollins.

'What you two did up there today was very commendable,' he continued more seriously. 'I wish you the best of luck.'

I couldn't believe what I was hearing. The man fronting the firm that threatened our very existence was now offering us encouragement. It was a surreal and unimaginable end to the day, and our minds began to buzz with ideas and possibilities.

13

Ben

We came home from the planning inquiry fairly sure that our twelve-acre field was safe from development, at least for the foreseeable future. But any elation we felt was quickly followed by a deep intake of breath, the kind you need before you take the first step up a very big hill.

Talk on the farm now turned to us taking over the tenancy with a view to buying the farm sometime in the future. I was starting to see the possibilities of my actually taking over Fordhall and farming it the way I wanted to. Only a few months ago it had seemed like an impossible dream, but now there seemed to be a narrow window of opportunity. Of course, the landlord held all the aces. If he saw a better offer he would no doubt take it. We knew, however, that he couldn't do anything while Fordhall's future as a working farm hung in the balance, and the results of the planning inquiry weren't due until August. Surely there couldn't be any harm in us putting a proposal forward in the interim, and seeing how we got on?

But we still had the eviction date of the end of March looming ahead of us. If the landlord wasn't going to change his mind, we needed to know sooner rather than later. We would have to find a new home that would be comfortable for Dad. And we would have to sort through years of paperwork, old clothes and toys, and a library of newspaper and magazine clippings on subjects as far apart as Permaculture and Princess Diana. There was no way everything we had would fit into a three-bedroomed council house in Market Drayton – if we were lucky enough to get one.

It was time to start badgering the landlord for a meeting. We wanted to be in on one of the regular get-togethers of the trustees who looked after the estate that owned Fordhall, or at least get ten minutes with the landlord himself whenever he could spare the time. Through Mr Godsal we tried several times to arrange something, but with no result. They were either ignoring us completely, or being very careful about when they would actually speak to us and what they would say. In short, we couldn't work out what they were up to, and so we had little choice but to remain in the odd situation of preparing to move out while planning for a new future at Fordhall.

While the landlord had yet to show his hand, there was movement within the Fordhall Project. Mike, the man who had had a vision of something other than a run-down farm and its odd inhabitants when he first came here, announced that he would be leaving us to go to Germany with Dagmar. They were getting married, and she had always wanted to go back to her native home. We were sorry; Mike had been a good advisor and a great friend, and he had got us to a place we never thought we'd be. Dagmar too had kept up Charlotte's spirits during some of the trickier moments of the past few months. We would miss them both, and we were sad to lose their invaluable help and good advice.

We did, however, have someone else we could turn to. Richard was a professional fundraiser whom we'd first met around Christmas, after he'd read about the farm in the local newspaper. He impressed us with his knowledge, and he was keen for us to meet up with the landlord to get across to him an idea of what was going through our minds. He offered to draw up a business plan and give us advice on setting up the farm business in return for future payment for his services when we could afford it. This meant we could use his experience and business skills right now, even though we had no money. He also suggested that a big clean-up of the farm would help us convince the landlord that we meant business. It was something we already knew, but had so far shied away from. Getting rid of all the scrap metal and abandoned vehicles was a massive task, but if we were serious about drawing a line under the past it had to be done. We also had to tackle the house, an even more difficult job than clearing the farm yard because we knew we would have a fight to part Mum from her clutter. The farm was in such a bad state it was impossible to know where to start. It seemed that whatever you did there would always be some other mess or crumbling building nearby that overshadowed the work you had just done.

But start was exactly what we had to do. The next two weeks of February 2004 were spent on a massive clean up. Charlotte and I worked like Trojans in startlingly cold weather to get rid of all the eyesores that reinforced the general view that the Hollins family could no longer manage Fordhall, and therefore had to go. In part, this was a cosmetic exercise to show the landlord we were serious about running the farm.

But it was also about breaking with the past; our parents had farmed and farmed well, but they could farm no longer. We wanted to be in charge now, and we wanted to prove to ourselves that a new era was beginning. I borrowed a tractor from Clive, a neighbouring farmer I worked for at weekends, and a big trailer from Danny O'Sullivan, and literally dragged all the scrap metal – cars, caravans, oil drums, broken farm machinery, everything – off the farm and to the nearest scrap-yard. We scraped together enough cash to pay a contractor to cut all the hedges around the farm – no mean task – and we hacked a path through the nettles. After two days scything and mowing we eventually saw our gorgeous garden once more. It was the first time anyone had cut the grass there in two years. The last person to do it was Charlotte, who had simply cut a small, person-sized circle in the middle of the garden one summer and had lain there lazily reading in the heat, undisturbed amidst the three-foot-high grass.

Despite the fact that my first-year exams at Harper were looming, I mowed the whole farm in February. The grass was two foot high from years of under-grazing and most of the grass at the bottom seemed dead, but it needed to be cut to tidy it up and show we were concentrating on really looking after the farm as well as tidying the yard. Besides, if we were to take over we would need some pretty good grazing to try and make money out of what few livestock we had. Cutting the old grass would make way for the spring's new growth and uncover the clover whose nitrogen-fixing properties we needed to help feed the soil. If nothing else it would make it easier to find the cows and sheep! During the summer the grass was often so long it was virtually impossible to see the few animals we had. Our six Suffolk lambs had free run of 140 acres – most of the fences were nonexistent or had big holes and gaps so it wasn't easy to contain them in one area. They had become almost like mountain sheep they were that wild.

Inside the house, Mum and Charlotte removed a huge collection of old newspapers from under the club-room table and took them to be recycled. They dusted and de-cluttered all the mantelpieces and put a new coat of paint on the walls. Mum even stayed up until 2 a.m. two mornings that week to help Charlotte finish painting the lounge. Finished, the rooms looked spacious, warm and welcoming. Mum also uncovered and polished the old oak table in the club room. She'd always had it covered with a tablecloth to stop it from getting scratched, but on this occasion she allowed us to show it off for what it was. A grand old dining room table that could comfortably sit ten guests for a dinner party.

We noticed the difference around the farm almost straight away. It not only looked better but it felt better too. Spring wasn't far away and there was something about all this hard manual graft that felt optimistic and energising. It was also very timely, because we heard that Mr Godsal had finally agreed to visit us in the early part of March. It was important that we and the farm set the right tone. He would take all the information he gleaned back to the landlord and his report would be crucial in determining whether we had a chance to stay here. We had one opportunity to look and sound good, and we were determined not to waste it.

As his Range Rover crunched up the drive and we heard him opening the gate, we dashed round the house one last time to make sure everything was in order. There was no way we were able to get it up to showhome standard, but we'd managed to take two carloads of old newspapers, tin cans and bottles to the recycling centre. We'd made a big effort every-where, and the ghost of a smile that passed over Mr Godsal's lips as he entered the farmhouse spoke volumes for our efforts. None of us had ever seen him smile before. To be fair, he'd not had much to smile about when it came to dealing with us. But it was there this time. Clearly, we'd impressed him. On this occasion Charlotte and I had decided to meet him alone, although we knew Mum was trying to listen from the other side of the door. We wanted to show him that it would be a completely new start and that we would be the ones pushing the farm's regeneration. From our achievements over the past few months we were trying to demonstrate that we could transform the farm if we were given a long-term tenancy.

'You have to leave on 26 March, you know. At the moment, that still stands.' The smile had vanished, to be replaced with the usual doom and gloom.

'We know,' I said, 'but you must be able to see we've made an effort here. You're right to say that Mum and Dad can't manage the farm any more. That's why we want to do it.'

'I can see that,' he replied, 'but what with?'

'We've told you all about the Fordhall Project,' Charlotte chipped in, 'and we're talking to a lot of people about finance. But it's going to take time. If we could take over the tenancy with a view to buying the farm in two years . . . '

'Yes, you've told me all that. But the fact remains that the existing tenancy runs out in less than three weeks and you have to go. I have to say, it doesn't look hopeful.'

'So there's nothing we could say or do that's going to persuade you otherwise, eh?' I could feel my temper getting the better of me. Why couldn't he see what was in front of him?

'I didn't say that,' replied Mr Godsal in a more measured tone. 'You know, if you had a cheque on the table now for £500,000 it might be a different story. I can see what you've done here in the last few weeks and I think . . . well, put it this way, I appreciate the fact that you've done it. But if you're truly serious about taking over here you'll need to convince the trustees by putting an amazing proposal on the table.'

'Well, we think we have a good one,' I said, 'and we just want the chance to show the landlord that ourselves.'

Mr Godsal paused for a moment while he took this in. 'Look, I think it might be worthwhile putting something in writing and getting it to me by Friday. Then I can have a careful look over it, and see what's feasible and what isn't. But I can't make any promises, I have to make that clear.'

In many ways it was the same story we'd heard time and time again. But there was a slight difference in his tone that we both latched on to. Was he secretly rooting for us? We thanked him for coming, held our breath as we showed him to the door, and breathed out again once we saw his car safely off the drive. We must have discussed the implications of his faint smile for at least an hour. It was a phenomenal thing to witness, and we both thought we might have discovered a chink in the armour he wore whenever he visited Fordhall.

'Oh no,' said Charlotte suddenly. 'Friday's the day we're supposed to be seeing the bank. I'll have to draft up this proposal today, then we can drop it off at Godsal's and go to the bank afterwards.'

We had an appointment to see someone from the bank about a loan, which would tide us over for a few months' rent and help us to buy some badly needed livestock. Without a few more cows and sheep we weren't much of a farm at all. We wanted £5000 from them, not a massive sum by any means. If we were students asking for a personal loan they'd have probably given it to us. But, so far, they hadn't seemed interested in two young people with a bit of get-up-and-go who wanted to set up a business.

We sat in the bank, feeling more demoralised by the minute as a woman with a bad haircut and corporate suit told us why we were too young, too ignorant and too inexperienced to run any kind of business, let alone the farm we had grown up on.

'I know we've got no collateral,' said Charlotte, hoping to turn this tough-looking bank employee around, 'but that's because we're a tenanted farm. We don't own it, we lease it.'

'Yes,' said the woman, 'but neither do you have any experience.'

'Of course we have,' said Charlotte. 'We've grown up there and worked on it all our lives. Ben's even studying agriculture at college. How can we have any more experience than that?'

'I'm afraid that "experience" in this case means paid experience. I'm presuming that you simply helped your parents out. Which doesn't count as experience.'

She consulted her notes for about the fifth time to make sure she was doing everything by the book.

'We've got plenty of people behind us, you know,' Charlotte went on, determined not to let this go. 'Ken Wood from Müller said he would help out with advice.'

'Yes,' the woman replied, 'but it still doesn't qualify you for a loan. You simply don't fulfil the criteria. You haven't ticked all the boxes and you don't seem to have any security.'

'But all we want is to be able to say on our business plan that we have access to a loan if we need it,' said Charlotte. 'Is there any other way of doing it? Any way at all?'

'You simply do not qualify for a loan. There is nothing I can do. I'm sorry,' she replied.

Needless to say, the meeting ended very soon after that. Charlotte was still angry about the woman's inflexibility that evening. We approached most of the high-street banks and found the same response from them all. We didn't even qualify for the small business loans scheme as we lacked experience and security. It was an extremely frustrating time. I knew we could do so much with that little bit of money. For a big high-street bank £5000 must be spare change, but it would have felt like a million dollars to us. Obtaining finance to start up in agriculture is a big problem for young people trying to enter the industry. The government is always promising to help small businesses and get young people into agriculture but as we discovered it is almost impossible if you just follow the conventional route. If we had been setting up a web design business they probably would have looked at us differently and thrown the money at us, but we weren't. Farming just doesn't give the returns on investment needed to service a loan or mortgage – well, not on a small scale like Fordhall, anyway.

We weren't deterred, though. We were still determined to make Fordhall Farm work. And we were sure that one day we would find a bank with vision who would be willing to take a risk. In the meantime we had to focus on the possibility of a face-to-face meeting with Mr Healey, the landlord. A meeting with him would be a very big deal indeed. Dad had only met him a handful of times; Mum, a resident at Fordhall for twenty-five years, had never even seen him. It was serious stuff for us to sit down with him and discuss the farm and our future, but if it was going to happen, it had to happen soon. If we hadn't heard anything by 26 March we would have to assume there was no deal on the table.

So we were pleased when Mr Godsal rang us to say he'd looked at our proposal. Not everything was to his liking. We wanted a long-term tenancy, perhaps three to five years, which would have given the legal protection of having a year's notice to quit. We didn't want a short-term, say twelve-month, tenancy as that would mean a lot of hard work and effort for us to lose it again after a year. That might put us in a worse position than we already were, and we had better things to do than get into deeper debt. However, it appeared that a short-term tenancy was just what the landlord wanted.

There were other bits and pieces that we had to take on board. Some we liked and some we didn't, but we felt Mr Godsal was doing his best to guide us towards some kind of agreement. Richard, our business advisor, helped us to formulate some intelligent questions that would make sure we were covering our backs as far as possible. We didn't want to commit to an agreement that would give us trouble somewhere down the line. Nevertheless, we didn't want to lose this chance in a lifetime through being inflexible. We would have to swallow some of the stuff we didn't like; what we were really opposed to we would have to fight against. Now we had a date for that fight, if that's what it was to be: Wednesday 24 March, lunchtime in the land agents' offices. We would attend with Richard, the business advisor. Representing the trustees would be Mr Healey and Mr Godsal. This was it. Just an hour and a half to present our case and convince a landlord who had wanted us out for the past ten years to give Fordhall Farm another chance, under new management. It was just two days before we were due to be evicted and we had no contingency plan if this failed. It was all, or nothing.

14
Charlotte

Looking back, I can see why so many people thought we were crazy. Dressed up in our suits, with our business plans tucked under our arms, we believed that we could make doors open and create opportunities in areas where doors had never been unlocked and opportunities were never offered.

I didn't really know what I was gearing myself up for as Ben, Richard and I drove to the offices of the land agents in Hadnall, several miles south of Fordhall, that morning in late March. Waiting for us were Mr Godsal and Mr Healey. One we'd met too often; the other was an unknown quantity.

I sat in the back of Richard's car, watching the banks of newly opened daffodils slipping by. It was one of those bright, blustery, cloud-filled spring days that make you feel like you've finally woken up out of winter's dark dream. A sense of sunlit optimism suddenly flooded through me; we had nothing, at least not in the bank, but we had passion. We were stepping into the light, and letting the excitement of new possibilities warm us through. I couldn't see that we would make it as far as meeting the landlord for him to then dismiss us with a wave of his hand and evict us only two days later. Surely that couldn't happen now? Then again, they had spent thousands of pounds trying to evict us through the courts. Why would they change their minds just as it looked as if they'd won?

During the car journey all our hopes and concerns played through my mind. We knew that our age could count against us, so we felt our best option was to turn this weakness into our strength. We would use our enthusiasm, energy and vision to convince the landowners that we were their best option and that we would do everything in our power to make it work.

Ben and I were putting ourselves in their hands. We had done all we could. We had fought through the planning inquiry, gathered support, begun to tidy the farm, and put time and effort into completing a business plan. It was now up to them to unlock the final door, so that we could really begin to make a difference at Fordhall. I was excited to have the chance to put our case forward in person – surely if anything was going to make a difference, it would be the personal touch. Just as it had worked with Dad when his father passed away and they were facing eviction all those years ago back in 1929.

The offices were located in a half-timbered, black-and-white Tudor-style building. I was thrown by its fairy-tale looks, and the fact that it was much smaller than I'd expected. It didn't seem to be the sort of place occupied by people I'd always considered to be bullies. The sense of disorientation continued as we were met by a friendly receptionist, who showed us to an executive meeting room and politely offered us a cup of tea.

Nevertheless, the surroundings were intimidating. Until now, I had felt confident about the visit, but as we entered the meeting room I suddenly felt my age. Twenty-one years old with my nineteen-year-old brother and here we were, trying to negotiate with powerful, assertive business people twice our age. I immediately felt small and out of my depth. However, there was a deep feeling of determination and stubbornness in us; neither of us intended to be defeated. Mr Godsal sat at the head of the table, looking stern. Whatever smile he'd let slip at our last encounter had now gone. It was no surprise to see him this way – he had a job to do after all. The surprise was Mr Healey. He looked personable, likeable even. Someone who would listen to us carefully without jumping to conclusions, not the harsh impersonal landlord we had envisioned him to be. Yes, he appeared every inch the serious businessman, and yes, I knew he was going to ask us some tough questions, but I felt he would actually listen to the answers.

We started to talk. I tried hard not to babble, but my nerves were gaining the upper hand. I wanted to show them how enthusiastic we were, how we could and would find ways of doing all the things we wanted to do at Fordhall. They wanted to know figures. We pulled out our business plan, and tried to counter everything they were asking, however negatively, with a positive. Mr Godsal was grilling us, but Mr Healey seemed to be holding back, offering us verbal lifelines with the occasional leading question and pleased expression; his eyes said that he was listening to what we were saying. They were challenging us, that's for sure, but it didn't seem to be malicious; on the contrary, I felt they were taking us very seriously indeed.

'Please try to draw a line under the past,' I said, trying to avoid us being drawn into the woes of the farm. 'We realise Fordhall's been left to deteriorate, and we know Mum and Dad can't cope with it any more. Think of us as brand-new tenants coming in to take it over.'

We tried to use our youthful enthusiasm to introduce a sense of opportunity in their thinking. We wanted them to feel that they were not only doing this for themselves, but that they were helping two young people fight for their home and realise their dreams. We wanted them to connect with Fordhall.

The farm had degenerated so badly, they argued, that it was barely viable, even for a new tenant. How would we raise money to buy livestock?

'I'm working off the farm when I can,' said Ben, 'milking cows on a dairy farm and doing a bit of parlour fitting. Charlotte's working at a nursing home. We can definitely cover the rent. We also have plans to set up a farm shop; selling our own meat direct to the public will provide us with an income. We've done all the calculations in our business plan.'

'Would it be a good living?' they asked.

'Well no,' I said, 'you can't really say that, but it would be enough to live off. But it's not just about making money, although obviously we have to make enough to live on. Farming is about more than that, it's a way of life. It's also the ethos and heritage at Fordhall, and the hope of opening it to the public to help people understand the connections between food, farming and the landscape. We can really make this work, we just need the opportunity to try.'

But could we? We were working on ideas and ideals, not hard-headed business models. I was out of my depth. But this was no ordinary project, and it required no ordinary thinking

Mr Healey seemed to want to hear that it would work. He was also keen to make the distinction between us and the past. However, he was giving nothing away about any plans for the future.

'If the farm was to be sold at some stage, could we have first refusal?' we asked.

They were non-committal, and I knew this worried Ben. He didn't want to put all his time and energy into building up a working farm, only to have the rug pulled out from under his feet when someone else made the landlord a good offer. He wanted the security of a long-term tenancy, five years at least, but I knew that the landlord was not thinking long term. They were certainly not looking to swap one long-term tenant for another.

A 'we'll let you know' ended the meeting. We had made the best case possible under the circumstances. Richard was enthusiastic and positive, but Ben and I sat in the car in near-silence, as flattened by the occasion itself as we were over the level of its intensity. Back at Fordhall we headed straight into the kitchen and put the kettle on. Cups and saucers on the boardroom table were one thing; all we wanted now were big mugs of farmhouse tea We had barely taken three sips when the phone rang.

'Hello?' I said, thinking it might be Marianne or Barbara, our older half-sisters, who had both offered a lot of emotional support throughout the farm's troubles. They knew where we'd been and were probably eager to know the outcome.

'Charlotte?' a male voice enquired.

'Yes?'

'It's Mr Godsal.'

My heart leaped into my mouth. They'd never rushed to tell us anything, except the date of our departure. Whatever news he had must either be very bad or very good.

'We've been talking. We were pleased you came in today and we listened very carefully to what you said. I suggested to Mr Healey that we offer you a twelve-month tenancy at Fordhall in recognition of your hard work so far and your energy to take things forward. However . . . '

My heart sank. Had they now decided not to offer a tenancy at all? It was characteristic of them to build up our hopes and then squash them in the same breath.

' . . . Mr Healey did not think that this was long enough. He suggested that we grant you an eighteen-month tenancy to, in a sense, "earn your stripes", and to provide you with more of an opportunity to build things up.'

My heart jumped back into my mouth as he went on. Part of me felt elated that we had succeeded in gaining further security at Fordhall, but I also realised that eighteen months was still not very long to make a difference.

'I have to stress that this new tenancy will provide you with no security or rights at Fordhall after the eighteen months,' he continued. 'The tenancy is also conditional on your parents winding up the old company, Fordhall Hollins Ltd, and signing an agreement to say that they no longer live at Fordhall Farm.'

I knew this meant Mum and Dad wouldn't physically have to leave, rather it meant that any rights they had at Fordhall no longer existed. I thanked Mr Godsal, saying that I would speak to Ben and call him back.

Ben was sitting next to me in the small farm office, the place where everything seemed to centre these days. 'So . . . ?'

'OK, they have offered us a tenancy. Originally it was twelve months but Mr Healey extended it to eighteen months. He said he wants us to earn our stripes.'

Ben fidgeted and instinctively bit his thumbnail. 'Oh, I'm not sure, Charlotte. That makes me really nervous. It's not long enough to feel like we've got any real security and the bank certainly won't offer any funding over such a short term. I'm worried that we will put everything into the farm and then have to leave in September 2005, worse off than we are now.'

I understood him completely, but I also wanted to do this

more than anything else in my life. I knew that they would not extend the tenancy for any longer than eighteen months. The Farm Business Tenancy (FBT) agreements, now standard among landlords and tenants, were not the same as the old Agricultural Holdings Act tenancy that Mum and Dad had had. Those gave the tenant a lot of security, whereas the new form of tenancy agreement favoured the landlord over the tenant. An agreement for less than two years required only one month's notice to leave, rather than one year's notice. I knew the landlord was keeping his options open, not wanting to tie himself up anymore than he had to.

'But if we don't try we'll never know, will we? All right, we might be out on the streets. But we'll be out on the streets anyway if we say no now.'

Council housing had been applied for but nothing had been confirmed. If we were to leave, then there was nowhere else to go.

'I suppose. I just don't want to get into debt. I'd rather go now if that's what'll happen,' Ben replied.

'We're not going to get into debt if no one will lend us any money, Ben. So, let's not worry about that. Anyway, who knows what might happen in eighteen months. Let's at least try, we can always leave before the eighteen months if we feel it's not working. We've got this far. We can't quit now.'

'All right, let's do it. But can we let them know tomorrow? Give me a chance to sleep on it.'

15

Ben

Securing the tenancy just 24 hours before our eviction date was a massive weight lifted off my shoulders. At the same time I felt the new weight of responsibility that replaced it. Taking over and being responsible for 140 acres at the age of nineteen while trying to study for a degree and hold down two other jobs was going to take a lot of strength and determination. My friends at Harper Adams realised this and, to offer me their support and to take my mind off my worries, they organised a big night out, starting with a curry at the local Indian restaurant. There's a tradition at Harper that says if you're holding a pint and someone starts to sing the Harper Drinking Song you have to down your pint in one go. The song begins 'He's from Harper, he's a true blue' but is pretty unrepeatable after that. As it was essentially my celebratory night out for 'getting the tenancy', that song was sung all evening and I can't remember much of what happened. But it was just what I needed – a break from the troubles of the farm and a new start, albeit a rather hungover one. And it made an enormous difference to know that I had the support of my friends at Harper to fall back on.

Charlotte and I had work to do, more than we'd ever had before. We accepted the tenancy in principle, but there were a couple of areas we weren't entirely happy about. A covenant in the agreement stated that once the tenancy was finished we had to hand back the buildings in good condition. Given that they were in a terrible condition to begin with, we didn't want to be landed with a huge bill for their repair, so there was a lot of to-ing and fro-ing before we actually put pen to paper on the agreement.

There was also the question of Mum and Dad. The landlord was adamant that we'd only get the tenancy on the condition that our parents wind down the company they had to run the farm, and sign a letter saying they'd left Fordhall and were not long-term tenants any more. This meant they would lose all the rights they accrued as tenants over the years.

Of course, there was no question of them physically leaving Fordhall, but the principle had to be upheld and as the new tenants we could have them at the farm as our 'guests'. It was an odd situation, but the landlord was determined that a fresh start must be made and, however strange we felt about it, we had to agree. We were nervous about them signing anything before we'd actually signed the tenancy itself, though.

Through our accountant, Mervyn Davies, formerly Mum and Dad's company accountant, we set up 'Fordhall Farm Ltd' in mine and Charlotte's names. It sounded grand, but it was necessary for us to do it straight away, because of the legal protection it gave us. I found that very reassuring, as I knew the state of the finances and, despite all Charlotte's positivity, I was still nervous about getting into debt. Mervyn was great and worked for us for free for a year to help us get off the ground. Without help like this we couldn't ever have got over the first hurdles of starting a business.

While we still worked closely and made joint decisions on a day-to-day basis, the granting of the tenancy was the beginning of more clearly defined roles for Charlotte and me around the farm. Charlotte busied herself in the makeshift office, contacting all those who had got behind the Fordhall Project to tell them the good news, and finding new leads and new ways to take the project forward. As I chased cows or sheep out of the garden, I would see her through the office window, pen in hand and phone clamped to her ear, contacting anyone who would listen long enough to hear her pitch about the farm, the tenancy, and how we needed help. But we were still a team – our mutual goal was to establish a viable business and try to gain enough interest to save the farm.

We weren't short on ideas, but we were very short of money. The rent was £8000 a year – not a huge amount, admittedly, but we had to cover it and all the bills by working elsewhere, which meant that our time spent working on the farm was somewhat limited, at least to start with. We'd also put in a couple of thousand pounds each from our savings, we had an overdraft if we needed it, and we also had the good news just after we'd got the extended tenancy that the Prince's Trust would lend us another £2000. There was no doubt that we would be bumping along the bottom for some time to come, but as this was a farm we considered it would be a good idea if we actually made it look like one by investing in a few cows and sheep.

Along with my other jobs off the farm and studying at Harper Adams, I was now running Fordhall Farm. It would have been extremely useful to be able to turn to someone at this point and get some practical help and good advice, but there wasn't anyone available. Dad was pleased that we'd got the tenancy, and on the days when his illness didn't dominate he was a gem to talk to, but those days were becoming few and far between. The rest of the time he was confused, or just silent. It was hard to see, and even harder to bear when his knowledge and an extra pair of hands on a farm that needed so much doing with it would have been invaluable.

I couldn't moan. There was too much to do to start thinking that way. I had a thousand and one jobs to get on with: mending fences, re-hanging the gates, fixing potholes on the drive, painting the buildings where the whitewash was coming off. It was like building a farm from scratch, and it took up a lot of my time. I also had to think about our decision to improve the livestock levels, and that would mean a visit to the local cattle market. It wasn't a day I was looking forward to with much relish.

I knew it wouldn't be worth us buying any breeding cattle, because by the time they'd had their calves and they were ready to sell, more than two years would've gone by, and we were only going to be here for eighteen months unless we found £500,000 or more in the meantime.

So it would make more sense to buy store cattle that we could fatten quickly and then sell the meat through the farm shop we'd planned to open by the summer. They'd also double as four-legged lawnmowers, cutting the grass that had grown like mad across the fields. It wasn't ideal, and I knew we weren't going to be able to afford the biggest and best-looking animals, but it would be a start. By selling direct to the public through a farm shop we would have the opportunity to create a viable business, a complete impossibility if we'd sold them through the cattle market or to the abattoir. Besides, having a farm shop here would encourage people to visit and have a look round, and that was the whole point of the exercise.

I prepared myself for a visit to the cattle market. I'd been with Dad a few times in the past, but I'd just tagged along and not paid much attention. Now I was going with both Mum and Dad but, although I hoped they would give me moral support, I would be bidding for myself, surrounded by older, more experienced farmers. It was very exciting to think I would be buying some new cattle after all the years of selling. I didn't know much about the prices before I arrived and I knew it was going to be difficult to stand up and bid.

Cattle markets are noisy places at the best of times. Trucks and trailers rolling up and taking off again, the auctioneer going at it nineteen to the dozen over the microphone, the animals grunting and groaning in their pens before stumbling around the ring as a stockman herds them about with the aid of a stick – it isn't a place for the faint-hearted, even if you're only observing. The scent of the newcomer is powerful, especially in farming communities that have grown up with one another, and, as you enter the shed where the auction is taking place, you feel the stares of the clan gathered around the ring, as if you'd walked on to the set of a Western.

The Hollinses were part of the Market Drayton farming community, but at the same time, not part of it. We farmed, but we did things differently, and Dad, for all his sociability, was never one of the boys in that sense. That's not to slight anyone else; it was just that Dad did things one way and they did them another. On the other hand, through the various articles in the press and appearances on TV, everyone knew who Dad was and, by now, they all knew who I was too. Or at least that's what it felt like when I first walked through the doors of the store ring that Wednesday morning, an empty trailer parked outside waiting to take delivery of my first purchases.

I decided to go over and introduce myself to the auctioneer. At least then he would be able to spot me if and when I put my hand up. 'Oh, so you're Ben Hollins,' he said, taking my outstretched hand, 'I've been reading about you in the paper.'

News of the tenancy had been in the *Market Drayton Advertiser* and the *Shropshire Star*, and we'd done a couple of radio interviews, too. Not very successfully, I might add, but we'd got through them and they'd been helpful.

'So what're you looking for today then?'

I told him I was after a few heifers I could fatten up, but I didn't have much to spend.

'Well, if you hang on here there'll be a few cheaper Herefords and Anguses in towards the end. They're not much to look at, mind. I'll keep my eye out for you and give you the nod when they come in.'

Mum, Dad and I took a place in the terrace surrounding the ring and waited for a chance to bid. I watched the other farmers closely to see how they did it. The auctioneer set off at a cracking pace, and I could hardly hear what he was saying, never mind keep my eye on who was bidding at the same time. There was the occasional nod from under a flat cap, or a jerk of the head behind me. Someone else would raise a finger so quickly that it was almost down before I'd seen it going up. Refusal to continue bidding was marked by a shrug of the shoulders or a shake of the head. Business was completed in the blink of an eye. It was totally confusing and I was becoming more nervous by the minute, knowing that I had to bring home the bacon, or the beef at least.

Finally, a selection of low-priced, skinny six-month-old Aberdeen Angus heifers was ushered in and I looked at the auctioneer. He nodded at me, and I knew it was time. I shot my hand up like an eager schoolboy and I swear I could hear the sniggers behind me. I was determined to get between six and ten, but I couldn't afford more than about £120 for each of them. They were the bottom of the barrel but we needed them badly. So badly, in fact, that I ignored the deliberately intimidating stare of a wax-jacketed farmer opposite me, who was bidding against me. He wanted me to mess up so he could get the Aberdeen Angus heifers at an even more knock-down price. I was having none of it; I needed those skinny characters, and I needed them today. I braved it out, and eventually loaded them on to my trailer. I was almost sweating with relief to get out of the place.

'Oi, you!' A voice behind me was demanding my attention. It was another farmer I'd seen around the ring, checking me out.

'Yeah?'

'You're Arthur Hollins's lad, aren't you?'

'I am, yeah, that's right.' My heart sank at the sight of this red-faced bloke with stone-cold grey eyes. I was about to get another lecture on the folly of organic farming.

'I used to know your father well. Everyone does around here. Bit of a legend. Bit mad, but a legend. Stubborn old bugger, too.'

He paused for a moment, working out how to say it.

'I just want to say well done for getting the tenancy. Can't have been easy, deciding to take over that place. Half the folk round here thought it were derelict a long time ago.'

'Cheers,' I said, unable to think of anything more interesting to say.

'Well, if you ever need any help or advice, give us a shout. I'm always here on a Wednesday.' He gestured towards my trailer, with its herd of waif-like, supermodel-thin cows, and grinned. 'You're not going to lose 'owt on them, are you?'

I had to agree, but they were a start, all seven of them. Did I say seven? I meant eight. In my haste to get them back to Fordhall, I hadn't counted the cows as they walked up the trailer. The following morning I had a call from the auctioneer. Could I come to pick up one scared cow that had spent the night alone in Market Drayton Cattle Market, waiting for its new owner to pick it up? You live and learn.

16
Charlotte

I stood at the bottom of the garden the day after we'd secured the tenancy, looking out at the fields rolling below me. I felt a huge sense of achievement; at just nineteen and twenty-one, Ben and I were responsible for the running of a 140-acre farm that was like few others we'd ever heard of. But I also knew that we needed help, because I was determined that Fordhall would not fall into chaos. When I was a sixth-former I'd had a job at a local supermarket and the lack of communication there between staff and employers, which resulted in an inefficient and often chaotic workplace, highlighted to me how crucial clear communication is for any business. I made a promise to myself to keep everyone connected with the project informed about what we were doing, and I wouldn't be too proud to listen to any advice that was on offer.

I sent out an email to all the people we had met and contacted during the run-up to the public inquiry, letting them know that we were here for the next eighteen months at least. I told them of our plans to open a farm shop and nature trail and I stressed the long-term aim of raising money to buy Fordhall, and putting in place the educational resource and ecology exhibition centre. More important, perhaps, was the plea for help; advice, time, muscle, machinery, brain-power – we needed it all. I had grown to learn that you have nothing to lose by asking; the worst thing anyone can say is no. And the embarrassment of all the 'nos' was forgotten when someone said yes.

In the stillness of those spring mornings I heard Ben stumbling downstairs at ridiculously early hours to feed his animals before he got ready for lectures at Harper Adams. Very few people of his age would take on two demanding and stressful roles but he was really putting his back into it. By 9 p.m., when most teenagers would be scrubbing themselves up for a heavy night out, Ben was going to bed shattered. He never complained about it; he was showing maturity and skill way beyond his years. I helped him to unload that first batch of store cattle, and I'll never forget the look of pride across his face as he told me how he'd bid for them successfully, despite a bit of jostling at the ringside. He knew and I knew that these cows were not of the best quality, but we didn't care. They represented our future here, and we would look after them as well as they would look after us. We knew that the grass on Dad's pastures would soon build up their strength.

With Mervyn, our accountant, Ben and I looked at various ways of securing the farm on the community lines that we'd planned. None of us had any experience of working within this kind of structure, which meant that a lot of the meetings seemed to be fumbling in the dark with ideas about charitable status and not-for-profit organisations being talked over again and again. However, Mervyn's knowledge lay with limited companies and charities. Even he was not aware of the diversity of not-for-profit community structures that exist throughout the world. We wanted Fordhall to exist as a community resource, but we also wanted the flexibility to run it ourselves and make the decisions we thought were best for the farm's future. As we found out when we started looking into it, the disparate elements of public resource and autonomy to make our own decisions never seemed to match up in any of the business models we examined. We had to find a new way of working, and we waited in the hope that something or someone would lead us in that direction.

The legal attachments to the Farm Business Tenancy that Ben and I had been offered caused the agreement to take longer than expected to sign. With Mum and Dad having to leave the farm and return as 'guests', it was a time of insecurity and apprehension. Without the new signed agreement, and with more ties to the old tenancy being lost each day, we knew we were in a precarious position. Thankfully these feelings of insecurity were eventually put to rest when pen was finally put to paper on 14 May, only three days after my twenty-second birthday.

Taking over the tenancy had been great, but we had little time to celebrate. There was work to be done, people to contact and rent to be paid. But towards the end of May we thought we could finally let our hair down and gather together as many friends and supporters as we could for a party. It was our way of saying thank you to all those who had supported us through the planning inquiry by writing letters to the council, and many of whom had never visited Fordhall before. One great thing about living on a farm is that you're never short of space for a party.

The barbecue coincided with Dad's eighty-ninth birthday.

All year his health had been failing; the prospect of losing the farm had really taken its toll and he was very weak. We felt it was a good occasion to honour him and mark his life and achievements; after all, it was the legacy that he had created that gave the farm its magical atmosphere and was the foundation for its future potential.

This barbecue also gave us the incentive to sort out the house a bit more. Mum was still finding life very difficult and was mentally at breaking point. We knew, however, that removing some of the clutter from the house would help her just as much as it would help us, even if the process was painful. And Ben and I wanted to make a good impression for the supporters who had not visited the farm before. We wanted them to see that we were already trying to improve the place and were determined to make Fordhall somewhere to be proud of again.

The garden looked much better already and the rubbish in the yard had gone, but we had barely touched the house. The lounge and club room had been spruced up for Mr Godsal's visit in March, but the bar room was particularly bad; the walls groaned under the towers of newspapers, magazines and paperwork leaning precariously against them, and the ceiling was black with years of accumulated soot from desperate attempts to keep the house warm during the winter months. You couldn't even get to the TV, never mind sit down on a chair. We could not leave it as it was. Mum eventually agreed to take some of the old papers for recycling. Once the room was relatively clear, Ben and I set to scrubbing the ceiling and giving it all a quick lick of bright white paint. This may sound like an easy job, but scrubbing the ceiling alone took over half a day, and painting it another half a day. The carpet was also removed and cleaned, the old rugs full of holes caused by sparks from the open fire were thrown out, the curtains were laundered, the curtain rail fixed, and the cast-iron log burner was dismantled, cleaned, polished and put back together. They were purely cosmetic improvements, but it took days. When we'd finished, it felt like a completely different place. Gone was the dust, clutter and soot and in their place was a light, airy and friendly farmhouse room, just as I had remembered it from the restaurant days as a child. It felt immensely satisfying to see such a change in the house after all these years. Almost instantly it was filled with new hope and opportunity. Now, it felt like progress was possible.

Around fifty friends old and new made it down that weekend, and for the first time in a long while I was proud of Fordhall Farm. You could almost feel the new energy being breathed into the place with the arrival of all these people. I showed guests round and talked them through the history of the farm – the dairy days and the organic heritage – and they seemed to revel in an atmosphere that I'd previously found hard to detect. They really loved the farm and the land and were utterly taken by its character and atmosphere. Despite its dilapidation, they could see how great it once was and they could tell that it could be great once again.

That weekend made me realise that other people also recognised why our home was special. During the evening, a friend from university whispered a confession.

'Charlotte, you know at uni when you used to go on about the farm and it being built on?'

'Yes?' I said cautiously, wondering what was going to come next.

'Well . . . it's just that . . . sometimes I really didn't have a clue what you were talking about. I thought you were a bit obsessed with it all, to be honest, and that you should stop thinking about it and have a bit of fun instead, you know?'

I did know. I probably talked about it a lot. It seemed to be constantly dogging my footsteps at that time.

She carried on. 'I can see now why you talked about it so much. Being here, it has this kind of . . . richness about it. I dunno what it is. You can see how hard it's been, but it doesn't seem to matter. It's like there's something magical about the place.'

She laughed, but I understood what she was saying. There is a pull under this soil that is hard to define. It makes people do strange things, like invent revolutionary seeding machines to till its fields and take on the powerfully large corporations that threaten it. That night, my university friend pledged to revisit and work to help us with the farm and the project. She wasn't alone. So many people said they'd come back whenever we needed them. Encouraged, I struck while the iron was hot, got out my diary and booked them in for a month's time. We would have our first ever volunteer working weekend, and it would mark a new phase in the project.

Dad enjoyed the barbecue and was visibly moved when we gathered to sing 'Happy Birthday' around a large piece of oak that had had holes drilled in for the candles. He spoke a lot that evening, about the history of the farm and the happiness he was feeling. He could see that Fordhall was moving on to a new level and he was elated that people were beginning to return to the farm, for it was people who had given it the energy it had during the dairy and country club days.

Dad had always been a very patient and wise man, and despite his illness that hadn't changed. He wasn't as physically able as he once had been and he needed more and more care on a daily basis, but Ben and I were always aware that he was absorbing everything that was going on around him, even though he did not always comment on it. He offered advice whenever he saw that we needed it, but he was content to sit back and allow Ben and me to start Fordhall's next phase.

'I am keen to see how you manage on your own. You will learn much better that way,' he told us.

In May, Ben also started to clear out a little tool shed at the side of the farmhouse to make way for our first farm shop. The word 'shop' is grandiose for what it was, as it just about fitted one customer and Ben or me in at a time, but it would be a start while we saved up to convert one of the bigger buildings into something resembling a retail unit. The working weekend had been arranged for 26 and 27 June and we would utilise the volunteers to help empty the old cattle shippon, in the hope that our farm shop would one day move there.

The Friday before that weekend, we called a meeting of key people who had offered advice and support. Along with Mervyn and Richard, we had Philippa and Jeff, from the Market Drayton 'Taste of the Town' food company, our old friend Danny from London and John from the Shropshire Wildlife Trust. We also invited Ken Wood from Müller, but he couldn't make it, and not long after that we heard he'd left the company.

The meeting was to air ideas and opinions and everyone was given the chance to speak. It was a gorgeous summer's day, and we hauled a motley selection of chairs out of the farmhouse and into the garden so the meeting could be held in the open air. We all sat in a circle in front of the old farmhouse, with the sun shining on our faces and the birds singing in the trees around us. You could not help but feel optimistic in those surroundings.

We listened to numerous suggestions for getting Fordhall on the map, including the possibility of linking up with the

Caravan Club to provide a site for their members. We also heard about a national art event called The Big Draw, held every October, and we thought we might somehow jump onboard to get people down to the farm. The issue of the tenancy was touched upon, and the ways money could be raised to buy the farm – if that option became available – after the tenancy was up. We even talked about reinstating the famous Fordhall restaurant.

Some of what we heard would work, some of it wouldn't. The point was that we were listening to everything, and the word we heard most frequently, at least from the lips of John Hughes, was 'experience'.

'The important thing is to give people an experience,' he said. 'Give them an experience they will enjoy, and make them come back for more, give them a connection to Fordhall. You've got to give serious thought to the business side of things. Fordhall's unique selling point is itself, so sell it!'

Marketing and branding has always left me slightly cold. I'm suspicious of being sold something that has had to be packaged up in a fancy box because it can't sell itself on its own. I didn't want Fordhall to become a brand but I knew John had a point. If we couldn't 'sell' Fordhall as something people wanted to be part of, we couldn't carry through all our plans and ultimately secure the farm as a resource.

'But that's the whole idea, Charlotte,' John countered. 'You don't need to dress it up. What will sell Fordhall *is* Fordhall. It's unique – all you need to do is tell people that. They'll like the fact that it isn't hyped or marketed, and that in itself is a marketing tool.'

It was clever, and it fitted in with how we felt about the farm. We didn't want it dressed up as anything other than a working farm and a community resource, and John seemed to be saying that's exactly what could happen if we were smart about it. I'd been conscious in press interviews that I wasn't getting the message across strongly, but if I thought about giving people a 'unique experience' here, I found that the soundbites just flowed.

John's enthusiasm struck a deep chord with me. No matter how large the challenge, John knew there was a way to achieve it. I came out of that meeting buzzing with ideas for an 'experience', but I also knew that I had to prioritise and take things one step at a time. A whole bunch of loose ends were flying around in my head and, although they were all exciting, none of them quite tied up just yet. There was a haphazard plan forming somewhere out there, but nothing would happen without the nuts and bolts of this project being in place. We had to get the farm shop organised and start to sell our meat, and we had to face the prospect of ten or so unpaid volunteers staying with us for a weekend at Fordhall while they helped us to get the farm back in order. Suddenly, it began to feel as if we were actually in charge and beginning to make a difference.

17
Ben

A t last, we had muscle. If they'd stayed for a month, it still wouldn't have been long enough to do everything that was needed, but we only had a weekend and so we had to think about what was most important. Just across from the farmyard was an old cattle shippon that hadn't been used for its original purpose for many years. It had a rotten corrugated-iron roof, green mould growing like grass up its walls and no door.

Like everywhere else on the farm, it was full of junk, and so we spent that first volunteer weekend clearing as much rubbish out of there as we could. We burned what was burnable. The rest went to the recycling centre or for scrap. The volunteers were brilliant – most of them were Charlotte's friends from university and we all got on famously. It seemed more of a social event than a working weekend and they didn't seem to mind sleeping on sofas or the floor. We dodged some heavy showers, and it was interesting to see that, despite people getting a thorough soaking, no one wanted to shout 'Stop it! I've had enough!' There was real camaraderie among the volunteers; they knew they were the first people to have ever done anything like this here and they seemed to be proud of that. So proud, in fact, that lunch was forgotten about as we hauled tons of rubbish across the yard, and by 3 p.m. some people were beginning to look a bit jaded. We'd promised to cook for them if they came, but in our haste to complete the work it had slipped our minds. There were jokey mutterings about 'slave-drivers' as we finally put our tools down and headed towards the kitchen, where Charlotte was waiting with a big vat of vegetable soup.

To make selling our meat on the farm a viable concern, we had to outgrow our first farm shop in the tool shed at the side of the house and we had to outgrow it quickly. The old shippon we cleared would make an ideal farm shop. Even cleared of its junk and spruced up, it needed time and money spending on it, but at least it was serviceable and it could be an on-going project while we sold our meat from the converted tool shed.

In July, after several evenings spent putting a new roof on the old tool shed with the help of Ade Birch, a builder friend of mine, we were just about ready to sell the first Fordhall products of our tenancy. We had a small chest freezer that just about fitted into the shed, a cashbox and a counter. This was the sum total of our enterprise. Some of the pigs we'd inherited from Mum and Dad were ready for slaughter and one morning we attempted to usher a couple of them into my trailer. They were free-range and really didn't want to go in. We had to tempt them up with corn. Once they were in the trailer I headed for the local abattoir. It seemed a significant moment. Our first animals were going for slaughter and hopefully the start of our business would follow. We would pick up the meat in a couple of days' time, so while we waited we made a chalkboard from some old timber, wrote 'Farm Shop – Open Sat!' on it and put it at the end of our drive.

The day came to collect the meat. Charlotte and I went together. We were excited, not only because this was where we would start to earn money, but also because we'd had a few orders for fresh meat already, which customers said they'd pick up on our return from the abattoir. We had our boxes at the ready. We were doing it our way – fresh from Fordhall Farm, not compromised by supermarkets or anything like that. Finally, it was all coming together. Sort of.

'Errmm, sorry to bother you . . . ' The butcher, Steve, at the abattoir in Ecceleshall turned round, a slightly pained expression crossing his cheery face. He'd been good about us packing our meat there, as we had no equipment to do it at Fordhall, and we wouldn't have had the space anyway. What we'd neglected to mention was that we barely knew a ham hock from a piece of topside.

Previously, it had all been meat to us. Dad cooked it and we ate it. We didn't ask questions. Now, we had large white spaces to fill in on the front of our packaging and we hadn't a clue what to put. Charlotte and I turned over the cuts of pork in our hands, trying to make educated guesses.

'You couldn't tell me what this bit is, could you?' I felt like the complete novice I was.

'This *bit*,' said Steve, repeating my words slowly back to me, 'is a cut of mid loin. You might like to advise your customers that they can roast, grill or fry it. Any other parts you'd like identifying?' He was struggling not to laugh.

'Yeah,' I said, holding up another slab of unidentifiable flesh, 'this one.'

'Forequarter,' he said decisively. 'Shoulder to you. Perfect for a slow-cooked Sunday roast.'

I muttered my thanks, and carried on labelling. I could just imagine that evening's conversation in his local pub. But he was good about it, and later we went through the same procedure with our lamb. I was learning quite a bit at college, about improving daily live-weight gains and the efficiency of intensive barley-fed bull beef, but not about the final product or identifying cuts of meat, so there was nothing like a little on-the-job training to sharpen me up, even if I did feel like a prize piece of chump.

We took the meat home, put most of it in the freezer, and waited. The people who had ordered fresh meat came to pick up their orders. At 10 a.m. the following day we opened for business and by 11 a.m. we had a queue of customers outside the tool shed. Only two people could fit in at one time, and one of those was Charlotte or me.

We didn't have a lot to sell that first day, and we probably did about fifty pounds' worth of business. It must have looked so unprofessional, but perhaps there was quirkiness about it that people liked because they came back, and within a month or so we were bringing in £200 a week. It seemed amazing to us that customers had seen our chalked sign and taken a chance on coming up the drive. It was as small-scale as you could get. We were looking at the farm business on a day-to-day basis, though I was finding that I had some spare cash to buy a slightly better class of animal from the cattle markets.

I was also starting a breeding programme at Fordhall. We had four breeding cattle that we'd inherited from Mum and Dad and the plan was that they would calve next spring. My problem was that I did not have a bull and a decent one could cost hundreds, if not thousands, of pounds. The solution was to hire one. I found a bull-hire company locally, and the man in charge of the operation said he had a spare pedigree Aberdeen Angus, which he offered to drop off later in the week. It sounded perfect as Dad had always told me that Angus cattle will finish well on grass, with no need for extra bought-in feed.

I'd decided to put the bull in the paddock behind the Dutch barn for a couple of days to let him settle down, and I was excited when the day came for the delivery. The driver of the cattle lorry reversed up to the paddock gate and dropped the tail board. Charlotte and I could not believe our eyes when a six-foot-tall bull that must have weighed a tonne strode arrogantly down the tail board and marched into the paddock. He was a monster of an animal, and I wasn't at all sure how I would be able to cope with him. There are two types of Angus cow – the traditional British breed, which is short and stocky with good conformation, and the Canadian strain, which tends to be taller with less shape. This bull was definitely the latter, which was not ideal, but we couldn't afford to be picky.

The lorry left and, still in shock, I went in for my dinner. I was sitting in the kitchen gathering my thoughts about the new arrival when I heard the most almighty roar outside the kitchen window. It was the bull, who seemed to have left his new home and had come in search of me. Gingerly, Charlotte and I walked him back to the paddock, to discover he had literally walked through a five-foot wall to get out. We put him back in, hastily erected a temporary fence, and gave him some corn to help him settle down.

The next day, while feeding the pigs, I heard a succession of banging noises. I went over to the bull and watched in amazement as he slowly put his head to the ground and walked into the paddock gate. The gate bent like a cardboard box and he casually strode out. This damn bull was wrecking the farm! There was nothing for it but to get rid of him, so I rang the hire company and they collected him that day. After this short but near-disastrous experience I bought a cheap bull from the market, and when he had served the cows we had to sell him again to make our money back, but at least this time the farm was left intact.

In five months we were ready to progress from the tool shed to the renovated shippon. We were doing well, and I saw no reason not to expand. I bought another second-hand freezer, obtained an old soft-drink fridge from a man in a petrol station who was throwing it out, and had a shop counter made from recycled wood, given to us by our friend Danny from the Leaside Wood Recycling Project. Danny also helped me to put a roof on the bigger building, and we moved in in November. We only seemed to occupy a minute corner of this building, but it was a step up from the tool shed and the customers certainly appreciated not having to wait out in the rain. We were also selling a bit of locally produced honey and jam, and some organic vegetables grown by a local lecturer at Reasheath College. We grew slowly and we had a lot of ground to cover if we were ever going to make a profit. Our customers knew that, and they stuck to us loyally. Strangely, our own loyalty to what we were doing, and to the whole idea of the project at Fordhall, was about to be put to a very difficult test.

18

Charlotte

By September 2004 Ben and I felt we were on the right
path. In the six months since the tenancy was granted
we had learned to survive, and stand on our own two feet.
Although we were both still working long hours off the farm,
our shop was making a modest profit and we'd had a couple
of successful volunteer weekends, proving that an interest in
Fordhall could be turned into something practical and worthwhile. Our confidence had grown and Fordhall was shedding
some of its years of hardship. However, our heads were still
spinning with the ambiguities of setting up a working structure to manage the farm and the project.

Then just as we were trying to clarify and organise all the
advice we had had in our minds, we had a visitor. Clive was
a stout, well-built man who had obviously spent plenty of time
on a rugby pitch. He'd seen the sign for the farm shop on one
of his regular visits to the area and decided to call in to find
out what was happening to the place he thought had been

abandoned years ago. Clive used to visit the farmhouse restaurant with his local rugby club in the 1980s. Mum recognised him straight away. Although he was older he had apparently retained all the bounciness of character he had displayed during those rowdy evenings in the restaurant.

We sat around the big club-room table with large mugs of tea and ginger biscuits. Clive told us he was now a wealthy property developer and, as we talked about what we were doing and planned to do at Fordhall, I noticed that a light seemed to switch on in his head. Between us, we told him all the goings-on over the past ten years, the fight against eviction, gaining the tenancy and the faint possibility that we might try to buy the place one day. The room seemed to be filled with positivity and opportunity.

'Have you had it valued?' he asked, curious to know more.

'Yes, we did a short while back,' I said. 'They thought we were looking in the region of half a million pounds, maybe slightly more, but that doesn't include any hope value for development on the land, which would obviously increase the price.'

'Really? You know, I might be able to help. I'm really, really impressed with what you're doing here. The whole organic thing is amazing, and what better time to be an organic farm than now? Everyone's talking organic. This is a seriously interesting project. How would you feel if I went away and gave you a buzz in a couple of weeks with a few suggestions?'

He was full of enthusiasm for something, but I wasn't sure what.

'What do you mean, "suggestions"?' I said warily.

'Well, you know, helping you to somehow secure this place. I know a couple of people who I might be able to talk finance with. I'm just keen to help, that's all.'

Clive seemed a straightforward sort of man and, as we talked, he showed a good understanding of what we were trying to do at Fordhall. We were pleased to have met him, and he cheered Mum up as she was keen to share some of her happier moments at the farm. His visit, random as it was, was an indication of the way the project had been progressing until now. We never knew what was going to happen next, or who would next knock on the door. Each day almost felt like a twist of fate in itself, and each day gave us new optimism for Fordhall's future.

A couple of weeks later I went to Preston to visit some friends still at university and we overdid it a bit one night. All the work I was doing at Cheswardine Hall and on the farm caught up with me at once, and I was hit by a big wave of tiredness. As I sat on Preston station, waiting for the evening train home, I had a call on my mobile. It was Clive.

'Look,' he said, 'I know you've only met me once but I was really buzzed about what you're doing. Which is why I'm going to say something radical to you now, so make sure you're sitting down . . . I'd like to put in an offer to buy the farm.'

I wondered if I'd heard him right. The tannoy was blaring out above me and a London–Glasgow express had just ground to a halt beside the platform I was waiting on. I couldn't believe what I was hearing, and I said so.

'I'm serious,' he said. 'I'm really excited about this project. I think we could work out something amazing between us for Fordhall. Why wait until September next year to find out what the landlord might do? We could put in a great offer now and have it all sorted by Christmas.'

I was beginning to panic, through excitement more than anything else. I knew he was a property developer, and so he must have meant what he said.

'Wow. This is amazing, and very generous of you,' I said. 'I'll need to talk it through with Ben, Mum and Dad and get back to you.'

'OK. Just give it time to sink in. Tell the others, but don't fret about it. I'll drop you an email tomorrow and we can arrange a time for me to come up again and talk it through.'

I pressed the button to end the call and felt totally light-headed. We'd got this far by ourselves, but to secure the farm now would be amazing. We could concentrate on the project and the farm business, and not worry about what might happen to us in a year. It was almost too good to be true and this made me instantly cautious. I had always recognised that the things that you worked harder for generally gave better results than those you achieved easily.

Clive came up to Fordhall soon after and talked us through his ideas. He was determined that we should continue to farm organically and he wanted Ben to run Fordhall the way he wanted to. He was also committed to the educational side of the project and he wanted to see this developed in whatever way we wished. It sounded like a dream come true. Then he mentioned the farmhouse. He wanted to live there. He wanted to do it up and bring up his family in it. In return, he would build Mum and Dad a bungalow somewhere on the land, and a house for Ben and me close to the centre of the farm. The new properties would be fully central heated, newly decorated, clean, tidy, easy to maintain – all the things that Fordhall Farm wasn't. He was confident that this would please us and that we would jump at the offer.

He assured us that he and his heirs would never want to take over the running of the farm, and that he would put clauses into the contract to say so. He simply wanted an inheritance for his children. He was a nice guy: open, honest and understanding of our situation. He wanted to help us, and in return he wanted to live in the farmhouse. It seemed to benefit both parties. It was a quick, easy and pain-free solution to all our troubles.

But, this house – run-down, dilapidated, sometimes depressing and claustrophobic – was our home. It wasn't a trophy house or a country mansion-in-waiting. Here was where so much drama had been played out over the years, and here was where we had grown up; where we had laughed, cried, fought and played together. The farmhouse was the heart of Fordhall and neither of us could bear to let it go. And Ben and I knew that Dad would not be happy in a centrally heated bungalow next door to his familiar home.

Furthermore, Clive saw Fordhall as a commercial enterprise that could make money. We wanted to do well, but we wanted to become more than just a profitable enterprise. There is a different kind of wealth at Fordhall that means more to us than hundreds of thousands of pounds floating through the till. It's the richness of life and the land, the richness of friendship and the joy to be had in simple things. We were adamant about retaining this at Fordhall. Although the farm had to be economically viable, we did not want that to become the main driving force in our decisions. Above all, we wanted to keep things real, and saying yes to Clive felt like we were selling out.

Both Ben and I discussed the offer at length after Clive had left, but came to the same decision quickly. Although taking up the offer would have secured the farm, we knew that we would not have been happy with it in the long term. It would be better to leave at the end of the tenancy without securing Fordhall than it would have been to see it go down a path that we were not happy with. We would simply have swapped one distant landlord for another who wanted to be very involved indeed.

I confess though that I did drag my feet telling Clive. I knew he would be upset, because he'd seen a way of helping us for a relatively small price and we could tell that had given him a warm glow. I felt bad about letting him down, and when I finally plucked up the courage to phone him he seemed both shocked and affronted at our response. I don't blame him; he must have thought we were insane. We still had a year to go on the tenancy, with no guarantee of a first refusal if the landlord wanted to sell. Dad was ill, and the chilly house and its permanent state of chaos can't have helped. We had every reason to say yes, but we said no for the best reason possible – if we couldn't live in the farmhouse, we didn't want to live here at all.

I remember seeing Dad years ago, trying to move a large metal roller in the yard one cold afternoon with a series of improvised levers. I was about sixteen at the time, and I couldn't have been much help. Still, I thought I could see an easy way of doing it, and I told him so. He was eighty-three, and he really shouldn't have been trying to move something so heavy. But he continued to manoeuvre the roller into position, enjoying every minute of the challenge he'd set himself. It wasn't the easy way out, but it was most pleasing to him and he felt most satisfied at the end of it. Even if we were to leave Fordhall at the end of it all, Ben and I and Mum and Dad were happy with our decision to reject the easy way out.

19

Ben

U ntil I realised that we needed them, I was very nervous when it came to meeting the press. I was always conscious of saying the wrong thing, or not getting my point across clearly. I still didn't feel totally convinced that we had to go along with media interest at all. I'd rather just get on with running the farm and making sure we could stay here, but to do that we had to get people involved. And to get people involved we needed the press.

It took a while before we were both confident enough to give press interviews without worrying too much about the end result. Once we figured out that as long as we sounded positive and optimistic and could be ourselves without trying too hard, we seemed to be able to get our points across.

It hadn't always been like this. In the beginning we had trouble fending off difficult questions. We still hadn't learned to steer the conversation round to the message we wanted to get over. In February 2004, just before we got the new tenancy, we were interviewed for Radio 4's *Farming Today* programme. This was a big deal for us, because it went into the 'On Your Farm' slot and it would be twenty minutes long. That's a lot of words to pack into a radio show and it meant we could really talk in depth about Fordhall and what we wanted to do here. A lot of people would be listening, too, and so it was a potential opportunity to get them on board.

The reporter came down and interviewed us at length. She was stern, patronising and noticeably shocked by the state of the farm. We gave her some old audio tapes of Dad talking about the dairy, and we also gave her the familiar walking tour of Fordhall. She was very sceptical that we'd ever make anything of it and she was quite forthright with her questions. 'How do you ever expect to make a profit here?' 'Why is there so much rubbish around the place?' 'What can two kids do to make this better?' I felt backed into a corner and, no matter how much I tried to persuade her that we would make it through, she didn't seem to want to hear, and picked up on yet another bad aspect of the farm to throw at us.

The result was as we'd suspected – a negative programme that emphasised just how bad the farm looked. But at least it was showing people the reality of our situation, one faced by many farmers across the country. The reporter didn't seem to have any faith in us and the whole show was all about the odds against us doing anything here. I was mad about it for a while, but we had to move on. There was enough to be getting on with here without worrying about a radio show.

As we expected, a fair number of people heard that show, and we had phone calls and emails from listeners giving us advice and offering support. A number of them told us to get in touch with the Soil Association. It was a good idea, not just because we were farming organically, but also because Dad had had links with them in their earliest days. In fact, I still have an original copy of the 1966 organic standards formulated during a meeting at Fordhall Farm in November of that year. So we contacted them and they replied very quickly. At that stage they couldn't see what they could do for us in practical terms, but they gave us a number of different leads and suggested we contact a man named Greg Pilley, who worked for them on community-supported agriculture programmes.

Charlotte rang him immediately, and by the tone of his voice she knew he was seriously interested in what we were doing. In the summer of 2004 he came to see what we were up to. He looked the very model of an 'earth father', if such a thing exists. He had a goatee beard and wore hard-wearing corduroy trousers and a woolly jumper. He was a great listener and was very in touch with the land, which naturally impressed us from the beginning. He told us that he was just about to start work on a new project that might really interest us – a community farm trust. He had already told us about community-supported agriculture schemes, which included initiatives like community-owned box schemes and, while we supported these, we didn't think they were quite right for Fordhall.

But we were keen to know more about farm trusts, and he outlined some ideas for us. People, it seemed, would invest in a farm that would be run on community lines and would be for the benefit of the community. It was about the de-privatisation of land and its removal from the dreaded 'hope value' that had plagued us for so long. It also helped farmers coming into the industry find affordable and useable land, as well as giving the community access to the land for educational or other purposes.

Greg told us that he was about to work with Martin Large, who was already involved in a land trust scheme in Stroud,

Gloucestershire. This was called Stroud Common Wealth and had already achieved results by identifying disused buildings and taking them over for community benefit.

The problem for us was that there was no model of a community farm trust around at that time, at least not in the UK. The idea was working in the United States, and had done since the time of the civil rights movement, when it was taken up by Dr Martin Luther King and used to provide access to land for black sharecroppers. And in the early 1990s a community land trust was set up on the Scottish island of Eigg so that crofters could buy back land from absentee landlords, but that was the nearest anyone had come to setting up a land trust on an agricultural model.

It was clear from Greg's conversation that he was interested in somehow adapting the land trust model for Fordhall, but there was a lot to talk about first and the timing wasn't yet quite right for him and Martin. However, he promised to come back with Martin, maybe later in the year, and put forward a number of suggestions once they'd done their homework.

For me, it was just another in a long line of meetings and ideas that attempted to tackle the problem of ownership of Fordhall, and how it might be secured in the future, but didn't come up with a definitive answer.

What we knew was important was making connections with people, at whatever level. We were committed to the idea of involving the community with Fordhall and we'd found that our volunteer weekends had been successful. Now it was time to see if people would come just for the sake of a nice day out and without having to commit to anything. We remembered the national art event going on in October called The Big Draw. The stretch of farmland that swept down to the River Tern was beautiful and the perfect subject for anyone handy with a pencil or paintbrush. People might also want to draw aspects of the farmhouse, or even some of the animals. We decided we wanted to be part of this. It wouldn't require too much planning, as there was already quite a lot of publicity, and it would be a simple way of letting people look round the farm, have fun and find out what we were doing. So we put some signs up on the main road and posters around town to let people know we were hosting an event.

Around seventy people came. It was a very wet afternoon. Grey clouds hung over the fields and daylight was in seriously short supply. In all, it was a terrible day for doing any kind of real artwork but no one kicked up a fuss. They dashed into the old shippon when the rain came down then went back out to their spot when it passed over. We got hold of crayons and paper and I got a barbecue going, and the mums, dads and children who came had a field day. The walls in the old shippon were still a bit green and the door was missing but no one seemed to care. They just sat around drawing scenes of the farm, chatting and generally enjoying themselves. Dad came along and talked to people who knew him and wanted to know how he was getting on. Some of them had been to the farm restaurant and remembered the great roasts he used to cook. He signed a few copies of his book, which pleased him immensely. We enjoyed the afternoon too. It was a true pleasure to see the farm and its buildings being used in this way. When everyone had gone we promised ourselves that we'd have many more of these events, and almost straight away we started to plan a Christmas Food Fair for December.

Greg finally brought Martin to the farm in late November. Martin was smartly dressed, and had a way of talking to you and staring right into your eyes that initially unsettled me. You had the feeling that he was a driving force in his field and a strong motivator. We went through the whole story and, after listening carefully, Greg and Martin told us about the research they'd done into community farm structures, particularly in the USA.

In America there were groups of farmers who worked collectively and were employed by the community who paid their wages, but as I listened I could once again feel the custodianship of Fordhall slipping away from me. We had just turned down the offer of a buyout from a property developer for what we saw as very sound reasons. Now we were listening to two men we knew very little about describing ways of putting Fordhall into community ownership. Moreover, they seemed exceptionally keen to start as soon as possible as it would be a 'model' project for them.

'Community ownership' . . . In my mind's eye I could see fields full of hippies and eco-warriors trying to plant strips of sunflowers and arguing over whose turn it was to feed the pot-bellied pig. For us there were always two strands to this project: an educational resource and a working farm. I wanted one to reflect the other, but not for the two to merge so you had a vague concept of a farm that wasn't really a farm, rather a series of decisions taken by a committee while the day-to-day running of the place went untouched. If there was one thing I really wanted, it was the freedom to run this farm the way I wanted to do it, following in Dad's footsteps, and for Charlotte and me to experience a feeling of security that had never been part of the Fordhall farming experience.

'Well,' said Greg, after I'd expressed my concerns, 'community ownership and an individual sense of ownership are two different things.'

'I know that,' I said, 'and I like the idea of community *involvement*. But it's the thought of handing over the reins to a whole bunch of people who maybe know nothing about farming. I don't really see how that would work.'

Out came the flip charts and the marker pens. They drew circles representing the farm and the community, and how they might overlap. Other circles were added, representing this trust and that trust who might actually own the place. All sorts of different interests were being thrown into the pot. It seemed too complicated and too ambitious. My head ached with it.

Greg and Martin tried, but that first meeting completely failed to convince me that some kind of cooperative was the way forward for Fordhall. Charlotte and I had come this far on our own. Why shouldn't we carry on the way we were and grow the farm our own way? At some stage I knew that a tough decision would have to be made about our tenancy and that we'd have to find a way of raising the finance to buy if we had the option to do that. But we were all right for now.

When the two men had gone, Charlotte and I returned to the club room where we'd had the meeting. I poured out my feelings to her and she knew me well enough to know that I wasn't going to budge. However, she had some ideas of her own.

'Look, Ben,' she said, 'this is a new scheme, right? It's never been done before. So there aren't any rules. If these two are serious about it, they'll find a way that suits everybody.'

'Yeah, exactly. Everybody. The world and his dog, all trying to stick their oar in. We'll never get anything done, because we'll be too busy answering questions. That won't be any good for us and you know it.'

'I do know, but what I'm saying is that it's all completely new. So we can say exactly what we want and they'll have to find a structure that fits with that. You want to run the farm your way, right?'

'Right.'

'And we want to secure the place so no one can buy it out and bulldoze it, right?'

'Yeah. Of course.'

'And we want to make the farm an education and community resource because we like the idea, and it's Dad's wish too, right?'

'Come on, make your point. I need to get to bed at some stage.'

'The point is, this is a new way of thinking. No one knows how it should work, so we don't have to have anything imposed on us we don't want. I think we can put it into community ownership and still have the final say over how it's run.'

I still wasn't sure, but I was damn certain that I wouldn't be led by the nose into something I didn't want to get into. We needed more time and more talking, and we decided to hold another meeting with Greg and Martin in February. This time, though, we would invite all those people in the local community who had stood up for us so far. They were Fordhall's closest friends and I trusted them. I wanted to hear what they had to say before we disappeared any further into the fields of sunflowers.

20
Charlotte

Everyone settled back as I closed the curtains in the club room and announced that we would now watch a short film. There were twenty-five of us squeezed in there, making it cosy, to say the least: Mum, Ben and me, Greg and Martin, Philippa and Jeff, Mervyn, John from the Wildlife Trust, and sixteen volunteers, customers and other interested parties to whom we'd now given the official title 'The Friends of Fordhall'. It was a chilly February morning in 2005 and the heat generated by all those bodies in one room together with a roaring log fire was a welcome change from the usual sub-zero temperatures inside the house in the winter.

We had invited our supporters from the local community to talk about the ways we might secure the farm. We were going to discuss charitable trusts, cooperatives, community trusts, listed building status, lottery funding and much more. It was the most important meeting held to date to discuss Fordhall's future and we had an agenda that would last the day.

After the film I was going to give a presentation about the current state of the farm, outlining the situation with the landlords, the tenancy and our hopes for the future of Fordhall. For the first fifteen minutes, though, I was happy to let someone else do the talking, someone who embodied everything we were trying to achieve. The film faded up from black to a shot of Dad showing the camera a Fordhall cowpat as he explained the importance of working with the natural systems of the soil to produce healthy pastures and healthy livestock.

Over scenes of Dad running through the long meadow at seventy-six years of age and enjoying a picnic in the garden with Mum, Ben and me, both of us under ten years old, came the presenter's voice giving us the history of Fordhall. Then it was Dad again, describing how precious the fields were and why it was important that they should be preserved against the development that was looming at that time.

I needed these moments to gather my thoughts and feelings. I had to keep focused but it was hard. Less than three weeks earlier, on 16 January, Dad had died. Although the Arthur Hollins who had passed on his vision, energy and love of the land to Ben and me was no longer with us, I felt his presence in the club room that day. I was hurting inside, but it was hugely comforting knowing he was there as I summoned up the strength to speak about Fordhall's future only a couple of weeks after his funeral.

When Dad passed away he was eighty-nine years old and very frail. Old age and a consistently bad chest had finally caught up with him. In the last few years of his life Mum and I had spent increasing amounts of time caring for him. His forgetfulness and confusion had become more noticeable over the last couple of years, in complete contrast to the energetic and eloquent man we knew when we were growing up.

Chapter 20: Charlotte

During the winter of 2004 he rapidly ran short of breath and could only walk short distances. One Saturday morning in mid-January, I could see he had deteriorated further; he was weak and finding it difficult to catch his breath. He needed help and this time it was more help than I knew I could give. I told Mum to call an ambulance. As we waited for it, I held Dad in my arms. I sat cross-legged on the floor, his head and shoulders in my lap. A deep feeling inside me said that I was saying goodbye to the person that I loved more than any other. The ambulance crew arrived at the same time as Ben, who had been working off the farm that morning and had dropped everything when we alerted him. Wrapped in a blanket, the paramedics gently carried Dad downstairs and into the ambulance. We were all in shock and extremely upset. All I wanted to do was cry, the kind of crying that comes from deep inside and consumes every part of your body. But instead I tried my best to hold myself together. I did not want to make Mum and Ben more upset, and I did not want Dad to see the worry in my eyes.

Mum, Ben and I prepared to follow the ambulance to hospital. But we'd forgotten something.

'Oh no,' said Ben, 'look. Look what's coming up the drive.'

A car was trundling along the rough track, just making it to the end and passing the ambulance as its driver gingerly prepared to negotiate its ruts and potholes.

It was Saturday. Farm shop day.

'Oh damn,' I said out loud, 'please not now. I don't know if I can face it.'

The car contained regular customers who would definitely buy something. Post-Christmas, business had lessened dramatically. We were going through a difficult period. We had piles of bills to pay and could not afford to close the shop.

The lady in the car opened her door and I immediately dashed into the shop. If I could switch on the pleasant sales assistant demeanour I might just get away with it.

'Is everything all right?' she asked. Even if she hadn't noticed my red-rimmed eyes and fixed grin, she'd clearly seen the ambulance leaving Fordhall.

'Yes, everything's fine,' I lied, hoping to pacify her quickly and stop her asking too many questions. 'Dad's just not very well at the moment.'

'Oh, I'm sorry to hear that,' said the customer, detecting more serious circumstances underneath my forced breeziness. 'Listen, don't mind me. I'll come back another day. You shut up shop and go with your dad. You've got more on your plate than worrying about what I'm going to have for my tea tonight.'

'No, honestly, it's all right,' I replied, 'take your time. There's no rush.'

'Well, if you're sure,' she said, hurrying herself along with her purchases. The poor woman must have felt terribly awkward, but she finished her shopping, and once her car was out of sight I slammed the shop door shut and headed off to hospital.

Marianne and Barbara joined us and we took it in turns to hold Dad's hand. He had very little energy, but he was making an effort to open his eyes and smile whenever he sensed one of us near his bedside. It was a very Dad thing to do, trying to be as positive as possible, even at the worst of times. In a gentle manner that was Dad all over, he slipped away from us peacefully the following day. It was the most painful moment of my life and I didn't want to leave his bedside in the hospital that Sunday afternoon. But even in his passing we knew he had happily handed on his most precious legacy – the richness of Fordhall's fields.

Chapter 20: Charlotte

The following day, I sent an email to all the friends of Fordhall informing them of Dad's passing. In it, I included a poem written by him, which expressed his whole view of life in words far more eloquent than any I, or anyone else, could employ:

There is no room for death
No decay can be rendered void
Surely, you are being and breath
What you give can never be destroyed

With wide embracing love
Thy spirit animates Eternal Years
Nature, Plant, Animal and Love,
Sustains decay, Create to Rear,

From the bondage of still life
Culture multiplies rising from the sea
From the soil to the air in strife
Human freedom is reached in thee

And may the spirit of thy being
Spread out to all our infinity
The rich joys of life is seeing
The steadfast rock of immortality

Nothing dies that is born through Love
God is Love, with us all He Lives
Humanity His Home, look not for Him above
We share, give and fail, and Love forgives

Arthur Hollins, 1915–2005

Dad's funeral was held at St Margaret's Church, Moreton Saye, the parish church nearest to Fordhall and the one he had known all his life Although he was eighty-nine and had lived a full and vibrant life, achieving more than most hope to accomplish in their lifetimes, we still grieved terribly for him and I dreaded the thought of the final goodbye at his graveside. As his coffin sat in front of us in the village church we stood and sang 'All Things Bright and Beautiful', that simple ode to nature and creation and a hymn Dad loved. The final hymn, 'We Plough the Fields and Scatter', is a true farmer's hymn, and it was fitting that it should round off what was essentially a celebration of Dad's life. I wept painfully as we walked to the churchyard and again when I saw the floral tributes the mourners had brought, but once we were back at Fordhall for the wake I felt a strange sense of elation. All that day, Dad's aura could be felt in every room. I knew that he had let go of life happily. Just before gaining the tenancy the previous March he had become very ill, but he had hung on somehow to see us through it. He had witnessed Ben and me attempting to make a go of the farm with some success, and he had seen people coming back to Fordhall with the volunteer weekends and events we'd been running. All this he had seen and he was happy for us and for the future of the farm. We knew he was content finally to let go.

The day after the funeral I went back to work at Cheswardine. I suppose I was still in shock, but as soon as I got to work I realised I had made a mistake and had to return home. I just wanted to run; to be somewhere else on my own and with my own feelings. I wanted to cry freely and from deep inside. I wanted all the hurt just to stop and disappear. However, when I finally got home, after a very misty-eyed drive of a few miles, I felt instantly better – and a little bit stupid for crying at work in the first place. I realised that I was not over Dad's death, but that I only mourned his loss when I was away from Fordhall, and doing that was just too painful for the moment. It was the same for Ben, but thankfully he was able to throw himself in to his farm work.

Through all this I had to keep going with the project; there was more reason to save Fordhall now than ever before. The farm was Dad's legacy. A couple of days after the funeral I had a meeting fixed with Ron, a business advisor who later became our treasurer, to talk about our business plan and how it might fit with the various schemes Greg and Martin were proposing.

'I'm sorry if I seem a bit quiet today,' I said when we'd sat down with a cup of tea and our paperwork. 'It's just that Dad died last week and it's been a bit of a shock.'

He looked at me as if he couldn't believe his eyes. 'Charlotte, we don't have to do this, you know. Not today. You should have told me about your Dad, then we could have rearranged. We still can rearrange, if you want to.'

'No,' I replied, 'it's OK. We need to keep things moving and I want to get this business plan sorted before the meeting. We haven't much time.'

We went through the plan and a wish list for Fordhall over the next ten years. Although Ron looked uncomfortable throughout the meeting, we pressed on and I felt that we had achieved something at the end of it. I certainly wasn't over Dad's death and I was hurting immensely inside, but the project gave me the focus I needed to get up each morning and face the day.

The February meeting could have been chaotic, with ideas being pitched in all over the place and opinions flying back and forth across the big table in the club room, but instead it was organised, civilised and extremely successful. My thoughts were with Dad, but also very much with the future of Fordhall, and to hear people discussing the most brilliant and innovative ideas was like having a huge dose of Vitamin C. The room crackled with energy as Greg and Martin encouraged debate and allowed the discussion to flow freely. Even Ben, who was determined that collective opinion would not force him to surrender control of the farm, began to look a little brighter and more enthusiastic as he listened to the opinions of those he trusted. Something was beginning to light up in that room and I was keen to grab its warmth with both hands.

We identified a number of key issues: that profitability was less of an issue in the short term, that time was a vital factor, and that land ownership was an essential consideration for the security of the farm.

Of all of them, the last point was the most pressing. If by the end of our tenancy in September we had come up with a sound scheme to raise finance and we could obtain first refusal from the landlord, we might stand a chance of buying Fordhall.

But how? A mortgage was out of the question. Ben and I did not have enough collateral or any spare savings for a deposit for us to get a mortgage ourselves, and even if we *did* have that we knew it was completely impossible to hope to pay off a mortgage on a farmer's income. This was precisely the reason so few people entered the agricultural industry. Faced with a room full of puzzled looks, Greg and Martin patiently outlined the types of structures we could implement and how they might work in relation to Fordhall.

The first was a charitable trust, which held the land and leased it as a cooperative to those running the farm and the project. The trust would invest money in the farm and profits would be ploughed back into the farm and the infrastructure.

The second proposal was for the Shropshire Wildlife Trust to buy the farm and lease it back to Fordhall Farm Ltd. This would enable Ben and me to direct and focus energy into fund-raising projects and the farm business, and it would include community involvement within specific activities of the project.

Finally, there was the option to create a community-owned society, a co-ownership between the local community, ourselves and an organisation like the Shropshire Wildlife Trust. The basis of this was an Industrial and Provident Society (IPS), an organisation set up for the benefit of the community. The IPS would raise the money to buy the farm and lease the land back to us under an agreement that incorporated the interests of everyone involved – Ben and me, the community and the Wildlife Trust. The community would buy shares in the farm and, although they would not be profit-making, the shares would give each shareholder a right to vote at an annual general meeting – it would give them a sense of ownership and involvement.

The third option was obviously Greg and Martin's baby, but they were keen to hear all opinions before any commitment was made. Options one and three were received favourably, but the majority felt they would take too much time to set up and organise into something tangible.

Option two was considered the most viable, though John Hughes made it clear that the Wildlife Trust did not currently have the money to buy the farm. However, they were happy to own the land on a short-term basis while other community-involved options were considered. They were also willing to be used as an umbrella organisation through which funds could be raised to buy the farm for option three. This was a great opportunity and really opened doors for us. With a credible organisation, such as the Wildlife Trust, supporting us, we had to have more luck.

Still, the lack of promised capital bothered me, and I could see this was unlikely to change while the months slipped away. Perhaps it would be better to look at the community land trust option again. I thought of Dad and his refusal to take the easy option. Raising money from the community to buy the farm would be an enormous task in the time we had, but nothing was impossible. Greg and Martin would be there to hold our hands, and they had made it clear that no structure could be set in stone unless we were completely happy with it.

But who were 'the community'? We'd had some support from around Market Drayton and from people in the wider Permaculture movement who'd understood why the farm was worth saving. But a handful of people, however well intentioned, would not have pockets deep enough to buy Fordhall Farm. And why would anyone else want to buy shares in a farm they could not make profit out of? An elderly couple in a high-rise in Birmingham? A postman with a large family in east London? A single mum on benefit in Stoke? Why would any of these people be remotely interested in two young people trying to save an organic farm in the middle of Shropshire? Not for the first time, and definitely not for the last, I posed myself this question and could not find an answer.

While I was pondering this there came a voice at my shoulder. 'Hi, I'm Sophie. I hope you didn't mind me coming along. I'm Jeff's daughter.'

Sophie Hopkins was as tall – or rather, as short – as me. The same age, and with an open and trusting face, Sophie had come along to the meeting with her dad because he'd told her that two young people needed support, and there weren't enough other young people supporting them. He also mentioned that there was a free lunch! She had just come back from travelling and was planning to work before she studied for a PGCE.

'This is amazing,' she enthused. 'I can't believe I've lived here all my life and never come across this place. What a great story you've got.'

We went through our respective histories. We'd been to different schools and, while Market Drayton isn't a big place, our paths had just never crossed. But we were glad they had done so now.

'If I can be of any help at all, just give me a shout,' she said. 'I'm looking for a job at the moment so have lots of spare time. Anything you want doing, just ask.'

She gave me her mobile number and even before she'd reached home, I'd text-messaged her.

Would you like to help me organise our summer fair event?
We're also designing a leaflet if you have some time to give a
hand?

She arrived at Fordhall the very next day. I had a good feeling about Sophie.

21

Ben

Midwinter can be a very depressing time of year on a farm. Everywhere is wet, cold and dead-looking. It was an even bleaker January than usual in 2005, because that was the month Dad passed away.

Rushing home after I received Charlotte's urgent call, I was shocked to see how quickly he'd deteriorated. Dad was lying on the floor, with Charlotte and Mum beside him. He had an oxygen mask on his face and the paramedics were gently lifting him into a chair to carry him downstairs. My eyes instantly filled with tears and I had to run outside to get my breath back. I sat on the concrete slabs around the old overgrown herb patch, watching them carry Dad out to the ambulance. He was sitting up but looked blank. I didn't even consider he wouldn't be coming home again. I thought he would be back burning his toast in the kitchen in no time.

The next day was frightening and the end, when it came, was more painful than I could ever have imagined. The only comfort came from knowing Dad had been able to stay at Fordhall right up to the end and that he had seen the beginning of its regeneration with his two youngest children at its heart.

My next visit to the cattle market was an emotional one. One of the drovers approached me as I was looking at a bunch of Angus heifers. 'I knew your dad, Ben,' he said. 'He was a good bloke, and he would be very proud of what you and Charlotte are doing.' Dad dedicated his whole life to the farm, so saving it from development was the least we could do to preserve his legacy.

Libby, our Gloucester Old Spot pig, decided to time the arrival of her first litter of pigs to coincide with Dad's funeral. He would have appreciated the symbolism of death and rebirth, and no doubt he would have had a good laugh at a parade of mourners traipsing past a 300-kilo pig, grunting and groaning as her labour began.

Libby was one of the first pigs to arrive at Fordhall after we took over the tenancy. We were approached by a neighbouring farmer who wanted two pigs off his hands. They were both about a year old and had been brought up as pets, but one was tamer than the other. The less tame one was dispatched to the abattoir to be converted into sausages for the farm shop, but the other pig we kept, and called her Libby. I was pleased to have her as a breeding sow as she had a nice temperament and, so far, I hadn't had a great deal of luck with pigs.

From Mum and Dad's tenancy we had inherited six pigs, one known as Nancy. In most respects she was a good pig – she had good conformation and was long, so would make good bacon. However, she had one major fault – she did not like males. Boars she could tolerate, but two-legged males she hated with a vengeance. It was frightening for me because she was a big pig and I had to quite literally gird my loins whenever I dealt with her.

Nancy was pregnant around the time we took over the tenancy but she had nowhere in which to deliver. I noticed that Clive had two old pig hutches in the field next to his dairy, where I was working at the time. I asked him if they were going spare and if I could have them for a pregnant pig about to give birth. I picked them up for £20 and brought them home, hoping that Nancy would settle happily in them and that she would forgive me the crime of being a male.

Danny was at Fordhall at the time, helping out with some of the more demanding physical jobs around the farm. Always handy and adaptable, he was willing to come within striking range of Nancy so that we could get the hutch up and persuade her to go in it.

When he saw the pig and the hutch in close proximity, he sucked his teeth. 'Ben, you're never going to get her in there. It's too small and she's one massive pig.'

It was true. Nancy was a big girl and suddenly the hutch looked like a chicken coop in comparison. I felt stupid and defensive about my misjudgement over Nancy's sheer bulk.

'Course she will,' I replied stubbornly. 'We might have to give her a hand, that's all. If we put some corn in she's bound to stick her head in. Then it's a case of shoving her in after it.'

'First one to jump back over the fence is a chicken, eh? All right, let's have a go.'

We climbed the fence and, while Danny distracted Nancy, I filled the hutch with corn and laid a trail of it back to where she was standing, looking mean and ready for action. A whiff of corn under her nose soon had her grubbing around in the mud for the rest of it and within a few minutes her head was through the hutch door.

'OK!' I shouted to Danny. 'Get ready . . . one, two, three . . . SHOVE!'

We pushed hard on the pig's wobbling flanks, but it was like heaving a Range Rover out of a clay pit. Nancy was not having any of it and dug her heels in. We pushed harder. Suddenly, she somehow released her grip and did a rapid reverse out of the pig hutch. We bolted, terrified at what might happen if the pursuing pig caught us before we could make it over the fence.

Out of breath and out of reach, we leaned on the gate and watched Nancy pace around the pig hutch as if it was an unexploded bomb. 'She might have a go if we're not around,' suggested Danny. 'Come on, we've got plenty to do. Let's pack it in for now and come back later.'

It was a good idea. We left Nancy alone and checked on her again a few hours later. She was still prowling around the hutch, which seemed to have moved five feet. She'd obviously tried to get in, and shoved it with her shoulders so hard that she'd bulldozed it from its original position. She wasn't going to fit, and there was nothing for it but to cut a bigger hole in the side. Even that didn't seem to persuade her, so eventually we pulled the whole side panel off and, grumpily, she hauled herself in for the night.

She never did have her piglets in there, though. There just wasn't enough room, and so we had to fix up a heat lamp over some straw bales in the paddock once the piglets had arrived. If I attempted to put the piglets nearer the heat lamp for extra warmth, Nancy would go for me, so Mum and Charlotte had to get in close while I directed operations from behind a hay bale. She trusted those two so implicitly that she would allow Mum to stroke her head and talk to her as though she was a child.

Chapter 21: Ben

Nancy had another litter of pigs the following year, but her temper where men were concerned never improved. If anything, it got worse, and her viciousness became more noticeable. By then, there were more people knocking about the farm and we couldn't take the risk of her getting out and attacking someone. We decided not to breed from her again and she went into the paddock under the oak tree to be fattened up.

The early part of 2005 was a busy time for the farm. In addition to Dad's death and the shock of not having him around any more, there was a lot of discussion about how we might actually manage the business we were building up in terms of the farm, and how that would link in to a community project without compromising the day-to-day decisions I needed to make. I had felt a little more confident since making my voice heard at the meeting with Greg, Martin and the others in February. I could now see we were moving forward with a structure that had plenty of room for manoeuvre and flexibility, and I was happy about that.

The Suffolk ewes we'd bought the previous spring were due to lamb. This would be a new experience for me. I didn't relish the thought of getting up in the freezing early hours of a February morning to deal with a struggling, pregnant ewe on my own, never having done it before, but I had no option. I took advice from some of the lads at Harper Adams who had grown up on sheep farms and knew what it was all about. By and large, though, I was feeling my way through a new situation. It was in keeping with a lot of challenges we faced at Fordhall during that time. If we didn't know, we asked; if we didn't get an answer, we carried on and did it anyway. You usually muddle through these things. While it was nerve-racking, the lambing went better than I expected. Seeing the first ones born at Fordhall Farm for a long time was a real joy, a sign of spring and a new beginning. It also marked our achievement, too; this time the previous year we had been fighting to keep Fordhall's land away from developers, and we had no idea whether we would be able to stay here. The arrival of the lambs signified a solidity at Fordhall that had been missing for many years.

We had managed to keep some of the heifers back from slaughter in 2004 and put them with the bull once they were big enough. They were not the best-quality cattle but they were the start of our breeding programme. A handful of calves were also born that spring. I dreaded this more than the arrival of lambs. A cow in distress with a stuck calf can be a nightmare, but I'd had a bit more experience of calving, both from helping Dad at Fordhall and from the local dairy farms I'd worked on, certainly more than I'd had with lambs, so I approached it with more confidence.

But I'd never tried to calve a lively Angus heifer in front of twenty shop visitors, which was the unusual situation I found myself in one day. I had the cow in a primitive holding crush. A crush sounds brutal but it isn't – it's a small pen that holds the cow still so she's under minimal stress, allowing me to deliver her calf safely. But it all relies on holding her head in the front gate.

The cow was in and I fetched a bucket of water to clean my hands and the equipment. Next I had to secure two ropes to the calves' front legs so I could pull it out. My hands were inside the mother and the first rope was on and the second nearly there when the heifer jumped forward with so much force that she broke the crush's front gate and ran out into the car park, the gate still attached to her head. My heart sank; I couldn't bear to look. The heifer was running round distressed, desperately trying to shake the gate loose. I was terrified that she'd damage an expensive car or harm a visitor. She charged frantically round the car park, shaking her head from side to side as she tried to free herself from the gate. I couldn't believe how close she was to the cars. Luckily one of our volunteers was close at hand and managed to calm the heifer down. I held her tail so he could knock the bar open, releasing her head from the gate. Thankfully the worst was over – she walked calmly back to the barn and the calf was delivered safely. But the experience was extremely stressful and one I wasn't keen to repeat.

After the previous year's experience with the monster bull I'd hired, I realised I needed to have my own resident bull. Money was still short at this point, but I went to the cattle market every week hoping I might see one going cheap. One Wednesday, a local farmer from Norton-in-Hales had a small Aberdeen Angus bull in the sale. It was a nice-looking animal, but to me it didn't seem big enough so I didn't bid on it as I thought it wouldn't be able to perform its vital function well enough. I spoke to the farmer afterwards and he invited me back to his farm to have a look at two little pedigree Hereford bulls. When I got there they weren't much bigger than the Angus, but they were only £600. I picked the biggest and took it home. Charlotte and Sophie quickly nicknamed him Barry the Bull, I think because that was my nickname at college. I'm not really sure why I was called Barry – I think it must have been because there were no less than three Bens in our class, and there had to be some jokey way of identifying each one.

I got the bull home and turned him out with the cows in the cottage field. Poor Barry only stood half the height of the cows and I suddenly thought I'd made a big mistake and he wasn't going to be up to the job. Unfortunately, there was nothing I could do. I'd just spent £600 and couldn't afford to buy or hire another. Luckily, as it turned out, Barry's height was no barrier to his fertility and he managed to perform effectively and on time.

As well as the farm shop I had to look for other ways of selling our produce and getting the Fordhall name known outside Market Drayton. Like a lot of local producers who aren't interested in going down the supermarket route, I started to look into farmers' markets. They fitted in well with the organic and free-range element of Fordhall and it would also be a good opportunity for me to meet other producers, make contacts and pick up ideas.

We had become members of Heart of England Fine Foods, an organisation that promotes good food and its producers around the Midlands region. Through it we found out that a farmers' market was being set up in Shrewsbury in March 2005. It was local to us, it was new and, as we hadn't done one before, it seemed to make sense to go, if only to find out whether it was a viable way of selling our stuff. There was only one problem, though: we had nothing to display our packed meat in and no way of being able to afford a new chiller cabinet. Solution: look on eBay.

It's true, you really can get everything on there, even a second-hand display cabinet to show off your finest cuts of prime Aberdeen Angus beef and lamb and mint sausages. There was one listed for £46, but it was up in Leeds. Still, a bargain's a bargain, and while it was going to cost me another £40 in diesel, it had to be worth seeing. I drove up there, and found a small, slightly tatty but completely serviceable cabinet that had previously displayed cans of drink in a Bradford corner shop. I bought it and booked my stall at the farmers' market.

It was a bitterly cold Friday in March, with an icy wind that could tear off a layer of concrete. Not a day you'd want to be browsing around a farmers' market, but I'd put down the money for my spot. A couple of volunteers, Elaine and Bryan Hunt, who were also part of Stafford Soil Association, had said they'd come with me to help set everything up and provide moral support.

I selected the meat I was going to take, loaded my new bargain-basement display cabinet into the car, remembered to take the box of leaflets describing our plans for the farm, and set off for Shrewsbury. When I arrived, I instantly wished that I'd done a bit more homework. There, setting up in front of me, were stall holders in smart white aprons with their logos on them. They had big plastic banners that hung behind their stalls and they were pegging their leaflets to pieces of string so the wind wouldn't blow them away. Their display cabinets were three times the size of mine. In comparison, I was completely disorganised and felt as green as I did on my first visit to the cattle market.

'Never mind,' said Bryan, sensing my feelings of inadequacy. 'From little acorns and all that . . . Let's get these leaflets blu-tacked down. And if they look like they're going to blow away we'll have to stick a big piece of steak on top of them.'

I laughed. We looked amateurish, but it was a farmers' market and there were plenty of woolly characters around who didn't care a damn for appearances. All they were interested in was the produce. I knew that if they bought ours they would find out how good it was. You can be marketed to the hilt, but if your produce doesn't come up to scratch people won't come back for more.

The stall was set up and I was ready to unload the meat we'd brought with us. It wasn't a large amount, but it would be a decent start if we sold most of it. I arranged it carefully into the cabinet. When it was done I asked Bryan to plug it in for me.

'Where's the socket, Ben?' he asked.

'Er, I dunno. We might have to use the exten . . . oh *balls*!'

'What? What's up?'

'The extension lead. I didn't bloody bring it, did I? Great. We might as well pack up and go home now. We can't have warm chunks of meat lying around everywhere.'

Just then, I heard a voice to the side of me. 'You looking to plug in somewhere?'

'I *was*,' I said, turning to face a burly man, who wore a pristine green and white striped apron. 'I've forgotten my extension lead, though. So I'm a bit stuffed.'

'Don't worry,' he said, ferreting through a big plastic box, 'I've got a spare. Always carry one in case mine blows. Or someone forgets theirs.' He grinned, and stuck out his hand. 'Alan Ball, Bings Heath Smokery.'

'Ben Hollins, Fordhall Farm.'

'Nice to meet you, Ben. You ever done one of these before?'

It was a ridiculous question. It was blindingly obvious that I hadn't. Alan, who ran his smokery from premises near Shrewsbury, pretended not to notice. He'd been selling his smoked fish, meat, poultry and game at farmers' markets for a while, and over the course of that cold afternoon he gave me plenty of useful advice about selling. It turned out he'd been following our story in the *Shropshire Star* and seemed to know everything about Fordhall. It made me realise that people do pay attention to the articles in the local press. Alan also knew my father, as his mother had gone to school with him. We had a lot to talk about that day and we got on well.

As it turned out, we didn't do too badly for a first attempt. A few leaflets blew away in the harsh March wind but we gave plenty of them out as well. I was happy to chat to people who wanted to know more about what we were doing. We also sold most of our meat, and when I counted up I discovered we'd taken £150. Initially I was pleased, but when I knocked off the cost of the stall (£70), the diesel used getting there (£10), and knowing that our margins were quite small anyway, I realised we'd barely broken even, not even taking into account my time packing and preparing all the meat.

It was worth going, though, if only to meet Alan and spread the word about Fordhall. And to pick up one particular invaluable piece of advice from Alan that I took on board for next time.

'Those sausages you've got there,' he said, pointing to a box of unsold packets as I handed him back his extension lead at the end of the day. 'What are they?'

'Those are Gloucester Old Spot and I've also got some lamb and mint.'

'I'll bet they taste better than they look,' he said.

'Yeah, they do,' I replied, puzzled. 'Why do you ask?'

'Because at these type of events customers tend to follow their noses rather than their eyes,' he said. 'You should bring a frying pan and a grill next time, cook a few of them up fresh. Then cut 'em up and put 'em out for free samples. See how many you sell as a result.'

I tried it the following month. The smell of slow-cooked sausages wafting across the town square brought customers in like bloodhounds. As a result, I almost doubled my profits that day. I love advice. Especially when it's that good.

22

Charlotte

E ven though the landlord was being typically elusive on the subject, all the talk at Fordhall in the early part of 2005 centred on the purchase of the farm. If, as we fully expected, North Shropshire District Council were going to delete the twelve-acre field from the local development plan, we saw no reason why a conversation with the landlord about the purchase of the farm – if only hypothetically – should not now take place.

We still didn't have an accurate valuation for the farm. Over the years, we'd had estimates of somewhere between £500,000 and £650,000, but all these valuations looked at the farm as a whole business and did not take into account the hope value that would automatically attach itself if it went on the open market. The twelve-acre field for example, was perhaps worth £40,000-£50,000 as a piece of agricultural land. But while it was in the local plan, with the words 'suitable for development' stamped on it, its hope value took it as high as £1.2

million. In this context, you can see why so many landowners sell their land for development rather than agricultural land. The temptation is simply too great.

Shropshire Wildlife Trust offered to commission their own survey of Fordhall's value, so that we could accurately assess the challenge ahead. The Trust's land agent came to the farm armed with a clipboard and spent several hours walking the fields, staring up at the buildings and noting down everything with care. His report was the most in-depth done on the farm so far, and it spared no blushes. The house, he said, needed serious renovation; in his opinion around £250,000 would have to be spent to mend the floors, wall coverings and ceilings, repair the roof, the main beams and joists, re-wire and re-plumb the whole building and solve the extensive damp problem that plagued the house every winter.

That in itself was a huge sum, but it was not the end of the story. The agent had completed his task with great attention to detail and had come up with a list of comparable properties and tracts of land in the area plus their selling prices. Using those figures, and national trends in property prices, he estimated that Fordhall Farm and its land, if used for agricultural purposes only, would be worth somewhere in the region of £550,000 – almost identical to the figure we'd been quoted in the past. If, however, it was to be sold with the expectation that it would be broken up into lots for a variety of developments (stabling horses, for example) it might realise just over £1.1 million. This didn't include the hope value of the twelve-acre field, which he estimated to be £1.2 million at current market value.

We felt we could safely disregard the twelve-acre field as we expected it to come out of the local plan. Even so, £1.1

million for the rest of the farm was a daunting figure, especially when money was so tight at the time and spending £20 on stamps and envelopes felt extravagant. It irritated me that it was so high simply because of its potential to be broken up into lots. This land was meant for farming, yet the planning system had taken it out of reach of any farmer. But we had no choice but to abide by the rules of local government in an open market economy. This was the new price of land and we were powerless to do anything about it. We had to work with the system.

The figure for the renovations to the house came as a shock, but not as a surprise. We knew exactly what state it was in, and that it would take a considerable amount of capital to put it right. Even so, there was no way we could include renovation of the farmhouse in the budget. What improvements we could make would have to come much later. Our most immediate concern was securing the farmhouse and the rich meadows that encircled it. As usual, I was defensive about the farmhouse, and this came out at one of the regular committee meetings we were now holding at Fordhall with Greg and Martin.

We were discussing the Wildlife Trust valuation, and the ridiculously big task of renovating Fordhall. 'You know,' said a voice, 'for that amount of money, it might just be worth considering knocking the whole place down and starting again.'

I was incensed. 'No way! That house is the heart of the farm.' My anger was exacerbated by one of my constant gripes – the way we in the western world so often throw something away without first trying to fix what we had to begin with. It seemed such a waste to me to lose the farmhouse, which still had so much worth keeping within its walls.

'It's only a suggestion, Charlotte,' said Greg, attempting to pour oil on to troubled waters, 'no one's saying it should happen. It's just something to think about, that's all.'

'I can understand where you're coming from, but there is no reason to pull down the house. It simply needs renovation and that can be achieved over a number of years.'

'We know that, of course,' Greg continued, 'but it's just the cost . . . '

I was becoming agitated. To talk of pulling the farmhouse down was sacrilege to me and flew in the face of everything we were trying to achieve. I apologised for my sudden flash of temper, but they had all seen how passionate I was about this house and, thank goodness, its demolition was never mentioned again.

At least progress was being made on the legal structure for the farm. Emails between us and Greg and Martin flew back and forth. Slowly, and not before time, a way for Fordhall to continue the work of our father and to look forward to a new future was emerging. It was to be some kind of community ownership, for sure, but we needed to identify the 'community'. I was still writing to a group of targets from various rich lists, all the time trying to target those who would be most sympathetic with our cause. I had high hopes for two letters in particular: one to Edward Goldsmith, the founder of the *Ecologist*, and the other to Trudie Styler, wife of rock star Sting and someone who was heavily involved in the running of her own organic farm in Wiltshire.

The good news we had wanted but had not dared to pin too many hopes on finally came in March. Fordhall Farm's twelve-acre field, the subject of so much contention and family distress over the years, was deleted from the local plan. Additionally, Müller was granted permission to extend their factory on a site on the other side of the A53, nowhere near

Fordhall's fields. I wanted to find out whether there was any chance that the field might at some stage go back into the development plan. While I was told by North Shropshire District Council that it would not, they added that anything like this was always subject to change. But still, the official confirmation lifted a huge weight from our shoulders and we felt it dramatically increased our chances of negotiating with the landlord. That field, out of the plan and out of reach of developers, dropped in value from £1.2 million to £50,000, in theory at least. But as John Hughes pointed out, the very fact that it now lay in some kind of 'grey' area – neither in the current development plan, but not one hundred per cent guaranteed to be saved from development in the future – still gave it some hope value. In that respect, he said, he felt it likely that the landlord would continue to have some hold over Fordhall, even if it was just this twelve-acre field.

What we needed now was clarity. We had to find out exactly what the landlord intended to do with Fordhall after September 2005. So far, the option to buy the farm had been based on speculation and assumption – ours. There had been no indication from the landlord about whether he would sell, and if he would, to whom. It was time to meet the trustees again and see what plans, if any, they had now that the field was safe. I would make the call to Mr Godsal and see if I could get an indication of their thoughts.

Meanwhile, we were working towards our biggest event so far, a summer fair and family fun day to be held at the farm at the end of May. Market Drayton's annual carnival had been cancelled due to organisational problems and we saw this as the perfect opportunity to get local people down to the farm and to experience Fordhall at its most colourful. Thanks to a number of well-attended working weekends that spring, our nature trail and picnic area were ready to be used. With the help of Sophie, who was being seen around the farm more and more since the February meeting, we came up with a number of activities for the event from welly-whanging to guessing the weight of a pig. We wanted it to be the kind of traditional, low-tech event that older people would remember from their childhoods, but that would still appeal to a new generation of children. We wanted to use the resource of Fordhall as the attraction rather than fun fairs and loud music.

This event was the first big task that Sophie was involved in and her energy and commitment to it was phenomenal. She and I were hitting it off very well and in her I could see a kindred spirit; someone who enjoyed getting something done, even if it wasn't always the easiest and most convenient route to take. She also wasn't the kind of person who took no for an answer. Although she didn't have a background in farming, her people skills more than compensated for that. Like Ben and me she had little experience in project management, but her personality and motivation were what counted, and what she didn't know she was willing to learn. As time went on, she became absolutely invaluable to the Fordhall Project, but for now she was happy to look into the ifs, buts and maybes of nature trail quizzes and tugs-of-war. The project was turning into an educational journey for us all and it was being led with enthusiastic young people at its heart.

A couple of weeks before the event, on my twenty-third birthday, I finally received the call I'd been waiting for. The landlord had reached a decision about our tenancy. They had been impressed by the efforts we'd made since March 2004 and they were keen for us to stay. Through Mr Godsal, the landowners offered Ben and me a year's extension from September 2005. If we were to take it, the rent would increase from £666 a month to £1000 to compensate for the capital costs of the countryside stewardship work that we would have to accept as part of the terms of the new tenancy. We were in no position to argue; if we wanted the extended lease, these were their terms and we had to either take them or leave them. Of course, we took them and although the issue of purchase was still vague, I read between the lines to assume that September 2006, when our new tenancy would expire, was crunch time for Fordhall. I felt it unlikely that they'd keep offering extensions to the tenancy ad infinitum. They wanted it off their hands, and they would wait until September the following year to see what might happen. Maybe they'd wait to get a good offer, like Clive the property developer's. Maybe they'd somehow persuade someone to buy those twelve acres for big money. Maybe, just maybe, they'd see what Ben and I could come up with. We had never hidden anything from them in terms of our hopes for the farm's future. A million pounds or thereabouts was a lot of money, but sixteen months in which to get it was more feasible than four.

The family fun day would mark an unofficial start to the climb up the fund-raising mountain. We worked like mad in the weeks leading up to 30 May, the Bank Holiday Monday on which the event would take place, and we contacted as many local groups as possible that might otherwise have joined in Market Drayton's cancelled carnival for sponsorship. We attracted a good number of enthusiastic stall holders representing a variety of businesses in the town and we organised plenty of fun events, live music, games, stories, competitions, guided walks and demonstrations.

Around 2000 people turned up to enjoy the fun, the largest number of people Ben and I had ever had on the farm. At times I almost had to pinch myself to make myself believe that we'd organised this right here at Fordhall, the farm that had come so close to dying. Everywhere I looked mums, dads and children were enjoying themselves; it was a glorious summer's day and they were making the most of Fordhall's natural beauty. It was simple and effective. There was a problem, however, with the widely advertised 'hog roast' – there was an awful lot of 'hog' and very little 'roast', and I still laugh about it to this day. To be honest, something had to go wrong somewhere; we had never arranged an event as big as this one before and we had done it completely on our own. Sophie and I had been as organised as we could have been: we even joked that we had made lists of lists! And the hog roast too was something we thought we had planned meticulously. We were all really excited about it – the first full Fordhall hog roast.

Ben had never cooked a hog roast before, but he'd been advised to start early and roast slowly. So he switched on the hired gas spit at 4.30 a.m., got the pig in the correct position over the flame and left it to turn slowly. He had a thousand other jobs to do that day, so he trusted the spit to carry on doing its work without too much monitoring. As he walked away, Murphy's Law – what can go wrong, will go wrong – kicked in and when he returned three hours later to check on the progress of the pig, he discovered to his horror that the gas had somehow gone out. He'd missed a few hours of cooking and the idea that the roast would be ready for lunchtime disappeared in the wind. He immediately turned it back on and announced the delay to the visitors on the tannoy at lunchtime.

No one seemed to mind too much, so I was pleased when, about forty-five minutes later, Ben turned up to tell me it was ready. That wasn't too much of a delay, I thought, and got on the tannoy to tell everyone the good news and advise hungry customers they could start queuing.

As the line started to form, I got a call on my mobile. Ben's number came up on the screen.

'Charlotte,' he said, sounding out of breath, 'I'm sorry about this but I've just had a proper delve into the meat and it's not ready yet.'

'Damn, I've just told them to start queuing.' I made another announcement. 'I'm sorry everyone, but I was mistaken. The hog roast is not yet ready. It'll be another half an hour. Sorry for the delay.'

Everyone in the queue laughed and returned to the activities. Thankfully it didn't seem to be too much of an issue.

Thirty minutes later Ben rang again to say it was ready. I asked him if he was sure, as I had already misled people once. 'Yes, definitely,' he said. I ran to the tannoy to let everyone know.

'Attention everybody. The hog roast is now on its way to the field. Please start queuing under the marquee.' As soon as the words left my mouth people began to queue. And at the very same moment my phone rang again.

'Sorry Charlotte, it's not ready yet. Don't announce it.'

I couldn't believe it. 'You're kidding,' I said. 'I've just told everyone for the second time. Do I really have to tell them to go away again? How long this time?'

'Another thirty minutes and that will be it. I promise!'

I was furious and embarrassed, and I could sense disquiet among the crowd. The only refreshments to be had were tea, cakes and small slices of quiche. The hog roast was the culinary highlight of the day, but it was now 2.45 p.m. and the event ended at 4 p.m. You don't invite 2000 people for a barbecue and keep them waiting this long, not unless you want them to vote with their feet.

Finally, at 3 p.m., Ben called again. It was ready.

'Are you sure?' I said.

'Sure I'm sure. Go on, tell them. It's here.'

'Not until I see you in that field with your pinny on, carving the damn thing.'

'Honestly. It's ready.'

'No. Not this time. I have to see you first.'

I watched as Ben made his way across the field and waited until I saw him unfurl the large carving knife and fork from the wrapped cloth he was carrying them in. He stuck the fork into the hog's flank and on that signal I made the final announcement. As I suspected, the queue wasn't as big as it had been a couple of hours earlier. People had started to go home and that hog roast fed us and the volunteers for several days to come.

Hog roast horrors aside, it was an extremely successful day. Our visitors had enjoyed themselves and so had we, even though the day had passed in a blur. We spent that evening with a group of volunteers, counting up the funds from each activity: welly-whanging, tug-of-war, guess the weight of the pig, guess the name of the lamb, the cake stall, the stall holders' rental, the donations boxes, the car washing (which the Market Drayton Scouts generously helped us with) and of course the hog roast. After totalling everything up we were totally amazed. We'd raised almost £2000 towards the community project pot. It was a long, long way from the £1.1 million figure hovering over our heads, but we felt cherished and supported, and that counted for just as much. We had been so busy in the weeks preceding the event that we hadn't had time to absorb the enormity of the task we had taken on. It all sunk in that evening, as Ben, Sophie and I, and the many volunteers that we had counted on throughout the day, collapsed with exhaustion.

Chapter 22: Charlotte

'I can't believe it,' I said over and over again. I didn't know what else to say. 'I just can't believe that we achieved that, when we had no idea what we were doing. We have no experience. How crazy is this?' Fordhall was no longer a forgotten, dilapidated farm; it was alive in people's minds. If someone had told me two years before that we would have organised an event at Fordhall that attracted over 2000 people I would have laughed at them. But that's exactly what we had done. Undoubtedly, we could not have done it without the enormous volunteer support we had from university friends and local supporters, but there was definitely a new confidence in our own abilities to bring Fordhall back.

A community had turned up here and had gone home knowing more about that small farm at the bottom of the town, and why some people thought it was important that it stayed just the way it was. If we could harness this support nationally as well as locally, there was no reason not to believe that we could raise the money to save Fordhall. If we convinced ourselves of that fact, we could convince others too.

23

Ben

It's a good job corporal punishment was banned by the time I got to college, or I think I might have suffered the same fate as Dad, beaten and verbally abused by the masters for his habit of dropping off to sleep in lessons.

Like me, he had an excuse: farm work. Luckily, I didn't start my habit of afternoon naps until I got to agricultural college and was running the farm single-handed. I'd get up early in the morning, see to the animals or drive to the abattoir to drop off livestock or pick up my meat. Then I'd come back, grab a quick shower, get changed, throw some breakfast down and head off to Harper Adams.

I can't imagine many other students get such a rudely busy awakening every day, unless they have an early morning job, and that hardly goes with the student lifestyle. Still, I would almost always make it into college, even though I was shattered, and I'd manage to get through the morning lectures just about unscathed.

At that point my mind was all over the place. I was sitting in lecture theatres learning how to be a farmer and when I came out I hung about with college friends who also wanted to be farmers. At the same time I had the enormous responsibility of actually running a farm and trying to scratch a living, pay the rent, all the bills, look after the animals and do all the maintenance. I was in the strange position of formally learning about things that I'd taught myself, or had somehow stumbled across, days or weeks earlier on the farm. No wonder my head sometimes spun with it all.

'Ben!' An urgent whisper in my ear, followed by a sharp jab to the ribs. 'Ben! Wake up!'

'Uh. What?'

'Wake up, Ben!' The same voice, dragging me out of a dream about a hedge-laying operation at Fordhall. The student next to me was shaking me by the shoulders, trying to coax me into an upright position.

'Come on Ben, pay attention . . . ' A different voice, booming from the front of the room. The lecturer. 'Now, taking into account next year's VAT return and the possible effects of a cut in subsidy over the next six months . . . '

Why did business management lectures always seem to knock me out faster than a round or two with Lennox Lewis? To be fair, it wasn't the finer points of single farm payments and herd movement records that sent me to sleep. They just happened to coincide with the tricky time of day when the adrenalin that has seen you through the morning has run out and the carbohydrate bomb you had at lunchtime is just settling nicely in your stomach.

I fared better than Dad, who regularly had his ears twisted by cruel masters who didn't understand what it was like to cram a morning's farm work into a couple of hours before school. When Dad was falling asleep in chemistry lessons, the fumes from the Bunsen burners contributing to his state of drowsiness, it was because his father had just died and he suddenly had a hell of a lot more work to do at home. Dad had been determined to take over Fordhall and reverse its fortunes, but the effort needed to pull it back from the brink of bankruptcy had dragged him down. I was luckier in that I had lecturers who understood what I was trying to do and made allowances for it, but I know how Dad must have felt.

And when I wasn't running the farm or studying part time for a degree, my life was filled with meetings, meetings and more meetings. The bane of my life. Endless conversations about structures, land trusts, community buyouts, support groups, shareholders, business plans and legal obligations. I was learning a lot about agriculture at Harper Adams, but nothing about any of this. It was the one area the lecturers were vague about, but I don't suppose there was much call for a module on how to buy a farm for a million pounds when you've only just turned twenty-one.

In truth, I didn't really talk to that many people at college about the financial bird's nest we were trying to unravel. It was too complicated to explain and the bottom line – that we needed a small fortune, and soon, to save our farm – was one of those statements met either with a blank look of disbelief or a stifled laugh. Most of my fellow students came from farming backgrounds and owned at least 500 acres of land, so our fund-raising project and small organic farm must have seemed a long way from their experience. Besides, the course itself focused on the necessary growth of farms in order to spread costs and increase their efficiency with more machinery and less labour. This was completely the opposite of what we were doing at Fordhall, so I was busy learning one thing during the day and doing the opposite when I got home.

By the time we'd had the summer fair and I'd clumsily mastered the art of the hog roast, we'd pretty much agreed on a structure on which to base the future of the farm. Greg and Martin had gently guided us in the direction of setting up as an Industrial and Provident Society. They were excited about this because they saw Fordhall Farm as paving the way for similar farm-based projects in the future. In other words, we were guinea pigs, but we were undergoing the experiment willingly, and for me it was an opportunity to build the structure in a way that meant everyone was happy as we were not following any set guidelines. In fact, we were making our own. Many hours spent reassuring us (and me in particular) that the farm would not be run by a committee had made us feel much more confident about the agreement we were entering into.

The actual structure document was complex and ran into several pages of legalese. In layman's terms, the main points were that the Fordhall Project would incorporate into an Industrial and Provident Society (IPS). This society would be made up of shareholders, both from the community and from larger organisations, who would raise the money to buy the farm and lease it back to Fordhall Farm Ltd: i.e. Charlotte and me. The shares were non-tradeable and non-profit-making, but each shareholder would have one vote at an annual meeting to elect board members. We would have the final say in how the farm was managed, though the rules of the IPS stated that we had to commit to access for the community by providing a chemical-free educational and social resource on the farm.

In effect, we would be tenants of the IPS, but that tenancy was secure for ever, well, one hundred years anyway. This was something the Hollins family had never had before. We had farmed at Fordhall for generations, but only ever as tenants and, especially over the past ten years, increasingly uncertain about the future. This new agreement looked as if it could save our farm for ever, for us and the community – it almost sounded too good to be true. When all the debate dried up and everyone had had their say, the IPS seemed the best and most straightforward option to secure the farm and ensure its survival. After a long period of worry and uncertainty about how this structure might work, I was finally convinced of its value. But until we were actually in a position to buy the farm I was not one hundred per cent convinced about just how well it could work.

By June it was obvious the landlord was clearing the path to allow us to make some kind of offer. Charlotte had had a meeting with Mr Godsal, during which she'd told him about the land trust structure and how it would work at Fordhall. He made it fairly clear that the extended tenancy the landlord offered us would be the last one. They wanted the farm sold. In September 2006, once our tenancy expired, the farm would go on to the open market and, under the terms of the trust which held the land, it had to be sold for the best possible price.

Charlotte continued to approach Mr Godsal. We wanted him to know we were serious about buying the farm, but we had to tread carefully. We knew they wanted to sell it, but we didn't know who their favoured buyer might be or how much they wanted to sell it for. We had valuations for the farm and a structure allowing us to raise funds to buy it, but we didn't want to offer the landlord a price above what he might propose, particularly when time was so short. It was extremely frustrating not to have a goal to aim for. And throughout all this, the fund-raising and the campaigning to create awareness went on.

This strange business of circling round one another lasted until early July. That afternoon I was spending a couple of hours trying to mend several broken fences between the Hall Meadow and the Little Meadow. As with most of the old stock fences on the farm, the posts had rotted at the base and the weight of cows leaning over them had squashed them into the ground. It was a gorgeous summer's day after a period of unsettled weather and a few thunderstorms over Shropshire. I'd taken advantage of the sun to get this work finished and make sure our animals didn't accidentally take a tour of the Hall Meadow's lush grass, which we were saving for the autumn grazing. Striding towards me in the distance was a wellington-booted figure. The half-run, half-walk was instantly recognisable: Charlotte. Always on the go and always at the double.

She marched up to me and I wondered what she was going to say. Her breathlessness and red face made it clear that it was very important news. Or had I left the pan of soup I'd had for lunch on the stove, burned it beyond recognition and was about to get in trouble for it? It was hard to tell, but as she got within fifty yards she shouted out something in garbled English.

'Who's been what?' I said, failing to catch her words.

'Mr Godsal's been on the phone,' she panted as she reached me, putting her hand on my shoulder to support herself. She was exhausted.

I never liked hearing those words. They always produced a sudden sickening jolt in my stomach and I wondered what I was about to hear.

'Oh yeah,' I said, 'what does he want now?'

'He's come back with a figure. Eight hundred thousand and

we've got first refusal,' Charlotte replied, an enormous smile lighting up her face.

'Bloody hell! Right. So that's it, then.'

'Yes, that's it,' she replied, slowly getting her breath back. 'He's offered us a contract of agreement to sell. They'll put it in writing that they'll sell the farm to us if we can raise £800,000.'

'By when?'

'By 1 July 2006, next year.'

'And what happens after that?'

'If we raise the money, we get the farm. If we don't it goes on sale on the open market at the end of September. But the twelve-acre field isn't for sale. They want to hang on to that as it has too much future potential,' she said, still slightly breathless.

The last bit wasn't a surprise. That field wasn't safe yet, developmentally speaking. There was still hope that it could sell for much more than it was worth agriculturally. That they would hang on to it was worrying, but they were still offering us 128 acres, which was the vast majority of the farm.

'So it's serious. Would he negotiate on the cut-off date?'

'No. I asked him. They're sticking to 1 July. Just a year away; we haven't much time. But this is the opportunity we've been waiting for! We now have a figure and deadline to aim for. We must try to get the IPS structure complete as soon as possible.'

'Sounds good to me. When do you think we should tell people?'

'Now. We've had the conversation, so no point waiting around. I'm heading back to the farm to get on the email. See you up there. Hey, I forgot to say . . . '

'Say what?'

'Do you know the date today?'

'Um. 2 July?'

'No. It's 4 July. Independence Day. Coincidence or what?'

Charlotte turned on her boot heels and set off at the same pace she'd arrived. She wasn't going to waste a minute in the search for every penny of spare cash she could lay her hands on. I thought back to two years ago to the demoralising conversations we'd had then about the state of the place and what would happen when we left. In just a short space of time everything had changed, and so had we. Together, we'd strapped ourselves in for a roller-coaster ride to rival anything at Alton Towers, the theme park just up the road. Charlotte and I had been through everything together: facing eviction, getting the tenancy, trying to make the farm pay, seeing people coming back to Fordhall, experiencing the painful sadness of our dad's death. Now, we were about to steer into the final stomach-turning bend. Two years is nothing over a lifetime, but I felt as if I'd come a thousand miles. I was running my own farm and making money from it, but it still wasn't secure. This was our final chance to do what generations of our family couldn't: make Fordhall safe from the plans of others for ever.

I watched Charlotte striding back over the brow of the hill in the House Field and I realised that, while we would always be shoulder-to-shoulder in the long battle ahead of us, from now on we would be fighting on different territory. Charlotte would be the driving force of the fund-raising campaign. Her determination to hook in anyone who showed the slightest flicker of interest in what we were doing naturally qualified her for the position of project leader. With Sophie, she would drive the campaign faster than Michael Schumacher, and I knew she would not rest for a moment until every penny of that £800,000 was securely in the bank. We had a year – just a year! – and even then, as she slammed the farm gate shut and went back to the computer screen in the office, I knew she would either pull it off, or die in the attempt. It felt like a massive achievement for us to have got a figure to latch on to and a date to reach it by. No doubt many people would think we were crazy to even attempt it, but this was a goal we just had to hit.

I came out of my reverie and looked round me. The fence I had been working on was almost finished. I had a hundred other jobs to complete before the presence of the bats that flitted under the eaves of the farmhouse would tell me it was time to stop for the day. The farm was doing well, but it could do better. All along, we had insisted that Fordhall remained a place of work. I never wanted it to be a toy farm. It had to be real and my role now was to build up our business and prove to the people who might invest in us that we were actually farming, not just playing at it. I needed to convince customers to find out more about Fordhall and visit us by producing enough high-quality meat to sell in our farm shop. I needed to be selling enough to pay the rent. I needed to be out on the road; at farmers' markets, agricultural shows and local food events, selling our stuff, talking to people, getting the message across. Wherever possible I had to join Charlotte in speaking to the press, something I'd not always enjoyed in the past, but something that would be difficult to avoid once we got the campaign started. I had to tell our story and look confident and convincing, not awkward and tongue-tied. Most of all, I just had to keep my cool and go on believing that we would do it, right up to the very last moment. If we didn't make it, at least we would never regret not having had a go. It had to be worth it just for that reason. All we could do was try our best.

And aside from all those minor concerns, I still had my bloody display fridges to worry about. Through my gadget-lending friend, Alan Ball, I was invited to display our wares at the West Midlands Agricultural Show in Shrewsbury that summer. I was still half-asleep when it came to getting ready for these sorts of things, but I was much better prepared than I had been just a few months before. This show was a big deal in terms of us getting our names around the region's farming community, but it was also £250 to hire a stall, money that could be better spent elsewhere, like trying to save the farm, for example.

Alan talked me round, telling me that the sales we'd make and the publicity generated would more than compensate for the loss of a couple of hundred pounds. Moreover, he said he'd give me a hand doing it, which was music to my ears. I'd been to hundreds of agricultural shows in the past, but only as a punter. Doing a big show like this was a new thing for Fordhall. We couldn't afford to look like amateurs, especially not now when we were hoping to part people from their cash to save the farm.

Sophie helped me draw up a checklist of items we had to take so I wouldn't have to run around trying to borrow what I had left behind when I got there. She even put the checklist on the checklist just in case I forgot to take it with me! I ticked everything off and headed towards Shrewsbury, confident I'd prepared properly. I arrived and was waved towards the Fordhall stall by a man in a flat cap and brown overcoat. Thinking that he'd made a mistake, I leaned out of the window of the truck and asked the marshal to point to our stand.

'It's that one there,' he said, pointing to a stand, the size of which wouldn't have disgraced a display of JCB trucks.

'It can't be,' I said, 'it's bloody huge, that one.'

'Well,' he said, consulting his plan of the showground, 'it says here that it's yours. Fordhall Farm.'

It was massive. It made our little display fridge look like a cool box. If I'd known how huge our stand would be I'd have brought double the amount of meat to sell. But maybe I could still do that – a plan was forming in my head. I got on the phone and rang a farmer friend who worked a stretch of land close to Fordhall. Martin was a pig farmer who sold all his pork direct to local restaurants and farm shops, and had already gone through similar stages to us in marketing his own meat. I knew he'd understand my predicament.

'All right, Martin,' I said, 'it's Ben. I'm at the West Midlands show and I've got a problem. Are you using your display cabinet today? The big one? Any chance of borrowing it for a day or two? Yes, I can collect it. Cheers, you're a pal. I'll set off now.'

I left one of our enthusiastic volunteers in charge of the stall while I raced back home to pick up the display fridge. Just as I was leaving, I saw Alan Ball approach.

'What's up?' he shouted. 'Forgotten something, have we?'

'Sort of,' I replied. 'I'll fill you in when I get back.'

I rushed back to Market Drayton and, with Martin's help, I hauled the display cabinet into the back of my rusty cattle trailer. He waived the modest sum I offered him, telling me I could rent it from him next time. This time it was a freebie. Cheered, I called in at the farm to load up with more meat before setting off down the A53 again.

That display cabinet was invaluable. I was able to give our produce a really good show and, as I had thought, we sold double the amount we would have done without it. At the end of the show it felt as though we'd moved up a league as a business. We'd sold well and we'd attracted lots of interest from people who'd already read bits and pieces about us in the local paper. Moreover, there was a great sense of cama-raderie among the producers. Such selfless support gave me a huge boost and further proved the benefit of selling direct on a small scale.

I gave Alan the latest update about the fight to save the farm. He sucked his teeth hard when I told him how much money the landlord wanted.

'Bloody hell, lad,' he said, 'you're going to be needing a few more display cabinets full of meat if you want to get up that much money. I'll tell you that for nowt. Still, stranger things have happened. Best of luck for the launch, Ben . . . because I think you're gonna need all the luck you can get.'

24

Charlotte

I was exhausted. Although I was still enjoying the work at Cheswardine Hall, and I needed to be there for the money it was bringing in to the farm, the hours required to work on the Fordhall Project were growing and I was getting less and less sleep. This began to interfere with my paid work – I was literally falling asleep on duty. I would work a twelve-and-a-half hour shift at Cheswardine Hall from 7.30 a.m. to 8 p.m., come home, have a bite to eat and get on with project business until the early hours of the morning. A short sleep and I'd be back on duty at the nursing home again.

My work colleagues were always very supportive and sympathetic about my lack of energy, and gave me the jobs that required slightly less running around. But their good intentions sometimes backfired. I loved talking to the residents in the Hall; they had had such interesting and rewarding lives and had often been through tough times themselves. I was often asked to assist those who needed a helping hand when they ate – a perfect opportunity for a chat – but as soon as I sat down I would become overwhelmed with tiredness and begin to drift into a heavenly sleep. Residents waiting for their lunch would soon wake me, but I felt guilty that I was not putting in as much work as the rest of the staff.

Still, a number of threads were tying together that summer and, while I didn't wholly forgive myself for doing so, I had reason to work late into the night. Excitement was a big part of it. Finally, we were nearing some kind of resolution for the land trust structure. It was new and innovative and it energised me just to think about it. The structure seemed to suit everybody. It gave the community involvement with the farm, the ability to help the cause, and the opportunity to use the farm as an educational and social resource; in fact, everything we had talked about in that early February meeting. In addition, the structure gave the Hollins family security at Fordhall through a long tenure agreement and it allowed us to run the farm business under our own control.

The last piece of the jigsaw was the landlord. That phone call from Mr Godsal in July took a huge weight off my mind. It was a giant step forward for the project.

The price they were offering for 128 acres seemed fair – it was obviously much higher that the £550,000 that the farm had been valued at, but much lower than the £2.3 million with hope value included. More to the point, ours was currently the only offer on the table. They had obviously considered their options very carefully and this was their most preferred. If nothing else, we were giving them free advertising for the sale of their asset. But for us, we now had a target and something we could focus on.

A stroke of coincidental luck came our way that summer and, like the other examples of good fortune we've had at

Fordhall, this one paid dividends in so many different ways. Ben and I went to a social event in Market Drayton in mid-July, organised by the Market Drayton Taste of the Town company. Jeff and Philippa, the people behind Taste of the Town, had been very good to us and we liked to support them whenever they had a function. At this gathering we were introduced to Christopher Hope, the business correspondent at the *Daily Telegraph*. We had not had any experience with the national press before, but we knew that it was necessary if the colossal sum of £800,000 was to be raised in less than a year.

Ben met Christopher first as I was deep in conversation with some local food producers. It was a time when Ben, Sophie and I were continually trying to gather support and telling everyone we met about the project. We were always quite upfront about it, but Ben in particular did this in a very humorous manner.

'Charlotte, come over here!' he called me over to where he and Christopher were sitting. 'This is Christopher Hope and he's going to write a story on Fordhall for the *Telegraph*.'

'Well, erm, maybe,' was the reply from Christopher. 'Ben tells an interesting story. We'll have to see.' He said it with a smile on his face, knowing full well that Ben was gently but firmly pushing him into saying yes.

Ben's confidence had grown tremendously since we had begun fighting to save Fordhall. In the early days he'd found it difficult to speak to the press or local people about the project, partly because of his embarrassment about how the farm looked back then. Over the past year, however, he had been concentrating on repairing fences, buying new gates, and building up his breeding herd and farm-shop business. The farm had become his baby and he was now proud to show off what he had achieved and the potential that he too believed could be realised at Fordhall.

'Maybe you'd like to tell me more about it some time,' Christopher went on. 'Look, why don't I get in touch next week and we'll discuss it in more depth? If the IPS structure really is the first of its kind in England, then I think we'd be interested. I can't promise anything, but I'd like to hear more.'

Details were swapped and, true to his word, Christopher contacted Ben via email soon after. He wanted to find out more about the land trust plan and was keen to contact our solicitor to pin down the nuts and bolts of it. He asked to hear more about our point of view, so we set it all down in writing and sent it off to him. We desperately hoped he would write something about us in the paper, but we didn't want to push too hard. We were both pleased, though, when, in his email, he described us as 'an inspiring pair'. It could only bode well for our chances of appearing in the national press and broadening the fight to save the farm.

As soon as we had the green light from the landlord, we booked the Festival Drayton Centre in Market Drayton for the launch of the campaign. The date would be 28 September 2005 – a year to the day before our current tenancy expired and nine months before our fund-raising deadline. At the launch, we would explain the concept of the land trust as comprehensively but also as simply as possible and convince every person in the room, plus the members of the press we were inviting, that Fordhall was worth investing in and saving for ever. One of the first, and most important, things we had to do was to fix a price for the shares. Ben, Sophie and I talked about it at length. We wanted a figure that was affordable, yet represented something of value. Ten pounds would have been too cheap and would not have covered the administration cost of processing the share. A hundred pounds would cover everything and leave some spare as a contingency, but we did not want to alienate those who could not afford it. Eventually, we settled on £50. It seemed an accessible figure, but it also represented something worth having. In addition, it would cover the cost of administration of the certificate issue and the annual paperwork to which each shareholder would be entitled. We were conscious that these were life-long shares and could be passed on through a will, giving us a continuing administration burden, but we hoped that other funding streams would help to balance this out and shares would continue to be sold to keep the project sustainable. And, of course, the rental income from Ben and me would help.

At £50 a share we would need 16,000 people to hit our £800,000 target, 6000 more people than the total population of Market Drayton. However, we didn't think it was unachievable. Some people would buy more than one share and we would continue to source grants, donations and loans. We took this figure to the interim board of the still-to-be-incorporated IPS and they all ruled in its favour.

Unfortunately, our incorporation as an Industrial and Provident Society (IPS) had taken longer than expected, and so we knew we could only advertise shares on the day of the launch, not actually issue them, which wasn't ideal, but better than nothing. Sophie and I set to work inviting as many people as we could to the launch. We drew up a wish-list of those we'd love to see present. Many were local councillors, MPs, environmentalists, academics, schools representatives and people from food-based organisations. Others were celebrities we'd like to be involved: Monty Don, Jamie Oliver and Prince Charles, among others. We had doubts about their availability, but even a word or two of support from them would be good for us on the big night.

The press were beginning to respond to our constant requests. We had a piece in *Living Earth*, the Soil Association magazine, which commemorated Dad's life and the work he had done at Fordhall. It concluded with a few paragraphs on what Ben and I were trying to achieve. It was an intelligent piece and we had a very enthusiastic and supportive response from it, but we needed to reach a wider audience, not just preach to the converted.

With a pile of new jobs mounting daily and none of the old ones disappearing from the list, I thought it sensible to get away for a weekend. There were too many distractions at home and we *had* to get this launch right. As Ben took care of the farm and continued to build up the farm shop, Sophie and I escaped to her parents' small cottage in Kendal for a few days.

We hoped to go for long walks to clear our heads and then return to the cottage to work, but the campaign launch dogged our Birkenstock-clad footsteps as we tramped across the foothills of the Lake District and almost every waking moment was given over to thinking about and planning the launch. While we were there, Sophie designed a logo for the project and we talked about names. We had been the Fordhall Project for a while now, but on reflection we realised that it didn't say anything about who we were or what we were doing. It also sounded very short term. And, more importantly, it didn't make any reference to the unique structure of the organisation.

Legally, we couldn't have the word 'trust' in the title, so that was out. With wine and chocolate close to hand, we brainstormed into the night.

'Fordhall Friends, Inc?' Sophie suggested.

'No. That sounds like a film.'

'How about . . . Fordhall Community Farm?'

'I can't see Ben going for that. It'll bring back his recurring sunflowers-and-hippies nightmare.'

Sophie pondered this then said, 'OK. What about this – The Fordhall Farm Initiative?'

'I like "initiative". I like that a lot – using your initiative to get things done. That sounds like us.'

'It would be good if we could get the community in there somewhere as well.'

I thought for a moment, then it came to me. 'Let's make it the Fordhall Community Land Initiative.'

'Wahey! Pass your glass over while I fill it up. I think we should drink a toast to the new name!'

So that's what it was: 'Fordhall Community Land Initiative'. A few more syllables than we might have liked, admittedly, but if we shortened it to FCLI we found it tripped off the tongue much more easily. A bit like CPRE. Or maybe that was wishful thinking. But we really felt that our objectives and vision for the future of the farm were summed up in those four words.

On the Sunday we packed up the car again and left the peaceful idyll of south Cumbria to return to the mayhem of north Shropshire. On the journey back we talked so much about the jobs we had to do when we arrived home that we both began to feel physically sick. Were we taking on too much? Were we reaching for something beyond our means? Did we have the skills and energy to match it? Our holiday had given us time to reflect but, in so doing, we were in danger of being utterly overwhelmed by all we had to think about. As we stared out of the car window at the passing views the southbound M6 gave us, the despairing silence was broken by my mobile phone. It was a London number.

'Hello, Charlotte speaking.'

'Hi Charlotte. It's Christopher Hope here, from the *Daily Telegraph.*'

'Hi Christopher. How are you?' It was good to hear from him. He'd sent a photographer to the farm a week or so previously but there had still been no indication of when the article would go out.

'It's going well, thanks. I just thought I'd let you know when the article's going to be in the paper.'

'Oh brilliant. When?'

'Tomorrow – 22 August.'

In shock, I finished the conversation as best I could and hung up. We were going national! This was really it. By the morning, a few hundred thousand readers of the *Daily Telegraph* would know about Fordhall Farm. Both Sophie and I felt even more sick. We knew that if we were bombarded by phone calls and letters over the next few weeks we would not be able to cope. We had just over a month before the campaign launch and there was already more work than we could focus on. I quickly rang Ben to tell him the news.

'That's amazing, Charlotte!' he shouted down the line.

'Even better, Christopher told me that his sister-in-law works for BBC News 24 and they're interested in doing a story around the time of the launch.'

The following morning I got up early so I could collect a newspaper en route to Cheswardine Hall. I flipped through every page until I reached the business section and saw the headline 'Shares Issue Aims To Save The Good Life'. Christopher Hope had done us proud. It was a great story; full of the positive energy that we'd always tried hard to transmit whenever we talked to the press. There was even a quote from Mr Godsal, which praised the 'great deal of determination' we had shown since taking on the tenancy, explaining that was why the landlord wanted to give us the opportunity to buy the farm.

It was fantastic. Finally we'd had national newspaper coverage. It proved that we were being taken seriously and that ours was a story worth covering. Now we needed to hold the press's attention. Christopher's words had given us hope that a broad cross-section of people, particularly those from non-rural backgrounds, would find our story appealing and might be inspired to help in whatever way they could.

As August turned into September we held a couple of events at the farm – a nature trail walk with a picnic and an organic exhibition to tie in with National Organic Week – any excuse to get people to see what we were about. The launch, however, was the priority. Almost 150 invites were sent out, which we followed up with emails and phone calls. Our persistence was paying off. Close to one hundred people, including MPs, councillors, people from Market Drayton and the wider area, farm customers, potential shareholders and environmentalists, had told us they would be coming.

The *Telegraph* article had ignited other press interest. We had articles in the *Birmingham Post*, the *Shropshire Star* and on the BBC Action Network web page, and we had interest from and promises of future appearances in *Shropshire Life*, *Countryman*, *You Are What You Eat* magazine and the *Ethical Consumer*. There was also the upcoming appearance on BBC News 24 and BBC *Midlands Today*. In terms of press interest we couldn't have asked for anything better.

The agenda we'd set was tight, but by now I was much more used to public speaking. It was crucial that I pitch this just right. We could have all the positive press coverage in the world, but there was still a lingering suspicion that Ben and I, and now Sophie, were just kids playing farms. If, out of a group of ten people, nine told you it was going to work and that you were doing a great job, and one person cast doubt on the whole thing, it would be that one voice that would stick in your head. I was determined that our guests should understand the underlying importance and significance of what we were trying to achieve at Fordhall; I would not come across as a silly, incompetent and inexperienced girl with a fairy-tale idea.

We were going to put up displays showing the history of the farm, the new projects we'd planned and how people could get involved. We wanted people to be able to see our vision. Photographs of our volunteer weekend and social events would hopefully show that Fordhall was very much alive and already playing an important role within the local community. We threw *everything* at the launch.

At 7 a.m. the day before the launch, the office door was pushed open gently, so it would not creak and wake anyone, and a head peeped around it. It was Danny, one of our most loyal supporters. He had been staying at the farm to help us with the launch and was getting up early to start work. But to Sophie and me, who had started work at 8.30 a.m. the previous day and were still at it, it was very, very late indeed.

'Good morning,' he said, with his characteristic smile. 'What're you two doing?'

'Laminating,' I said blankly. I was bug-eyed with a combination of adrenalin, caffeine and over-tiredness.

'Oh, naturally,' Danny replied, laughing. 'It's what all the best people do at seven in the morning these days. It's much more trendy than yoga.'

Danny gently ticked us off by reminding us that if we looked like we did then at the launch, people would be too scared to buy shares. We took the hint and grabbed ourselves a few hours' sleep.

The day of the launch finally arrived. We buzzed with excitement as faces old and new crowded into the venue. The first part of the day was spent meeting and greeting, listening to people's memories of the farm and explaining to others how they could become involved. Ben was welcoming people at the door with his foot placed on a chair, not because of any nonchalance on his part but as a result of a minor operation he'd had earlier in the week. This had knocked him out of his usual farm duties, so we'd swapped roles for a while – in addition to preparing for the project launch I'd fed the pigs, cows and sheep, while Ben helped in the office.

Before I knew it, it was my moment to make the opening speech. Row upon row of expectant faces stared up at me, waiting to hear all about this good idea to save a farm. I felt flushed with a mixture of embarrassment and fear. But if there was ever an opportunity to shine, this was it, and I was going to grab it with both hands.

'Ladies and gentlemen,' I said, hesitating slightly, 'thank you so much for coming here tonight. You don't know how much it means to us to see you here. My name is Charlotte Hollins and I live and work at Fordhall Farm. The reason we're here tonight is to tell you why we want to save our farm from development and how you might be able to help us do that. First, though, let me explain a little bit of the background to our campaign. It all started . . . '

I was off, and anyone who has met me will know that once I'm on a roll I'm hard to stop. I had to keep checking my watch surreptitiously to make sure I didn't talk too long. I finished my speech to a warming round of applause and sat down, my heart pounding, feeling I'd run a marathon. Sophie leaned over and gave my arm a squeeze and Ben mouthed a 'well done!' in my direction. I had to concentrate hard on what Martin, the next speaker, was saying because my adrenalin level was taking time to subside. Gradually, though, I began to relax and enjoy listening to these articulate men talk about Fordhall Farm with such affection. I felt a huge burst of pride and I so wished Dad was there to listen to his legacy being praised so fulsomely.

Towards the end of the speakers' session, Sophie announced from the stage that shares were now on sale, although we had to wait until incorporation before we could bank cheques and issue share certificates. The flutter of excitement that went round the hall when Sophie said we were open for business was palpable. Within seconds we heard the pound-pound-pound of feet running towards the stage. It was Graham Sedgley, a local businessman and one of our most enthusiastic supporters.

'I want to be first!' he said breathlessly as he strode towards me, chequebook in hand.

We all laughed as we handed him an application form, which he filled in at lightning speed. He was indeed our first shareholder, and clearly very proud to be so.

He wasn't the last that night, either. We sold a good number of shares and I was both pleased and relieved. All day I'd worried that the idea of buying a share in a farm would be widely misunderstood. Earlier in the afternoon, as we'd guided members of the public around the exhibition area and talked about the sale and the shares and the community, a man had taken me to one side. Middle aged and well dressed, with a strong public school accent, he had a keen way of looking at you as you talked. He was clearly nobody's fool.

'I understand about the organics, and the heritage etc.,' he said. 'What I don't quite follow is why I should spend money to save your farm and not get anything in return? Answer me that.'

He was referring to the non-profit, non-tradeable status of the shares. It was a fair point, and one that would be raised many times in the months to come.

'OK,' I said. 'You see, the value is in the share itself, and in membership of the FCLI. It's a philanthropic investment in the future rather than a financial one. As a shareholder you would become part-owner of Fordhall Farm. The shares are an investment in the future in our farmland, of our natural landscape and in the future health of our food production systems.'

'So, as a shareholder, would I have control over what you farm?' he asked.

'No. Ben and I will manage the farm as tenants of the FCLI and we will pay a rent to the society. You wouldn't have direct control over how we farm, but we will have to farm the land in accordance with a management agreement drawn up by the FCLI and its shareholders. Essentially, this specifies that the farm has to remain chemical-free and accessible to the community.'

'But have you had any experience of running your own business?'

'Yes. Ben and I are already doing this through the company we set up when we took over the tenancy – Fordhall Farm Ltd. This is a commercial limited company that will hopefully provide Ben and myself with a salary when the land is fully stocked and the business is at full capacity. The income generated from our farm shop increases livestock levels and pays the rent to the FCLI. In essence, Ben and I will be substituting one landlord for another, or perhaps I should say thousands of others.'

'So what exactly will the society do?' he replied, beginning to look interested in the novelty of the idea.

I explained that one of the primary reasons for creating the society was to remove the enormous barriers that exist for new entrants to farming. The idea was that this society would not only help Ben and me, but that it would exist to help other young farmers in the future and might even be a model that could be replicated elsewhere in the country.

'The society is also obliged to utilise Fordhall Farm for the benefit of the community,' I went on 'in order to fulfil its aims and objectives set out in the society rules. Primarily, these objectives refer to the promotion of biodiversity, conservation, healthy living, organic farming, heritage and community land trusteeship.' I ticked off all the points I knew so well by heart now on my fingers.

My interrogator was making me sweat a bit, but I didn't mind. He was right to ask hard questions. It was an unusual set-up and it needed a sound explanation. The relationship between the FCLI and the tenant farmer is complicated, but essentially they both share a common aim and they both rely on the close connection between the community and the farmer on the land.

The man stroked his chin for a moment while he considered what I'd said to him.

'I've done very well out of stocks and shares,' he said eventually, 'very well indeed. That's because I've always played to win, even if I've sometimes lost. I've never played for fun.'

'OK,' I retaliated, 'so you won't get any financial reward, but you'll be helping to preserve and sustain something valuable for the future. Your share is worth much more than money alone.'

Once again, he thought hard before he spoke.

'Well . . . part-owner of a farm, eh? That would be something to talk about, wouldn't it? More interesting than part-owning a racehorse, which everyone seems to do these days. I might just have a flutter on your shares. Though I will call in on you now and again. I like to check up on my investments.'

'Be our guest,' I said smiling. 'You're welcome any time. Especially when the farm shop is open for business.'

He smiled back and shook my hand.

'Very well,' he said, 'I'll do just that. It's been a pleasure to meet you. Good luck with it all.'

He wandered off to look at one of our exhibition stands. I sighed with relief. He was a cynic, but I'd got the message across and he had seemed convinced. Only 15,999 more people like you to persuade, I thought.

25
Ben

We were burning the midnight oil more and more often these days. Well, Charlotte was. After a long day's work and a big evening meal, I'm not fit for any other purpose than going to bed. Charlotte's the night owl whereas I'm the lark – happy to get up at the crack of dawn and get going straight away after a cup of tea with lots of full-fat milk.

In fact there were quite a few occasions when our paths crossed – me getting up at 4.30 a.m. to load animals for the abattoir, with Charlotte just off to bed. It must have been a huge relief for her when I set up a system of gates in the barn so I could load the animals for the abattoir by myself and not have to wake her at silly o'clock in the morning to help coax a big heifer into our little trailer.

That said, I like a lie-in when the very rare chance of one presents itself. I'd had a minor operation on my foot in the week leading up to the FCLI launch and had to keep it strapped up and off the floor, which meant that I couldn't squeeze it into a mud-encrusted boot and haul it around the farm for a few days. So Charlotte had to do the morning shift with the animals while I snuggled under my duvet and savoured the rare treat of a lie-in. She was happy to help, but not so pleased to find that on the day of our big BBC News 24 interview – the day after the launch – I was still soundly snoring in my bed.

As she pointed out, standing with her hands on her hips at the door of my bedroom, using a tone of voice she usually reserved for bank officials who refused to lend us any money, she had been up since 6 a.m.

'And not to do any of my own stuff, even though I've got plenty to do! Oh no. I had to get up to go to the abattoir and pick up the meat, then get it all sorted out to go in the fridges. Now I come back and I find you're still in bed, nothing's been done in the house and the BB-bloody-C are coming in an hour!'

I guessed the lie-in was over. With a heavy sigh I pulled on my jeans and jumper and opened the curtains.

This is going to be a very long day, I thought, as I started to clear a pile of unwashed pots out of the bar room. We'd never done any TV before, so it wasn't surprising Charlotte was jumpy. I didn't feel too good myself about appearing in the nation's living rooms, but there wasn't a lot I could do about it so I just tried not to think about it. I know now that if you've been on the TV, even on the most unwatched programme at the most obscure hour of the day, someone who knows you will have seen it and will tease you mercilessly for it. And BBC News 24 is a very widely watched programme.

I had a broad idea of what they would ask us and by now I felt confident enough to talk to the press without worrying about every word falling out of my mouth. Television, though, was different. For a start, you had a very limited amount of time to get your message over. Although we'd done some radio interviews, by and large we weren't used to giving soundbites; we preferred having the time and space to explain what we were doing so we could get our message over correctly. This time, what we said would have to be snappier, and we'd have to make sure the reporter knew what she was talking about. What we did know was that the journalist coming down was Victoria Panton. She'd been in touch with us and Charlotte had explained the story to her, so we were confident she'd be able to get the message over properly.

Victoria was lovely, patient and understanding of our situation. She made allowances for the fact we were nervous, and she carefully coached us before the cameras started rolling so that we didn't look totally silly when the piece went out at the weekend. She did a fantastic job, too; while we looked slightly ill at ease with the situation, we didn't come across as the TV virgins we were. We both spoke and we tried to tell the story as clearly and simply as possible. The explanation we gave about the shares, and why they weren't money-making but were worth buying, was a bit long-winded. After the interview was over we agreed we'd have to work on a way of getting this message across more succinctly.

When the show was broadcast the following Sunday morning, Charlotte cursed herself for not mentioning where you could get the shares from. She'd talked about the farm and the fund-raising, and all the other details, except for the most vital one. Even so, it wasn't too disastrous. People could always use the Internet or directory enquiries to find us at the farm.

Seconds after it had finished and the programme had cut back to the studio for the next item, I had a two-word text message on my mobile. It was from a friend at Harper Adams. All it said was 'TV Superstar!' I was both embarrassed and proud. I certainly hadn't enjoyed seeing myself talking on camera and had been tempted to put a cushion in front of my face whenever I appeared on screen. But I also realised that I had to do this sort of thing in order to keep the farm going, which was what I wanted more than anything else in the world. If that involved being a kind of celebrity farmer, even in the most minuscule way possible, so be it.

26

Charlotte

The long days and balmy nights of summer – always a gorgeous, life-affirming period to spend at Fordhall Farm – had given way to the harsh cold of autumn and winter and the all-consuming reality of fighting a tough campaign to persuade people to part with their money. The first rush of share applications immediately after the launch and the appearance on BBC News 24 had been fantastic, and we'd felt overwhelmed by the generosity of the public. It was a great start to the appeal and it really helped to allay my fears that people with little interest in agriculture or organics would simply ignore us.

Some prospective shareholders wrote short letters explaining why they wanted to be part of FCLI. They were beautiful and touching. Many were from people who had had some connection to agriculture or rural living in their past, but had somehow become disconnected from it. What we were doing seemed to strike a chord with many about a way of living that had been

lost in the rush to modernise, maximise and produce intensively. Ours was a slower, but more holistic way of operating.
In a world where everything seems to move at double speed,
people appreciated the pace of Fordhall.

Those first few letters were very encouraging at a somewhat
bleak time of year. And we were doing exceptionally well with
our press coverage: after BBC News 24 we had coverage on
the BBC Midlands Today regional news programme and on
the second Sunday in October there was an article about us
in the *Observer* newspaper. Juliette Jowit, the paper's environment editor, wrote an excellent piece, which described the fight
for the farm as a 'David and Goliath battle'. I liked that, not
just because it made reference to the developers who had
directly threatened the future of the farm in the past, but also
because it symbolised the battles faced by all farmers in almost
every aspect of their working lives, and particularly their
attempts to attain a fair price for their produce from supermarkets.

Even so, this article had happened somewhat by accident,
and Sophie and I couldn't help feeling a little guilty about it.
After seeing Tom Oliver, the head of rural policy at the
Campaign to Protect Rural England (CPRE), in a TV interview talking about their latest report 'Your Countryside, Your
Choice', Sophie had contacted him to see if he would provide
any support for our project. He was only too pleased to help
and offered us a quote, plus a mention in a press release he
was to send to the *Observer* about the CPRE report. As it
turned out, the majority of the *Observer* article was about us
and Fordhall Farm, with only a paragraph or two at the end
mentioning the CPRE report. We were embarrassed about it,
but thankfully Tom was fine, and simply happy that his report
was given press.

This article did more for us than we could ever have expected. The Monday following the article we had six different production companies call to arrange meetings at the farm to discuss the possibility of following our story for a TV documentary. This burst of enthusiasm felt a bit surreal and we were careful not to jump at the first offer we received. We met all the companies and eventually went with the BBC Midlands *Inside Out* team. They were the only group that we trusted not to twist our story and overdramatise the events. We were sure they would make it real. Furthermore, they were able to do a two-part documentary, the first of which would be aired in February, which would be in time to give the campaign a boost. Helping the fund-raising was our main priority and we couldn't afford to give up time to filming if the programme was going to air after our July deadline.

All the press and media interest, locally and nationally, was bringing in more and more share applications, and there seemed to be a never-ending mountain of paperwork to be done. We weren't complaining, but somehow Sophie and I had hit a bit of a wall. Maybe the weeks leading up to the launch had burned us out; maybe it was all the previous months of ups and downs regarding old tenancies, new tenancies, planning inquiries and the rest. I was still working full-time off the farm, as was Ben, so we were switching hats with exhausting regularity. There was some good news, though; after a lengthy funding application to the European Union's 'Leader Plus' programme, we were finally able to offer Sophie full-time, paid employment at Fordhall Farm as Project Manager. Our age and lack of experience eliminated us from many grant applications so our success with this one was a huge relief – we were over the moon.

Sophie's new role was no less than she deserved. She had

put her heart and soul – not to mention her precious time – into the Fordhall Project and there was no way we could have managed to get so far without her.

Help for Sophie and me came in the form of Sue Corkett, a woman with warm, twinkly eyes. A retired teacher, she now had time on her hands and a determination to fill it with good things. She had read about us in *Living Earth* and was keen to do something to help. She emailed us to say she had a spare couple of days a week and could she fill it by helping us at Fordhall Farm? Of course, we said. But there was one problem; she lived in Kidderminster in Worcestershire, which was a good hundred-mile round trip to Market Drayton and back. We didn't think she could possibly come here, do a day's work and drive home again the same day, but her energy was incredible and she dismissed any of our fears with a teacherly flick of her hand. She was to be our first in-office volunteer after Sophie and we loved and admired her.

We had another Big Draw art event planned for the end of the month, and a fund-raising concert by a local folk group in Market Drayton for the beginning of December. There was plenty to keep us going through the increasingly short days, but I was finding the mountain of paperwork tough, especially the amount of time I had to put into dealing with the first-refusal contract from the landlord. This was being bounced back and forth between their solicitors and ours, and there seemed to be a problem with us using the land for anything other than agricultural purposes.

The whole ethos of the FCLI was to create a resource for the community. But under the terms of this contract there would be no bunkhouse, no seminar room, no teashop and no exhibition centre. There wasn't even room for a farm shop. It was ridiculously irritating, and it needed to be changed.

Chapter 26: Charlotte

Luckily our solicitors at MFG were amazingly helpful and negotiated on our behalf. Iain Morrison was the solicitor dealing with our case and he offered to complete the land purchase agreement for the FCLI free of charge. It was very generous and we were extremely grateful for all the help that he and the rest of his colleagues gave.

An old acquaintance of Dad's then lent some support to us in an unexpected but exciting way. He was Peter Cheeseman, a stalwart director of the New Vic theatre in Newcastle-under-Lyme. He himself had campaigned for years to raise enough funds to rebuild the theatre when it was going through a difficult time. After Dad died he kept in touch with us and keenly followed our progress. One day he rang and said he had something interesting to run by us. He was friends with the actress Prunella Scales, well known for playing Sybil Fawlty in *Fawlty Towers*. She had grown up on a farm and for several years was president of the CPRE, so her interest in agriculture and land usage was strong. Peter said she might be interested in our campaign and he would speak to her on our behalf.

She replied with a lovely quote, which she gave us permission to use: 'I support with all my heart the Fordhall Community Land Initiative and wish them every success for the future.'

She also said that she would be at the New Vic theatre in May 2006 to take part in 'An Evening with Queen Victoria'. Perhaps, she said, that might be a good time for us to meet up and talk about ways she might be able to help us further. I was excited by this, not least because we had our first celebrity backer with a real interest in farming, conservation and what we were trying to do. We wasted no time in putting her quote on our literature.

The share applications dripped in; three here, four there, occasional days when we had six, seven, eight. The demand wasn't huge, but it was steady and the fighting fund was growing all the time. By early November we had taken cheques totalling about £20,000, though we were still unable to send out share certificates due to the delay in incorporation. I was adamant that we would not sign the agreement until the rules could not be improved any further. We had to think of every eventuality. The rules had to work for the next generation and the one after that, just as much as they should work for us. Thankfully, our prospective shareholders were patient, but I was getting increasingly worried that certificates would not be ready for Christmas. I thought we were doing quite well financially, then I would compare the money we'd raised so far to the £800,000 in front of us, and the colossal difference between the two loomed like an impassable brick wall. On my fingers, I would do a quick calculation of how many months we had to go, and how much we needed to raise each month to hit the target. It was at those times when I began to feel physically sick and drained.

Sophie and I went to a farmland trust conference in Stroud organised by Greg and Martin early that winter, at which we were the star attraction. Greg and Martin were already holding Fordhall up as a model project, and it became clear that all eyes were on us to succeed. The pressure was huge and if any of us stopped to think about it we would find ourselves spinning into a minor panic. We had to make this work. We had to succeed and raise the money and buy the farm, because if we didn't there would be no hope for other similar projects in the future, never mind what happened to us and Fordhall Farm.

Fortunately, this pioneering spirit was more often exciting, challenging and energising than not. But on the days when it was all just too much, I confided in my diary before I went to bed: 'I am not sure if I can continue with this, it feels too hard at the moment. I am not sure if I have the energy to carry on.' Not surprisingly, however, after a good night's sleep I was mentally back on form again, with the doubts of the previous night completely out of my mind.

One morning, a couple of days after I'd given Ben a hand moving some shop fixtures and fittings into the recently re-floored farm shop, I was sitting alone in the office going through the post. Normally our volunteers and board members, Bryan and Elaine, would be doing that but, as the postman had arrived early, I had decided to do it myself. There were a couple of applications for shares, which I put aside to be dealt with later, and a letter postmarked Wiltshire. I opened it and a cheque dropped out. I read it and my legs turned to jelly. It was for £2000. I read and reread it, to make sure it was for us. It was from The Lake House Trust.

There was a short letter enclosed, thanking us for our correspondence and informing us that a donation of £2000 had been made. I was so astonished that I didn't seem to hear the phone going in the club room. It stopped ringing and after a couple of minutes I got up to listen to the message. It was from Elaine, a kind, gentle lady from the Stafford Soil Association group who had supported us from the early days.

'Hi Charlotte,' she said, 'I don't know if you've opened your post yet, but you might find something exciting in it. I followed up on your letter to Sting and Trudie Styler and they've replied.'

The penny dropped. The £2000 had been from Sting! I repeated this over and over, trying to make it sink in. I'd almost forgotten about the letter I'd sent to Trudie Styler and although I knew Elaine had tried to reach both her and Sting a couple more times, we'd heard nothing. Until this. An amazing early Christmas present and the single largest cheque we'd had so far. When I told Ben his smile stretched from ear to ear and Sophie was as elated as I was. It was moments like that, when we reached the people we thought were unreachable, which made us really believe we were moving forward with the project and there was hope out there. Days like that gave our energy levels and enthusiasm a fresh and much-needed boost.

We knew the donation would make a good story and prove a powerful tool in helping to convert the sceptics. So we told the local press who went crazy over it. But in interviews I was also conscious of thanking the many other ordinary people who had donated to the cause. They were the backbone of the campaign to save the farm and we needed their support more than ever.

As we expected, the run-up to Christmas was very busy for us all, with people catching on to the idea of buying a share in an organic farm as a present and Ben dealing with increased orders in the farm shop. Finally, on 6 December 2005 we were registered as an Industrial and Provident Society and we were able to issue share certificates just in time for Christmas. The pleasure of being able to fill an envelope with the long-awaited certificate, write an address on the front and put it in the letter box was immeasurable. At last we were able to say to people that a small slice of Fordhall would be dropping on their doormats very soon. But we didn't have much time to meet the Christmas post deadline. Generously, North Shropshire District Council had offered their franking service to help speed up the process. Ten days before Christmas, Sophie and I raced to the council offices in Wem with 321 share certificates, hoping they would frank them before they went home for the day.

Chapter 26: Charlotte

'Wait!' shouted Sophie, just as I was about to hand the envelopes over to the receptionist behind the desk.

'What's wrong?'

'We've forgotten the Christmas cards!'

We had printed Fordhall Christmas cards for all our new shareholders to say thank you for their patience as we waited for incorporation. But crucially, we had forgotten to put them into the envelopes – they were still in the boot of my car.

'Damn it! It's OK, we can put them in now.' We hastily re-opened all 321 envelopes, added the Fordhall Christmas card and resealed them, hoping our shareholders would appreciate the festive gesture. I think the ladies behind the reception desk found the whole escapade extremely humorous, but at least our job was done. Such crazy methods, challenges and adventures were all part of our everyday life at Fordhall and they have given us memories that will last for ever.

Back at home, Ben was busy getting orders ready for our customers' Christmas meat and needed our help. He was really excited as sales in 2005 were set to double those of 2004. We had made a modest profit in our first year of trading, which surprised both us and our accountant, but for Ben to even begin thinking of quitting his jobs away from the farm, we had to do a lot better.

We had worked on the farm shop jointly for the first year, but as things had begun to progress with the project, I had passed full responsibility for the farm shop and business to Ben. I simply did the VAT return each quarter and, of course, kept my eye on the chequebook. Sophie and I would often watch Ben moving livestock or putting up fences from the office window – seeing him at work brought the outside world into our office, where we seemed to be spending more and more of our time. The new responsibility had done wonders for Ben's confidence and he was thriving on the challenge, always looking for new ways to sell his products while watching the fields carefully so that he could manage the winter grazing. Dad would have been so proud.

After the last post had gone and the final Christmas order had been sent out, we had just enough time to plan a relaxing Christmas at Fordhall, a time to rejuvenate ourselves before what promised to be a momentous year ahead. That year we held Christmas at Fordhall. It was to be the first Christmas without Dad, so it felt right to stay at the farm instead of at Marianne's, where we'd spent it for the last ten years. The deterioration of the Fordhall farmhouse and the overshadowing court cases had created a negative atmosphere that we strove to avoid at what should be a joyful time of year. But the Christmas of 2005 could be the last at Fordhall. The old creaking house felt warm and welcoming that Christmas Day. Ben had got up early to light all the fires and we had even splashed out on a bag of coal so that he could keep them going all day. We wanted to make it as special as possible and it was.

We had a late, three-course, fully home-cooked meal, and in the traditional Hollins family way, left the presents until just before dessert. However, before we got that far, something magical happened. Just as we raised our glasses to toast Christmas, Fordhall and Dad, our old grandfather clock, which sat in the corner of the room and which had not been wound up for years, chimed. The timing was perfect and it felt as though Dad was in the room with us. Whether it was him or some kind of reserved energy in the spring, we will never know. But we felt he was there and that was what counted.

Chapter 26: Charlotte

It was a wonderful Christmas and our thoughts of Dad gave us the energy to tackle the year ahead. Whether we saved the farm or not, we were going to ensure that everything we did, we did to the best of our abilities.

27

Ben

The farmer's year seems to have no beginning and no end. You don't mark time like everyone else, with Christmas, Easter, Bonfire Night and the rest. Instead you mark time with lambing, calving, silaging, harvesting and weaning, and because the seasons are always turning, bringing new demands as well as requiring you to do certain things at certain times, there is never a natural break. If you need to take time out you have to make double, treble sure that all your work is covered for the period. You're managing nature, which is unpredictable at the best of times, and so any slackness on a farm can lead to disaster.

While Charlotte was celebrating the welcome arrival of cheques from rock stars, I was dealing with the newly born lambs. They arrived early, just two days before Christmas. There were many more to follow, and all over that Christmas period I was keeping a close eye on our Suffolk ewes, who all seemed to be popping out lambs like shelled peas. Between the lambing and the various farmers' markets, which started up again once the Christmas break was finished, I was experiencing a very busy start to 2006.

Still, I thought it was important that Charlotte and I showed a united front at the Soil Association Food and Farming Conference in early January. Although I'm always nervous whenever I have to leave the farm for more than a day, this conference would be an excellent platform for encouraging new supporters. We had done well over Christmas with people buying shares as presents for family and friends, but we were still a long way off raising £100,000, never mind eight times that amount. We had a long way to go, but events like this one would help spread the word. Plus, it was a night away in a hotel in London, and while I'm no great lover of the bright lights, I do find that the occasional break from the relentlessness of running a farm charges your batteries massively.

We would be talking about the FCLI and our farming enterprises as part of a series of workshops looking at various aspects of farming. Ours was called 'The Next Generation' and focused on the challenges for younger people wanting to get involved with organic farming. If there were ever two young people who knew about the challenges of farming organically, it was Charlotte and me. When we arrived there seemed to be hundreds of people there, most of them standing due to the lack of seats.

Since standing up at the inquiry in early 2004 and making the speech that helped to get Fordhall's twelve-acre field taken out of the local plan, we had done various speaking engagements together, though not nearly as many as Charlotte had done on her own. I still found public speaking daunting.

I went on stage first and talked about the farm, the foggage system, the livestock, the farmers' markets, the rare breeds and the unique quality of the soil. I mentioned Dad and I touched on the tenancy, though I drew back from explaining the whole situation. That would be Charlotte's task. I finished, and sat down to an enthusiastic burst of applause. I listened as my sister, with the aid of a PowerPoint presentation, went through the structure of the initiative and the fund-raising campaign. Being part of the story I knew it inside out, so I took the opportunity to sit back and observe the way people reacted to what was being said.

Something extraordinary was happening in the room. People weren't just listening to the story and letting it wash over them, they really seemed to be engaging with it emotionally. By the expressions on their faces and the occasional intake of breath or shaking of the head, I could see that the story of Fordhall Farm and the fight we had taken up to save it was strongly affecting people. By now, our slot had definitely run its course and Charlotte was still taking questions, but the chairman didn't seem to mind. The audience wanted to hear more, much more, and we were happy to oblige.

Finally, the chairman called a halt to the questions, but as we left the room we were followed by a group who hadn't yet heard enough. We were surrounded by people who were brimming with enthusiasm for what we were doing. Some wanted to buy shares, others were interested in volunteering. Some just wanted to wish us well and urge us on to success. Of course, we were talking to the sort of people who would always be behind a venture like ours, but we really didn't expect such an overwhelming reaction, especially as we were only a small part of such a big conference.

The word must have gone round about us. We were approached by a constant stream of people who either had listened to us speak, or had heard about our project and wanted to know more. I was being buttonholed by people who were telling me that we were *the* topic of conversation that day. To get a break I nipped into the loo, but even in there I was collared by someone who said his whole table had been talking about us.

It felt very strange, generating such a buzz in an environment like this. We'd had plenty of support from people coming to the farm and, of course, in the form of the new shareholders we were picking up every day, but to hear yourself being talked about like this was weird. It was hard to gauge which bits of the story affected people the most; all we did was explain the situation up to now and let people make their own minds up. But we were touching a nerve, whether in getting people thinking about the way we produce or consume today, our 'David and Goliath' struggle against large-scale development, or simply the story of one man's fight to do things his way, a fight continued by his children, or all three, it didn't seem to matter. It wasn't us provoking such a reaction in people, it was the farm, this mysterious and beautiful place, that seemed to be winning people over. We just carried its story round with us and passed it on wherever and whenever we could.

28
Charlotte

We had expected January to be quiet as far as shares were concerned, and it was. Opening the post was still the highlight of the day though. You never knew what you were going to pull out of the next envelope and there was a secret hope, each time you began to rip it open, that there would be a fat cheque inside. Of course that never happened. But January did give us time to catch up on other jobs and time to plan for the next six months. We were looking forward to the challenges of 2006 and making that July deadline.

The farmhouse was still in a state of general disrepair, our office included. Situated in the old restaurant dining room, it was one of the largest rooms in the house. There was an enormous sash window, Dad's wonky old Welsh dresser filled with decorative plates stood against one wall, almost holding it up, and a large open fireplace. My desk, in the centre of the room, faced the sash window, while Sophie sat opposite me. It was an atmospheric room, filled with memories and stories, but it was excessively cold in these winter months.

We lit the fire as soon as we got up in the morning but this alone could not heat the room, in fact it often struggled to heat the dark office at all. It offered more of a warm glow to stare at for inspiration. In an attempt to save energy (and money) Sophie and I would wear tights, trousers, T-shirts, scarves, jumpers and more jumpers, the more layers the better. We even treated ourselves to some fingerless gloves that we could wear as we worked on the computers late into the night.

Our office was next to Ben's farm office. This allowed us to stay in constant communication with each other. He had a log burner, made by his godfather, Peter Rudd, out of an old Calor gas bottle and it radiated heat like an oven. I have to admit that Sophie and I were slightly jealous of Ben's office on occasion and we would sometimes sneak in to use his computer while he was out farming so that we could defrost.

Like the rest of the house, our office had peeling wallpaper and yellow patches where the damp had seeped through. But we did our best to brighten it up with photos of the farm animals and inspirational quotes that we had come across in our research. Bar Dad's dresser, everything in our office – all the desks, filing cabinets and shelves, even the laser printer – had been donated by North Shropshire District Council and supporters. It was stuff that would have been thrown out if we didn't take it – there is nothing more energy efficient than making use of other people's rubbish.

We had moved into this office in November 2005. By the end of December we had 321 shareholders and, although we were a long way from hitting our £800,000 target, we were moving in the right direction. To have raised £20,000 from nothing in just three months was amazing and we were focusing on this achievement to bolster us through the quiet months.

Plus, we were getting some wonderful words of support. Prince Charles, in several letters to us, made clear his encouragement, and we also had a message from Patrick Holden, the director of the Soil Association, after our talk at their conference in London. Patrick said there had already been 'one lost generation of the 1980s and we don't want to lose another one. Ben and Charlotte are a perfect example of how young people's passion can make a difference. They are an inspirational example to us all.' We were thrilled.

Messages like that kept us going, along with continuing support from volunteers and visitors to the farm shop. At the start of February we organised another volunteer working weekend. Fifty volunteers helped us mend fences, lay hedges and plant oak, alder and hazel saplings donated by Shropshire County Council. It was a productive and fun weekend and, as always, Fordhall came alive with the enjoyment of so many people.

Among the volunteers was a self-effacing, modest and quietly humorous man called Christoph. He was a writer from south London and he had bought a share in Fordhall Farm on the strength of the *Observer* article. He was inspired enough to take his shareholdership a little further and come up to see Fordhall for himself. Not only was he funny and enthusiastic about our mission, he was also a non-stop stream of good ideas that we might use.

'This farm just *has* to be saved!' he would say over and over again.

He spent time with Mum and they really enjoyed each other's company. He understood her troubles and the difficult journey she'd already been on. A fortnight later, Christoph came back with his entire family to show them the gate he had helped to hang on the volunteer weekend.

'Just because I'm proud of it,' he replied, when we asked him why. 'I live in south London and you don't get the chance to hang farm gates very often down there. You might think it's an everyday thing, but I'm telling you, it's deeply satisfying for a city person to be able to come here and do this type of work.'

His desire to help Fordhall had consumed him and he was telling everyone he met about our campaign. ' . . . And one of them works for the *Telegraph*,' he said. 'Her name is Sally Williams and she's an excellent journalist. I've been round and knocked on her door and told her that she needs to get in touch with you ASAP. You need to get another good national hit and I think she might be just the person to help. She's really enthusiastic about it.'

This sounded very encouraging and we waited to see if she would call. In the meantime, we were working on ways of improving the shares take-up and donations. After numerous calculations we came up with a strapline to attract people's attention – '32m sq of Natural English Countryside for only £50!' A bit like selling plots on the moon, except you could actually come and stand in your thirty-two square metres and survey all that you owned, if you so wished. A brainstorming session with some PR students from Wolverhampton University who were doing coursework on our campaign resulted in the idea of a charity dinner with an auction and a ceilidh. It was just what we needed, and we began to organise it at Harper Adams, where Ben was still studying. It would be a black-tie affair with tickets at £50 a head. One of the raffle prizes was donated by Prince Charles himself: a guided tour round the gardens at Highgrove House. It wouldn't be a cheap evening out, but we wanted it to be a very memorable occasion and raise a good amount of money for the FCLI.

Chapter 28: Charlotte

We booked Tom Oliver, the head of rural policy for the CPRE, as guest speaker. It was very kind of him to even want to attend, given our accidental hijacking of his *Observer* article.

As we waited to hear from Sally Williams from the *Telegraph*, we had our ten-minute slot on the BBC Midlands regional news programme, *Inside Out*, to watch. Ten minutes was a lot of airtime to fill and we were hoping that this would give the campaign the post-Christmas boost that it desperately needed. Could it help us win the hearts and minds of people right across our region?

Mum, Ben and I settled down in the bar room to watch it, full of the usual mixture of embarrassment and enthralment about seeing ourselves on TV. Halfway through Ben spoke up. I knew what he was going to say.

'They haven't mentioned the shares yet,' he said. 'Or anything about being community owned.'

'I know. Fingers crossed though. There's still about four minutes to go.'

We watched on. All the information about Dad and the organic ethos and even the educational side of the Initiative was there. But nothing at all about the shares. It looked as though Ben and I were raising money to buy the farm for ourselves; that we would be the owners. It was about as far from reality as it was possible to get and we felt hugely disappointed. This was the one aspect of the story we'd tried the hardest to get over. Ever since our launch some local people had found the community ownership concept difficult to get their heads around. So in every interview we had stressed and double-stressed the community involvement aspect of the project and how we would be tenants of a community land trust. It seemed the message had not got through to the documentary team and as soon as it had finished I was on the phone to complain. They apologised. Apparently, the share issue was too difficult to explain in a ten-minute slot. I just couldn't understand it, as News 24 and *Midlands Today* had both been able to do it very successfully in three-minute slots on previous occasions. It seemed they had simply not understood the most fundamental part of the campaign. I wanted them to broadcast a correction the next time *Inside Out* was aired, but they refused, and besides, the damage was already done.

We felt frustrated for days afterwards. It would take time and effort to explain the mistake to anyone who'd seen the documentary and gone with the explanation for the campaign offered by the BBC. It felt as if all the hard work we had put in to getting across the 'community-owned' message had been wasted in one fell swoop and this misconception could cost us the support of the local people, those from whom we needed support most. We put a clarification on our website, but that was all we could do, and we inevitably became more cautious of any press interest. There would be no more ambiguity. No journalist would leave Fordhall without a full and clear understanding of how the Fordhall Community Land Initiative worked or the benefits it would have for the public as well as for ourselves. We simply could not afford another mistake like this.

So when Sally Williams from the *Daily Telegraph* finally rang to tell us that Christoph had almost beaten down her door to give her a good story and that she'd like to see us, we ensured that we were fully prepared for her visit. Sally was a lovely person, interested in what we were doing and knowledgeable about the issues involved. She was also extremely hard to gauge; unlike the majority of journalists who visited us, she didn't give much away about how she might pitch her article. Other journalists openly voiced their support for what we were doing or their concern over the likely success of our campaign. With all previous articles, including the BBC documentary, we had been left with a sense of the story's direction, even if it was misplaced. Sally was different; although friendly, she retained an air of cool professional detachment as we explained the background to the campaign.

After the interview was over, as we watched her car rattle down the drive, I turned to Ben and asked him what he thought.

'I don't know,' he replied. 'I really, really don't know. I hope it's not going to show us in a bad light.'

'Me too. Do you think we got the shares thing over OK?'

'I can't see how we could have done it any better. We must have told her about eight times. Surely the message was clear enough?'

'You'd have thought so,' I replied. But in my heart, I still wasn't sure. If we ended up with a negative or incorrect article in a national newspaper, it could destroy the last few months of the campaign. I was desperately worried, but with numerous deadlines for grant applications and the charity dinner to organise, not to mention the Family Fun Day (now an annual event), volunteer events and more reporters to pester, I had to move on. We had submitted three major grant applications which, if successful, would be a huge boost for the campaign and take us close to our target. We had already been turned down by one organisation, but we had our fingers crossed for the other two. We had also entered into friendly dialogue with a bank at long last – the Bristol-based Triodos bank, which operates on ethical lines. They had followed our campaign from the early days and were keen to help. We knew that a loan or mortgage would have to be an option for the purchase so we hoped they'd offer us a favourable package should we need it. We had to cover as many bases as possible and could not rely on the shares alone to raise enough funds. Many of our supporters had suggested trying the National Lottery, but the time required to complete the detailed forms simply did not exist and it might be two years before we heard their decision. It was time that, unfortunately, we just did not have.

In March we had a board meeting to discuss the latest position. We had around 500 shareholders and had raised some £60,000 so far. No mean figure in itself, but light years away from our target. It was a somewhat fractious meeting. Some of our board members, quite rightly, pointed out that we had more than £700,000 to raise and only four months to do it in. What was Plan B?

'There isn't one,' I said. 'If we don't raise the money the landlord won't extend the deadline. We can ask them again, but I don't think we'll get much joy. We have this one and only chance to succeed.'

'So, what happens next?'

'We keep going. We just have to keep pushing. If 500 people so far are very passionate about Fordhall, then we only need a lot more people to be slightly less passionate about it and we'll get there. We've got to stick at it. We have no choice. I'm positive that we will succeed; we have simply come too far not to.'

One of our board members commented: 'Charlotte, if we draw a graph and plot the amount raised so far over time, and then draw an average line between those points . . . '

'Yes,' I said, knowing exactly where he was going.

' . . . and you then put that against the time we have left and the amount of money we still have to raise, I'm afraid it just doesn't add up.'

I was infuriated that our own board members could not

see the potential here. But I could understand why they couldn't see it. They were not in the office every day. They didn't hear people crying on the phone to us because they had been through similar situations and lost, or because they were so pleased that they could once again have a connection to the land. They could not see the passion that we were seeing when people found out about the project. All we needed was to get our story out to more people. It was a simple task, but we were working all hours every day to ensure that we achieved it.

Maybe they thought I was being stubborn and ridiculous. But I truly believed the path we had set ourselves on was the only way forward. We were talking about the possibility of a loan to cover a shortfall, but the majority of the money had to come from the shares issue. As we'd found out to our disappointment, we couldn't bank on getting a grant and, even if we did, there was no guarantee it would arrive on time. The only possibility of us hitting our target was through a public appeal and it would be ordinary people who decided our fate. Of that, I was certain.

At the beginning of April, much to everyone's relief, Tom, a friend of Sophie's, kindly volunteered his time and set us up as online traders – shares were now finally available online via our website. Perhaps the Fordhall magic was working again, because just a week later the *Telegraph* article came out. As luck would have it, our online sales service went live just as the campaign really went national.

We knew when the article was coming out – Easter Saturday, 15 April – and Sally told us that it would be about 1000 words long. But that was it. We had done the interview, the photographer had been down and all I was concerned about was that the article mentioned something about the shares. I was working at Cheswardine that Saturday and, just like the last time we'd featured in a national newspaper, I reminded myself to stop at the newsagent's on my way to the care home. At 7.15 a.m. I quickly picked up a copy of the paper from the bundle, paid for it and took it back to the car. I rifled through to get to the weekend supplement section, then froze. There we were, beaming from the cover of the *Telegraph*'s Easter Weekend Supplement. I could barely believe my eyes. We were on the front cover. There was a double-page spread, with a half-page photo. Numb, I put the paper down without actually reading a word, put the keys into my car's ignition and drove to Cheswardine on autopilot, completely stunned.

News travels fast, especially when you're the cover star of a national newspaper supplement. The early birds among the residents at the home had already seen the article and there was a real sense of 'oohh, she's here!' when I walked through the front door. A lot of them were *Telegraph* readers and they couldn't believe we'd made it on to the pages of their favourite newspaper. I finally had time to skim-read it and it was all there; Sally Williams had done a terrific job. It was the best piece of press we'd had so far, a fantastically positive story, and it mentioned every aspect of the fight in no small detail. Not only had she faithfully recorded our quotes, she had also contacted people like the Soil Association's Patrick Holden and the environmental campaigner Colin Tudge for their opinions. Christoph was in there, giving an example of what volunteering at Fordhall was like, and she had not forgotten the all-important share-buying issue, which she covered comprehensively but uncomplicatedly.

To say I was overjoyed is an understatement. If this didn't give us the push we needed, nothing would. I thought back to the last board meeting, when I said that 'something would turn up'. And here it was. Of course, it didn't guarantee a huge rush of sales, but it was about the best publicity we could get and it had all stemmed from that cold volunteer weekend in February. I had to ring Ben and Sophie straight away, to check they'd seen the piece. I could hardly punch the numbers in I was so excited.

I tried and tried to get through. Nothing would work. Their mobiles just rang and rang and the landline was always engaged. I was puzzled. They were both there that day, I knew. Ben was minding the farm shop while Sophie had come in early to catch up on some paperwork. What was going on? I ploughed through the rest of my shift, still enjoying the comments from the residents who were busily reading the article, and at 3 p.m. I left Cheswardine and drove straight home.

I walked into the office and was met by the sight of Sophie scribbling frantically on a large pad of paper, the phone clamped to her ear. I tried to ask her what was wrong with everyone's phones, but she quickly shushed me.

'Please could you hold the line a moment,' she said to the person on the end of the line, before putting her hand over the receiver, 'Charlotte, just give me a sec and I'll explain everything. Hello? Yes, sorry about that. Now, if I could take your postcode again and we'll get back to you as soon as we can . . .'

She finished the conversation and put the phone down. Immediately it started ringing again.

'Hello, Fordhall Community Land Initiative. Sophie speaking. Yes, that's us. I know, it's a great piece isn't it? I'm really pleased you enjoyed it. Yes, of course shares are for sale. They're on our website, but if you'd like more details I can put some information in the post to you? OK, if you could just give me your address?'

Another five minutes and she put the phone down. On cue, it rang again.

'Right, I'm going to leave this one to the answer machine,' she said. 'I've got to tell you what's gone on here today. It's been completely, utterly mad. That phone hasn't stopped ringing since 8 a.m. and Ben hasn't been able to leave the farm shop because there have been so many visitors. Neither of us has had time for lunch.'

'You're kidding? I can't believe it!'

'No, I'm not kidding. Ben and I have taken it in shifts to answer the phone and work in the shop. Every time we put the phone down we find there are about fifteen new messages on the answer machine. Honestly, Charlotte, it's been melt-down here.'

'And they're all talking about the article?' I was amazed. I felt as though a weight had been lifted from my shoulders.

'Yes! Seems like the whole country's seen it. If it carries on like this, we're going to need another phone line pretty damn quick.'

I looked over her shoulder and saw the pages and pages of names and addresses she'd jotted down. All these people, none of whom we knew, or had ever met, and they'd rung our home number to see if they could help us out. It was nothing less than extraordinary. I was astonished and almost moved to tears by people's generosity. Once again, the old question popped up in my head – what was it that was bringing people into our world? Was it the educational side, our commitment to organic farming, or the battle to save the dwindling English countryside from large-scale development? But I hardly had time to answer my own questions. The phone was ringing again and Ben and Sophie needed a break. It was my turn to be Fordhall's receptionist.

We went through the rest of that day and into the evening

working almost non-stop. Just after midnight I decided that I would drag myself to bed, tempted though I was to sit by the phone all night. Tomorrow was Easter Sunday, and we'd planned to have a quiet family day, just Mum, Ben and me and our half-sister Marianne and her husband Alan. After weeks of hard work we were looking forward to a rare day off, and a chance to catch up with one another properly.

Not a hope. By 10 a.m. there was a queue of cars down the drive, packed with people who wanted to meet us and find out more about what they'd read in the paper. We would have been foolish to turn them away, so instead we opened the gate and the farm shop, and welcomed all comers. It was a terrific day, though any thoughts of a lunch break were quickly put aside in the rush to serve people, answer the phone and talk to visitors who wanted to see the farm. Our brother-in-law Alan did his stint on the phone, and was surprised to find that callers were disappointed when they found out they weren't speaking to Ben or me. It was almost as if we had become celebrities overnight.

We also had to keep an eye on the massive number of emails we were receiving, just in case our computer crashed. As we always suspected, the Internet shares sales were very popular, so popular, in fact, that we raised £20,000 that weekend in online sales alone. PayPal even phoned us as they were worried someone was laundering money through our account! In total, we estimated that one article in the *Daily Telegraph* helped to bring in around £200,000 worth of shares sales, a phenomenal amount of money and a tribute to the words of Sally Williams and the kindness of those readers who responded almost as soon as the paper hit the streets.

The week before, Sophie and I had been working more than twelve hours a day every day and we could not see that we could physically do any more. But it's interesting how you fit things in when you have to. Our work rate seemed to treble overnight. Aside from the 300 or more addresses we had taken over the Easter weekend, there seemed to be a bulging mailbag full of new applications every day. Mum, Sophie and I sat up stuffing envelopes with share application forms and hand-writing envelopes until we could no longer keep our eyes open. It was clear that even between those of us already working at the farm, there was no way all the work could be completed. Fortunately, the cavalry was coming over the hill in the shape of our ever-loyal volunteers. After the *Telegraph* article we were inundated with help. People travelled from all over England. One volunteer came from Sussex twice and a young man from Leeds called Rob camped in the garden and opened the post for us every day for a month. It would take him more than eight hours to do that one job, such was the volume of mail. All he did was open each envelope, check the name on the form, stamp the application with the date and put it into a separate pile from the cheque for someone else to process. It was a marathon job and, under any other circumstances, mind-numbing. But Rob wasn't bothered, because the content of the letters he was receiving made every hour of his job worthwhile.

'You see the best side of human kindness when you do this job,' he would say, and he'd read out some of the more interesting or emotive letters for the rest of us, silently beavering away in the office, to hear. One very memorable letter was from a woman whose sixteen-year-old daughter was disabled and housebound. She was her daughter's sole carer, and had decided to buy her a share in the farm because it was a way of bringing the outside world into her existence. The woman would ring us occasionally during the campaign to find out how we were getting on and to talk about her life. She was pleased to hear that we enjoyed her calls and understood her reasons for buying a share. Maybe it was the case that a lot of city people bought shares for a similar reason, in that it was a way of bringing the countryside to them. But we had just as many buyers from the countryside itself, many of whom had seen how industrialised farming had become over the years and wanted to do something to preserve the natural way. Others seemed to be recognising the difficulties faced by young entrants to the farming industry and wanted to offer support. Whatever their reasons, we were pleased with and humbled by their response.

29
Ben

I watched with interest as rucksacks were hauled across the farmyard and into the garden. Their contents were spilled on to the newly mown grass and out came a kaleidoscope of coloured nylon, all tied up with bits of string, guy ropes and bungee cords. Excitement and anticipation filled the late spring air; it was another working weekend at Fordhall and it would be the first time this year that volunteers would take their chances under canvas.

I liked seeing people camp here. Not only did it give them the chance to experience a truly outdoor weekend, but a tent affords a bit of peace and quiet at the end of a day when you've been busy among so many other people. Not that there was much peace and quiet around Fordhall at the beginning of May. The *Telegraph* article had been the fuse that exploded the campaign to a new level and almost overnight Fordhall Farm had become very big news.

The difference was noticeable at the first farmers' markets

I did after Easter. No longer was I 'Ben from Fordhall', the amateurish young guy trying to make a go of a run-down organic farm. Now, it seemed, I was 'Ben from Fordhall – you know, the one in the *Telegraph*.' So many people would come up to the stall and say they'd seen me on the TV or in the paper. Others would walk by and whisper to one another: 'Look, there's Fordhall Farm.' I started to understand how Jimmy Doherty, of the TV show *Jimmy's Farm*, might feel when he went to market.

The reaction at the markets I was attending ran parallel to the cheques and share applications with which we were suddenly inundated back at the farm. Charlotte and Sophie kept a running total of how many letters we'd received and how much money we'd taken. It really was incredible to hear the totals. Just before the *Telegraph* article we had raised about £70,000, and at the start of the working weekend on 1 May 2006 we were close on £200,000. With just sixty days to raise more than £600,000 we weren't out of the woods yet, but the campaign had definitely moved up a few gears and we seemed to be on a roll. If we didn't make it, it certainly wouldn't be for lack of effort.

Our friends under canvas in the garden were full of optimism for us and their enthusiasm carried us through a particularly successful working weekend. We chopped logs, painted gates, shifted bricks and moved the picnic area to a more scenic location near our pigs who were shaded by the ancient oak tree. I was enjoying being in charge of these weekends with Sophie. Farming can be a lonely business sometimes but, when you've got a willing group of people suddenly working by your side, the tasks you find mundane or even boring seem to take on a new life. We built a sturdy stile over the fence to the picnic site and the level of satisfaction gained from that activity was very noticeable. The Saturday of that weekend saw some great weather, but it turned a little fresher on the Sunday and there were one or two damp volunteers in their tents that morning. They soon rallied, though, when they had the chance to see a cow giving birth – not an everyday occurrence for many of our city-dwelling friends. This particular cow was a Jersey, given to us as a thank-you gift by Joyce, who Dad had helped get into cheese making many years ago. Although not the ideal beef-producing cow, we had kept her for sentimental reasons. She later gave birth to a healthy, lively Hereford heifer – one of Barry's first calves.

The campaign was really starting to get going now and through the recent media interest we had accumulated a mass of support. But along with the support came extra work. I had a girlfriend at the time, Holly. We had been together for nearly four years, but the past few months had put a lot of strain on our relation-ship and I was seeing less and less of her. I would visit her in the evening after finishing my jobs on the farm and quite often I had only been there for ten minutes before I fell asleep on the sofa. It wasn't the kind of relationship a girl in her early twen-ties wanted. Most of our mates would be out drinking and partying on weekends, but I was busy packing meat for food fairs and feeding pigs while they were nursing their hangovers.

With the extra work caused by the mass of media interest, and the increasing commitments I was taking on at the farm, Holly and I decided it would be best to split up. It was a hard decision, as I felt forced to choose between someone I really cared for and the farm. It made me wonder whether all the hassle and energy that it was taking to save Fordhall was worth it. But I knew it would be in the end. It just wasn't fair on Holly to carry on as we were, so we went our separate ways but always vowed to stay friends.

The publicity had another side effect. Suddenly we were in

demand as guest speakers. Between Charlotte, Sophie and me, we did three in a week, which was exhausting but productive. The Stafford Soil Association group, to whom I spoke with Charlotte, were very keen to hear how we'd gone from nearly nothing in terms of livestock to where we were now – 50 cattle, 123 sheep and 20 pigs. It was the steady growth I'd always hoped to achieve at Fordhall Farm. As I spoke I could feel a small wave of pride wash over me for having got to where I wanted in such a short space of time. I didn't often feel like that. Farming is a hard job and you don't tend to stop and wonder at your achievements. You just get on with it. But when I tell people what was here when we took over in 2004 compared to what there is now, it's hard not to talk yourself up just a little bit!

In the middle of May, one of our first celebrity supporters fulfilled a promise made to us the previous year. Prunella Scales was making a scheduled appearance at the New Vic theatre in Newcastle-under-Lyme, and through our friend and New Vic director Peter Cheeseman, we were told she would be prepared to say something about Fordhall Farm at the end of the show. I don't admit to being a regular theatre-goer, but this was an event not to be missed. A group of us were invited along – me, Charlotte, Sophie and Mum – and we sat expectantly through Prunella's performance, wondering what she was going to say. Right at the very end, she came out of the Queen Victoria character she was playing. She fished out a piece of paper from somewhere and, as she did, the audience descended into a kind of puzzled hush. Only we knew what was going on.

It wasn't a long speech, but in it she praised the campaign and urged people to buy share certificates. 'In fact,' she said, 'if anyone wants to buy one tonight I'm very happy to sign their certificate, so enthusiastic am I about this project.'

She was as good as her word and, while she autographed

the newly purchased certificates, we stood outside the theatre and gave out as many leaflets as we could carry to the departing audience, telling them all about the farm, the initiative and the campaign.

We took the opportunity to invite Prunella down to the farm. She said she'd be delighted to come and, as she was in the area, would tomorrow be too soon? Not at all, we said, and the following day she joined us for a walk around Fordhall. She told us about her childhood on a farm and how she believed preserving land such as ours was vital to the health of the countryside. It was strange to hear the woman who used to bully poor Basil Fawlty on a daily basis talk about nature conservation and the importance of keeping traditional farming alive, but there it was.

'I have always had a keen passion for the landscape,' Prunella said, as we made our way down to the spring-fed pool, always a delight at that time of year, with mayflies and damsel flies hovering above it, occasionally dipping their tails in to lay their eggs. 'I find it disgusting to see how much green-belt land is being built over when there are perfectly suitable brownfield sites,' she continued. 'There's so much beauty here.'

She stopped for a moment and gazed over at the hawthorn hedges, which had just burst into bloom after a few nights of heavy rain. 'It's only a small part of England,' she mused, 'but I'm sure your project will succeed. It has too much to give not to.'

Her enthusiasm was infectious and we were delighted that she'd made the effort to see Fordhall, even though it was an unseasonably overcast day and she probably had a hundred other things to do.

Prunella's wholehearted support gave us the impetus to look around for more celebrity backing. We didn't want to become a celebrity 'cause', and we understood that the vast majority of our shareholders were people who had nothing at all to do with television, theatre or music. But we realised it did our credibility no harm at all to pick up support from famous people, particularly those who in some way were connected with or had a passion for the land, organic farming or countryside preservation. In the same month that Prunella visited Fordhall, Charlotte travelled to Shrewsbury to hear Dr David Bellamy speak at a conference. Afterwards, she introduced herself, but before she could begin the by-now-familiar speech we gave to anyone who might not have heard about us, he stopped her with a wave of his hand.

'Oh, don't worry, I know who you are,' he said. 'You're Arthur Hollins's daughter, aren't you? I'm familiar with Fordhall Farm – the past as well as the present.'

It turned out that he owned Dad's book, so he was aware of Fordhall's history. He'd also kept abreast of the latest goings-on at Fordhall and Charlotte hardly needed to ask him whether he would support us. Of course he would, he said, and he promised to write to as many influential people as possible on our behalf, to widen the net.

Generous support like his was such a boost. We were also in contact with Jimmy Doherty, who was interested in the structure of the initiative and was looking at it as a possible means of securing his own, more famous farm in the future. Charlotte and I were also invited to gardener Monty Don's new project in Herefordshire, a small farm employing young people who were serial offenders as a means of taking them away from their old lifestyles and allowing them to find themselves through outdoor life and farm work. We were greeted by a very enthusiastic chap about my age, who told us how great the farm was and what they'd all been doing to grow vegetables and even breed pigs. His new-found passion proved to me how important it was going to be to make the farm accessible for people and to make a space where people, particularly those from deprived or inner-city homes, could come and learn about farming and where their food comes from. This young chap had gained so much from working on Monty's farm, that I felt there must be lots more people out there in a similar situation who could benefit from visiting Fordhall. I could see that our land was valuable in so many ways.

After the disappointment of the BBC Midlands *Inside Out* programme, which gave most of the West Midlands the idea that we wanted them to buy the farm so we could own it and run it for ourselves, they contacted us again. They wanted to do an update and possibly follow us right up to deadline day.

At first, we said no. We couldn't afford a repeat of the first programme, which had utterly failed to grasp the issue of shared ownership. But the researcher was new to the programme and she hadn't heard about the difficulty with the first short documentary. She admitted that she'd seen that programme and hadn't grasped that the farm would be community-owned.

'Exactly our point,' we said. The researcher said she felt something should be done to rectify what had happened and she rang off promising to take a closer look at the issues. A couple of days later she rang back with a plan. The documentary team wanted to follow us through the final stages of the campaign, but they also wanted to take us to a community-owned piece of land in north Wales – Moelyci Farm. The idea was for us to meet the people behind the project and see how it operated in the context of our own community-owned structure at Fordhall.

This sounded like a very good idea and it couldn't fail to get the community-owned angle over. At the very beginning of June, both Charlotte and I took a rare day off from the increasingly manic activity around the farm and on a beautiful, early summer's day went up to North Wales to see the work at Moelyci. It was a very interesting project indeed, although it has to be said that it was less of a working farm and more of a series of allotments providing a community space. Still, the community had purchased this land and were using it successfully, both as an education and food-production resource. It was good to meet people who understood our situation and we took home a lot of valuable advice and suggestions we could follow up. They had shown us that these structures can and do work, and are valuable to the community long term.

It was obvious that Moelyci enjoyed a great deal of public affection and support, and the crop of tents that appeared on our lawn from May onwards proved that we could corral the same level of commitment from people who simply wanted to do something to help us. But would it be enough and would it be in time? As the June days passed by and the campaign countdown clock began to tick ever more loudly in our ears, we gathered all our forces for what would be the final battle in a long history of conflict and strife at Fordhall Farm.

30

Charlotte

Sophie had taken to wearing sunglasses inside, such were the hours she was putting in in front of her dazzlingly bright computer screen. But she was determined not to tear herself away from it. We sat up all night to get our first colour newsletter ready for the printers. We knew this was our last chance to hit our existing supporters and we had to get it right. It had to go out on time. It was now or never.

Sophie and I took it in turns to sleep. While one of us wrote and edited, the other slept, lying across two office chairs. It was a heavenly feeling, if a little unsteady.

We were driven on by the deadline and our urge to succeed, and Sophie's unusual fashion statement was evidence of our drive. We had almost £500,000 in the bank. This included a £200,000 loan from Triodos bank, but we were hoping that, with the shares and donations from the public we wouldn't need to draw on it. We were more than halfway there, but it had taken nine months to get to this point. We now had just four weeks to find the other £300,000.

We were asking people to offer interest-free loans (over a period of five years), make donations or purchase more shares. We knew that contacting our database of supporters could be our only hope of making the deadline in time. All the large grants we had applied for had been declined but, undeterred, we set ourselves a new aim – to reach our goal through public support. This would be a real achievement.

They say the darkest hour always comes before dawn and, on the frequent mornings that I woke early, overtired and over-worked from the day before, and the day before that and the day before that, I often felt as if we were so near, yet so very far away from the target. A voice in my head would tell me that we couldn't do it, it was impossible, that I would run out of steam, that I was being stupid.

Then I would open a letter from a supporter in Australia, Hong Kong, Bahrain or Norway who by some miracle had heard of the campaign and wanted to help. That someone so far away had bothered to send a cheque and a letter to a small organic farm in North Shropshire astonished and inspired us all. Other people tried to buy shares for unborn children and we had to explain that we could not legally issue shares for people that had not yet been born! We had a whole file of shareholders just waiting to take their first breath – we were amazed. When things like this happened, almost instantly I would put my demoralising introspection to one side. Of course we could do this, and we would do it. We had got this far and we were more than halfway. So what if we only had a few weeks left? To give up now was unthinkable; plus the administration involved in returning everyone's cheques if we failed was unimaginable. Whatever happened on 1 July we would at least get to that point without ever having surrendered the fight, knowing that we had put everything we could into saving Fordhall Farm.

The impatience in my bones meant that I was constantly running – running between the house and the farm shop, between the office and Ben or the increasing number of volunteers out in the fields. Sophie was the same and, while the office itself, now filled with volunteers, was an oasis of relative calm, we were two dervishes whirling in and out of all the measured and methodical work going into this campaign. Maybe it was because we'd become the touchstones for the whole project. If anyone wanted to know anything, they had to ask either Charlotte or Sophie. If the phone went and it was something official, they fetched Charlotte or Sophie. When all the volunteers had packed up for the day and gone, and the newsletter and the legal business had to be tied up, that was Charlotte and Sophie's job.

And yet, for press inquiries and requests for interviews, it was always Ben and I who were marshalled to step into the limelight. It was hardly surprising; after all, we were the brother and sister who had taken over their parents' farm to stop its destruction. That was the media's story and it seemed to be working. But we were always slightly concerned that we were being asked to take all the credit for the hard work. Many if not most of the volunteers were happy to let us fulfil this role, but I was concerned that Sophie was being unfairly over looked.

She worked just as hard as Ben or me. She had been camping on my bedroom floor for months because by the time she'd finished all her work it wasn't worth going home. She and I had become as close as friends could be, but when the media came calling and all the attention and praise was lavished on Ben and me, she was left out in the cold. To my shame, I didn't notice it for a while. At first I felt as though I was simply a vessel for the story of Fordhall and the farm, and that people weren't so much interested in me and Ben as personalities as they were in the farm and its history. But I was wrong, and as it became increasingly clear that the press interest was focusing on Ben and me as young people who had taken on this huge project 'on our own', I became aware that Sophie felt isolated.

She didn't express it out loud, but whenever we obtained a cutting from a newspaper she never seemed quite as elated as Ben or me. As Project Manager she was often interviewed by the particular journalist working on the story, but more often than not her contribution was missing from the final draft because it 'complicated the story'. It must have been crushing for her to read about the efforts made by Ben and me and not to see her own hard work acknowledged. Journalists who covered the story more than once – our local press and BBC *Midlands Today*, for example – were sensitive to Sophie's presence and would ask for and publish her opinion. She also featured in the crucial *Telegraph* article that set the ball rolling. But, more often than not, it seemed she just didn't exist.

It was hard to know what to do and I felt my newly developed people management skills were being put to the test. I desperately wanted Sophie to know how grateful Ben and I were for all her effort and all the hours she had worked and was continuing to put in. She had been planning to start a PGCE in September 2005 but had postponed it in order to work on the campaign. She'd even worked unpaid for us for the first six months. If anything, her commitment was even greater than ours. This was our home and our life; Sophie was an outsider who came here, discovered a passion and put her heart and soul into something she previously knew nothing about. She didn't have to, but she did, and for that I would always be grateful. But, unable to control what the press published or broadcast, all I could do was offer my thanks to her on a regular basis.

If her lack of inclusion in the press article grated on Sophie she certainly never let it affect her work. With less than a month to go before deadline day it was vital that we all stayed as focused as possible. In the middle of June we were going to hold our second annual Family Fun Day at Fordhall, which would be a great opportunity to pull the people of Market Drayton into the final stages of the campaign and let them see what they would lose if they didn't act now.

To reinforce the point, we designed a big 'countdown' board to be placed at the entrance to the farm on the A53. We updated it daily to show drivers how much – or rather, how little – time there was left to save the farm. In the farm shop we had a board that told our customers how much we'd raised so far and how many shareholders were involved – about 4500 at that point. Visitors would stare with incredulity at the target and the date. Some would make reference to it, perhaps to see if we really understood what we'd taken on.

'So,' someone would say, 'you've £200,000 left to raise and just a few weeks to go. That's a lot of money, isn't it?'

'Yes,' I'd reply, as brightly as possible, 'I know. It is a lot. But we'll do it. No doubt about that. We're getting quite a lot in interest-free loans now, so that'll really help.'

'Are you sure? There's so little time left and £200,000 is an awful lot of money.'

'I know, but don't worry. We've come too far for it not to succeed. We'll do it.' I was smiling hard now as my innate enthusiasm and optimism took over.

'Well, in that case, I'd better buy my share. Have you got a pen?'

We took a stand at the Staffordshire County Agricultural Show on 1 June. It was an opportunity both to sell our produce and promote the fight for the farm. We had banners, posters and leaflets all about Fordhall and the current struggle to save it. Most people were friendly and interested in what we were doing, asking about progress on the farm and offering kind words of support. One, however, came to our stall seemingly determined to pick a fight. He was a big local landowner and he started by commenting about the mess left behind after we'd laid hedges along the bottom of our drive. It was only brash – cuttings trimmed off the hedge – and when we had a minute away from the campaign we would do something about it. But this gentleman, dressed in traditional tweeds and with an attitude to match, seemed to think it a heinous crime. I knew he was talking down to me and it got my back up. I could sense what was coming next and that I would be defending the whole ethos of the farm on a day when I'd much rather be talking up its attributes. I tried to be as enthusiastic as possible, but he simply would not have it.

'No,' he said, almost smirking, 'you won't do it. You're having a go, and fair enough, but you won't do it. Certainly not by the deadline, anyway.'

I flushed with anger. 'How do you know we won't?' I countered. 'You can't say that for sure. A cheque for half a million pounds might come through our door tomorrow.' I was trying to remain calm and positive, yet assertive.

'I'm telling you,' he continued, even more forcefully and pointing his finger at me, 'you won't do it. Not a chance.'

He wasn't going to be shifted from his viewpoint and it was pointless to continue. He wandered off, smug in his certainty, and I felt ready to explode. His view was so shortsighted, so arrogant and so cynical. It held absolutely no room for opportunity or chance. This attitude was the reason that so many people didn't even try to fight for things they believed in any more. We had already shown, through evading our eviction notice, gaining first refusal on the land and already raising half a million pounds, that doors *could* be opened and the fight *could* be won when people gathered to support each other.

But strangely enough, I felt beyond anger. If anything, the words of this man had cemented my determination to make that deadline, come what may. If for no other reason, we would raise £800,000 by 1 July just to prove that one man wrong. I realised I had never been more determined or more focused in my life.

A rush on shares seemed to happen all of a sudden as the deadline drew nearer, just as several people, including the ever-wise John Hughes, had said it would. Most of these shareholders were local people who had perhaps exercised caution as the campaign got underway and decided to come in when it looked as if we had a fair chance of being successful. Whatever their reasons, we were tremendously glad to have them on board and delighted to see so many local people, more than 2000, at our second Family Fun Day. That year's event was focused on the farming side of Fordhall and the link between 'pasture' and 'plate' that we so wanted to emphasise in our educational activities. We felt the connection in Britain between farming and food had become, if not entirely lost, at least misplaced. Farms were places where people feared to tread, in case the farmer came out and fired his gun to warn you off. No longer was the farm at the centre of the community, as it once had been, a place where people both worked and played. So many people's working lives had become busier and this, coupled with the rise of pre-packaged, processed foods that bore no resemblance to the original product, meant they had lost touch with what a farm was essentially about. We wanted to help people re-establish that connection and for mutual respect for the land to be fostered once again. During our Fun Day we had willow-gate-making demonstrations, sheep-shearing, wool-spinning and traditional Shire-horse-ploughing as well as guided walks and information about the farm animals. Small beer, maybe, but the principle of opening up the farm and communicating the message about diversity and sustainability was being made. Plus, we raised £16,500 that day through stalls, shares and donations. Most certainly not small beer.

On 21 June we had our second big-hitting newspaper article in a paper we had been chasing for some time – the *Guardian*. It was exactly what was needed. The article conveyed the near-panic of having to raise £200,000 in two weeks and the paper's readers rose admirably to the occasion. We'll never be quite sure, but we estimate that the *Guardian* article earned the FCLI around £100,000 in shares and donations following its publication.

I was so, so tired. Sometimes I felt so utterly exhausted that I was unable to achieve the thing I most craved – a few hours of deep sleep. And even if I did manage to nod off at some unimaginably late hour, my dreams would be crammed with paperwork and phone calls, requests, queries and problems. I thought about all the thousands of shareholders I would let down if we failed now and I tried to stem the rising panic coming up from my stomach into my throat. This fire, the little but hopeful fire we'd lit three years previously, had now turned into a roaring inferno. My commitments felt unceasing and, if it was to go on for much longer, I felt I would break down. It was only the continual enthusiasm of volunteers and supporters that kept Sophie, Ben and me going in those final weeks and days.

The campaigning never ended. Wherever we were and whoever we were with, saving Fordhall was always on the agenda. I took leaflets to the pub and to the shops, and even got guests to volunteer when they were invited to the farm for dinner. I remember one evening we had invited the padre from Tern Hill Army base and one of Mum's friends for an evening meal. Not wanting to lose any time working on the project I asked if they would mind helping with a very small job before dessert. They agreed, despite my definition of a 'small' job being a little broad – well, it was certainly small in comparison to raising £200,000 in less than two weeks. They successfully counted 10,000 'Save Fordhall Farm' leaflets to insert in the *Ecologist* magazine and I think they thoroughly enjoyed earning their dessert by contributing to the cause. Their small job was no small job at all and brought in hundreds of share applications in the following weeks.

Our late nights working on the newsletter had paid off. Dave, the postman who had the increasingly onerous task of delivering the bags of mail to Fordhall, was a very cheery character who, having watched the farm falling into disrepair over the years, took a personal interest in the fight to save it. He had been amazed by the volume of letters received in the days after the *Telegraph* article and even more surprised when the correspondence kept on coming. And so were we; we'd half expected the flood to become a trickle, but it showed no signs of abating and we were taking tens of thousands of pounds in share applications every day in the last two weeks of the campaign.

The volume of mail eventually became so large that it had to be delivered by container rather than by hand. There was a collective intake of breath as the first box was levered through the office doorway. That day would be one hell of a busy day in a long line of very busy days.

With up to twenty volunteers spread throughout the house, share applications were being processed by the bucket load. The tension built as we inched ever closer to our total. At the end of each day, Sophie and I would run to the bank, quite often with only ten minutes to spare before they closed, to clear as many cheques as we could. Every minute and every cheque in these final two weeks counted. We had one chance to make the project succeed and, despite our exhaustion, we were getting too close to slow down now. We were running on nothing more than adrenalin.

Early in the final week of the campaign I sat down to make an accurate account of the money we had received so far. We had a fund-raising total on the website, but this was based on the amount of money cleared in the bank, not the amount we had received in the office. It had been a blisteringly hot day and even our normally freezing office had been too hot. It was now 1 a.m. and I'd been up working since eight that morning. As usual I was almost cross-eyed with tiredness. It took quite a while and there were a few recounts but I suddenly realised that we were just about to go through the £800,000 barrier. For the first time in my life I was speechless. As surreal as the last few months had been, that evening felt even stranger. I looked around the room – Sophie was quietly working away on her computer and Ben had just entered the office to see how things were going before he went to bed.

I asked Ben and Sophie to come over to my desk. Still in a state of complete shock myself, I whispered that I thought we had raised enough money.

'I've calculated the money we have received from the Triodos loan, the shares, the donations and the interest-free loans, and it looks like we have raised almost £800,000. I can't be one hundred per cent sure but we are definitely around that figure.'

'No way,' they said together – quietly, but there was no doubting their excitement. 'Are you sure? I can't believe it.'

There was no jumping for joy, no screams, no bottles of champagne. We were all in shock and, for a few moments, we sat there in silence and simply smiled to ourselves and one another. This was what we had been working so hard for and, although we had all been convinced in the final weeks that we were going to make it somehow, it's difficult to put into words how you feel when you actually do.

Mum walked in shortly after and when I shared the news her reaction was the same: total disbelief and relief. After years of fighting to save Fordhall herself and after losing her husband in the midst of it all, she couldn't believe the journey was finally over. I explained that I might be a little premature in my calculations But if we weren't quite there yet, then judging by the constant stream of post, it would not be very long until we were. To even contemplate not having to fight any more seemed alien to us all.

Our elation was definitely tempered by our complete exhaustion. We also knew that the farm would not be saved until the funds were cleared in the bank and the deeds were signed. All this had to be completed by the end of the week before we could rest in the knowledge that Fordhall was safe. Having the money was the second-last rung on the ladder, but a signed agreement would be what took us to the top.

There was one person we had to tell and soon. We had to get the contracts in order for the purchase. Obviously, as a twenty-four year old fresh out of university, I had never bought a house before and certainly never 128 acres of an organic farm. It was completely alien to me and I had no idea what I should do. The first port of call seemed to be the landlord's agent. I needed them to know that we were close so that they could start the ball rolling at their end. I rang them the next morning.

'Hello, it's Charlotte Hollins, from Fordhall Farm.'

'Hi, how can I help?' It was another land agent. He was relatively new at the offices and Mr Godsal had passed our case over to him to look after.

'I was just calling to let you know that it looks as though we will raise the money in time.'

'Money for what?'

'To purchase the farm!' I was taken aback by his lack of response, but pushed on regardless. 'I wasn't sure what the official process was. Do your solicitors initiate talks with our solicitors, or do we get our solicitors to talk to yours? I've never bought a farm before.'

'Oh right. Sorry, I misunderstood. So you think you're going to raise the money then?'

He sounded very surprised, as though he couldn't possibly have anticipated us ever raising that money. Suddenly, I felt horribly worried.

'Yes, I think we're going to do it. It's pouring in. Tens of thousands of pounds a day.'

'Oh, OK. Well, I'd better have a word with Mr Godsal. I'll get back to you.'

There was a silence at the end of the phone that hung in the air until I realised the conversation was over. The office had been full of joyful laughter just before I made this historic call. Now, a subdued hush had descended.

I got off the phone feeling sick. 'You know what? I don't

think they're going to sell it to us. They never expected us to make it. They're going to go back on the deal.' I felt like bursting into tears on the spot. We'd never actually signed the first refusal contract with the landlord. There had been wrangling over a deposit they'd wanted and various other legal to-ings and fro-ings, and the actual pen-on-paper moment had never happened. Legally, they weren't obliged to sell the 128 acres to us at all. There had only been verbal agreements.

It was Ben who broke the silence. 'No way,' he said, sounding resolute. 'No way would they do this to us now. They must have seen all the press. They aren't going to go back on it now. Imagine the publicity.'

He was joined by a chorus of volunteers, all offering reassurance. They were right. The fallout from such a volte-face would be massive. Besides, there was no reason for them to renege on the deal, verbal though it was. They'd named their price and we'd matched it. Were they going to get a better offer now? I decided not to look on the black side and nervously waited to hear their next move.

Thirty minutes later, the call came from their offices. It was the new land agent again. 'Hi, Charlotte. Sorry about the delay. OK, I've spoken to Mr Godsal. He's rung our solicitor, so you'd better ring yours straight away and we'll get this contract sorted.'

'Which contract are we talking about?'

'Well, both of them I expect. The option to purchase and the purchase itself.'

I came off the phone and almost fainted with relief.

The next job was to get on to Iain Morrison, our solicitor. He supported us and was delighted when I told him the news. He said he would get on to it straight away and, although he was based in Worcestershire, he promised to come to the farm towards the end of the week to oversee the signing of the contracts. But there were some important documents required first – proof of the Triodos loan and proof that there were enough funds in the bank. We also had to organise an automatic payment for the deposit. This had to be in the solicitor's account before the agreement was signed.

There was so much to do and only a few days to do it in, not to mention managing the post that continued to roll in each day, organising the volunteers in the office and trying to arrange press coverage for the announcement. To this day, I don't know how we managed to find time to fit it all in.

The press, of course, knew the deadline was approaching, and our volunteers were beginning to field anxious calls from reporters and producers wanting to know if we would do it in time. We really didn't want the news to leak out until the documents were signed; there were just too many things that could go wrong beforehand. But I was determined to have the end of the campaign covered in as big a way as possible. Our shareholders across the country would want to know what had happened, and we knew we couldn't afford the time or the money for a mail out.

Luckily I had a call from BBC *Breakfast News*. If they could come to cover us live on Friday, we'd be able to spread the word across the country. I told them we had almost got there and they asked if they could have the scoop on it. We would be able to tell the nation, live on air, that they'd helped to raise £800,000 to save Fordhall Farm. It would be a great moment.

On Thursday morning I rang our bank. We had been anxiously waiting for that week's cheques to clear so we could say definitively that we'd raised the money. Yes, they confirmed, there were enough cleared funds in the bank for the FCLI to buy the farm. I immediately drove to the bank to collect a print-out of the latest bank statement. The next document we needed was the proof of the loan from Triodos. That arrived by recorded post on the Thursday morning, just in time. All we had to do now was sign. In the afternoon, Iain Morrison arrived with two printed agreements. He laughed as he handed the FCLI treasurer and myself (as society secretary) a pen each and aked us to sign. 'In the whole of my career,' he joked, 'I've never had someone sign the option to purchase on the same day as they exercised that option. Let's just make sure that we sign them in the correct order!'

In the glare of the lights from the BBC Midlands *Inside Out* cameras we signed the two agreements on the table in the small farm office – the room that had seen over £800,000 pass through its doors and the room that had seen us stressed, elated and exhausted! My legs, arms and fingers shook as I held the pen and put my name to the document that now represented all our dreams, hopes, desires and frustrations. Watching us were Ben, Mum, our treasurer Ron, Sophie and Danny O'Sullivan. I should have been whooping with joy and celebrating like some gold-medal-winning athlete. But there were too many conflicting emotions going on to be triumphant. We were pleased, of course, but so exhausted too. The *Inside Out* reporter, Ashley Blake, asked us on camera, 'Have you now done it?'

'Yes,' we replied, 'we've done it. We've made it.'

He looked at us expectantly, waiting for a more emotive response, but we just couldn't give it. When the film was eventually broadcast later that summer we came across as rather flat. It was a shame, but it was such a big moment that any expression of our feelings could never accurately convey the drama of the moment itself.

It was a beautiful summer's evening. Sophie and I wandered off into the garden with a glass of champagne and, for a few moments, found the oasis of peace and quiet that had eluded us for so long. Neither of us could believe it had happened; the contract was signed and the farm now belonged to the FCLI. Yet we still had oodles of work to do. Share applications were coming in at a rate of knots and there were cheques to be processed and banked. But we had reached the defining moment.

The silence was broken by a volunteer shouting for me out of the window. 'Charlotte! Can you take this? BBC *Breakfast* wants to speak to you!'

I picked up the phone and spoke to a researcher. 'Hi,' she said, 'I'm just calling to let you know that something else has come up and we can't make it tomorrow. But good luck anyway. Bye!'

I was astonished. I'd emailed 5000 shareholders to tell them to watch the BBC on Friday morning and we had advertised it to thousands more on our website all week. Yet the researcher's tone was so laid back and flippant. We couldn't let our supporters down now. I rang them straight back.

'Listen,' I said, 'I know you're busy but I've just told 5000 people to watch BBC *Breakfast* tomorrow morning. It's a huge number of people you'll let down.'

The researcher told me to give her a moment while she spoke to her producer. They were obviously completely unaware, and not surprisingly so, of the scale that our campaign had reached and the sheer number of people it had touched. She called me back. 'Right,' she said, businesslike, 'I'm leaving the office for the station now. I'll see you tomorrow morning. We'll be there at 5 a.m. with the satellite truck.'

Fantastic – they were coming! I was delighted and I asked as many volunteers as possible to come in the morning. I had been told by Iain Morrison not to say anything until the landlord had signed his copy of the contract and everything was one hundred per cent watertight, but it was simply too late for that now. This was our opportunity to tell every single person who had helped in the campaign that their efforts had been successful.

At 5.30 a.m. the following morning I awoke to the sound of cables being unrolled, lights screwed on to their mounts and people talking into mobile phones. I peeped out of my bedroom window and saw the BBC *Breakfast News* crew setting up. It was a dull and overcast day. Shame, when we'd had such good weather up until now. Today – of all days – I would crawl back into bed and allow myself the indulgence of another hour's sleep. Ben and I wouldn't be needed for a while, and it was going to be an intensely busy and demanding few hours. They could manage without us for a little bit longer.

I was eventually woken by Ben banging on my door. The crew was almost ready to begin the live broadcast. As Sophie and I rushed downstairs, Ben told me the BBC had been trailing the broadcast by asking viewers, 'Did they do it? We'll find out later in the programme . . . ' The volunteers and crew had set up in the field by the pigs, and everyone was gathered round a couple of benches there. As the director counted down the seconds to the live feed to the *Breakfast News* we tried to contain our excitement, but it was almost impossible. Ben announced the good news to the nation while the rest of us giggled, cheered and generally messed around. There was a big sense of relief after the live broadcast was finished and, as one of the volunteers went off to make us all porridge for breakfast, we calmed down and prepared for the next live feed at 8 a.m.

It was the beginning of one of the most surreal days of my life. We felt like celebrities running from one interview and one photographer to the next. It was non-stop action and the bottles of champagne kept arriving. We could not believe how we had begun this project with so little and ended up enriched in so many ways. It was almost too much for us to take in within such a short space of time.

Meanwhile, back in the office, the phones were going as mad as they did on the day of the *Telegraph* article's publication. Elaine and Lesley were relentlessly manning the phones as shareholders rang to congratulate us, having seen the announcement on the TV. Others were emailing; one lady wrote to tell us that she had literally jumped up and down in her living room and screamed with delight as she watched the news that morning. I took the BBC reporter into the office to show her how busy it had become since the broadcast. She was amazed and very pleased that the decision had been made at the eleventh hour to cover the story after all.

Neither was our office the only place to receive calls; apparently the switchboard at BBC *Breakfast* was going crazy too, and the show's producers wanted more live feeds. So we did two more within half an hour. This was really big news, and aside from the TV, we were being asked for quotes from the press and radio presenters who had come down to find out what was going on. It turned into a carnival and, as I wandered round, I felt an unbelievable surge of joy rush right through my body, like the bubbles rising to the top of the champagne bottle I was clutching. The smiles on the faces of all those we had worked so closely with us over the preceding weeks and months, plus the phone calls and messages from well-wishers we had never met, said it all. There were even tears from shareholders on the phone. I was getting as much satisfaction from the joy others were feeling as I was from my own.

And, extraordinarily, we were getting calls asking if shares were still for sale. Even though we'd hit our target, people wanted to be part of the experience and the future of Fordhall. In fact, on the day we secured the farm the post went unopened, and when we did get round to it we had to wade through 600 letters all requesting shares. Actually, we did open one letter that day, chosen at random from the box. It's hard to believe that we picked on this one completely by chance, because it contained a donation for £10,000 – the largest single donation we had ever received.

At 9 a.m. on the Friday, I got a call from Iain Morrison, our solicitor at MFG – the people that had so generously carried out all of our legal work for free. There had been a slight delay in the exchange of paperwork between us and the landlord. He advised me not to talk to the press until everything was cleared up. But by that time it was too late and my brain could no longer accept any doubt. Whatever the problems were, I blindly believed that they would be sorted soon. In fact it was not until 5 p.m. that day that I got the phone call to say that contracts had been exchanged, accepted and signed by all parties. Finally, officially, it was over. We could breathe the fresh air blowing across Fordhall's fields and never again worry about what was in the wind.

After a day of intense celebrations, we thought it was only fair that we should allow ourselves another one the following day, Saturday 1 July – deadline day. We did spend a lot of that morning processing shares, but in the evening the first of the many people we'd invited to a celebration barbecue started to arrive at the farm, and by the early evening the party was in full swing. It was a bring-and-share event, so we all tucked in to each other's food and enjoyed the company of all the friends and supporters who'd seen us through the best and worst of times.

As the evening wore on, we lit a campfire, which drew in the partygoers wandering around the garden and provided a focus for the conversations and shared memories being passed around. I've always found that sitting by a fire helps to concentrate my thoughts and that evening was no exception. All Friday, I'd been asked questions about the one person I dearly wished could be here to share in the moment. I had tried not to think too hard when answering the questions; had I done so, I might have cried too many tears on this most celebratory of days. It would have seemed out of place and, in any case, it wasn't in my nature to let go so publicly.

We had raised the best part of £800,000 through the kindness of ordinary people and we were in a position to be able to live and work at Fordhall, utilising its pastures and the richness of its history for the good of the community, for as long as we wanted. Thousands of people had got behind us: friends, volunteers, shareholders, local supporters, farm shop customers, councillors, celebrities, journalists and fellow farmers. Together, a community united in its determination to join the battle for something worthwhile, we had fought for and saved Fordhall Farm for ever.

Here, beside the warmth of the fire and under the vast covering of stars in the night sky above, I could finally turn my thoughts to Dad – the visionary, the pioneer, the legend who had inadvertently turned this land into a priceless commodity that thousands of people thought was worth fighting for. His legacy was not in property, or money, or any of the usual things; what he left behind was the fertility in these fields and a philosophy that built the foundations of the Fordhall Farm we know today. He had left us a different and an invaluable kind of richness. I wished he were here with us, and in some ways, he was. If we'd lost the farm we would have lost Dad, too, but in the spirit of those people celebrating with us that night, and the many others who had contributed to the cause, he was still here. Far above us, a shooting star made its way westwards in a never-ending arc. Somewhere, Dad was looking down on us, and he was happy.

31

Ben

Just after BBC *Breakfast News* had left Fordhall Farm at midday on Friday 30 June I received a phone call. I expected it to be either another message of congratulations or a request for an interview. But it was neither of those. It was a call I'd been expecting, but had secretly tried to forget about. It was from my course tutor from Harper Adams University.

'Hi Ben,' he said, 'congratulations on the farm. You must be so pleased. I'll bet that's some party you're having down there today?' He had heard us on BBC Radio 4 news that morning.

'It is,' I replied nervously, waiting for him to get to the point.

'Well that's great, because you have another reason for celebration. I'm ringing to tell you that you've passed your degree.'

As he said it, a grin spread across my face and I could feel my forehead breaking out into a sweat of relief. I'd been dreading the results, but I'd done it. I had good cause for extra celebrations. The time taken up by running the farm, attending all the markets and shows and helping with the campaign had eaten into my revision periods; even on the morning of one of my first exams in June I had had to go to Stafford Agricultural Show to set up my stand. I got there at 7 a.m. after feeding the pigs and quickly set up the fridge and meat display in preparation for Charlotte taking over when the show opened, all before rushing off to Harper for a 9 a.m. exam.

So I was delighted with the news, even though it had slipped my mind with everything else going on at the time. Some might say that farming is in your blood and no amount of schooling will ever teach you all you need to know, but I found the course in Agricultural Land and Farm Management very useful and I was glad I'd made the decision to see it through to the end, despite the pressures.

Harper Adams was the venue for a black-tie dinner we held two weeks after the deadline expired. Originally this had been scheduled for May, but just as the final touches were being put to the planning of the event – then billed as a fund-raiser – the *Telegraph* article came out and suddenly it was all hands on deck as far as processing share applications and dealing with inquiries was concerned. Attention couldn't be diverted, so the decision was made to postpone the event to a later date.

We rescheduled for 15 July and sold one hundred tickets for the event. It was now more of a celebratory dinner than a fund-raiser, but we were still raising money at this stage and any extra, to help offset the loans and the Triodos mortgage, was very useful. It was a hard event to organise, in that we aimed to source as much of the menu as possible from local and organic suppliers. We wanted guests to know where each item on the menu came from. After a lot of effort and endless phone calls we managed to compile a menu that reflected the variety of local producers. What we couldn't source from the area – organic tea and coffee, for example – was donated by Waitrose, which sponsored the event.

In contrast to the home-made earthiness of events at Fordhall, this was very upmarket, especially for a bunch of organic farmers and their supporters. We all made the effort to look our very best, and the fun and the laughs we had that night reflected the trouble we'd taken to make this a special celebration. Charlotte was in particularly good form. Perhaps she felt the pressure, as far as the campaign was concerned, was finally lifted off her shoulders. 'This,' she whispered to me, as the guests giddily crashed into one another to the sounds of a ceilidh band, 'is exactly how it was meant to be.'

'How do you mean?' I asked.

'Just everything. The farm getting people together, having fun, friendship, sharing. All that. All these people getting on and joining in. It's just amazing. It really is amazing.'

People 'getting on' at Fordhall had, in some cases, gone a little further than the sharing of simple community spirit. A few of the regular volunteers had teasingly renamed Fordhall 'The Love Farm', after several relationships had been forged during the campaign. It was a tag that Charlotte, Sophie or I could hardly deny, for all three of us had found romance with volunteers over recent months. I met Marie-Anne on a working weekend, Sophie became close to Hugo after he arrived as a volunteer, and Oli and Charlotte had become an unbeatable team after he had driven up from Essex to volunteer. All of us found it hard to believe that we'd even managed to spare a minute in our busy schedules for the finer things in life!

The fun continued with an appearance on the TV show

Ready, Steady, Cook! Charlotte and I would be competing against each other and, given that she's always claimed to be the best cook at Fordhall, there was a general feeling that I would be on the losing side. When we arrived we were introduced to our celebrity chef partners. Charlotte was paired with Brian Turner while I was matched with Lesley Waters. She was pleased to see what I'd brought with me in the way of produce – our own Gloucester Old Spot bacon, a smoked trout from Bings Heath Smokery that Andrew, a volunteer, had caught for me, some sweet potatoes and a punnet of locally grown strawberries. We then met the show's host, Ainsley Harriott, who had obviously been well briefed about the fight for Fordhall, and he promised us he would keep mentioning the farm during the show.

Ainsley did his best to put us at our ease and make us laugh – and when he hugged Charlotte he lifted her right off the ground as if she were a little rag doll. Despite these familiarities, however, we were both very nervous and apprehensive as the filming started.

The competition was hot, but to my astonishment – and given that my only culinary claim to fame is sausages and mash – I won, beating Charlotte hands down. The first prize was £100, and when Ainsley asked what I would do with it I immediately told him that I would buy a sheep.

It wasn't a flippant remark. With the breeding season approaching and only having one ram to serve more than sixty ewes I was concerned that I would be putting the solitary male under a lot of pressure. It's usual to have one ram to fifty ewes but, only having sixty, I hadn't thought I could justify a second. But having two rams would mean the lambing period should be shorter as they would work faster between them! The £100 would allow me to buy a second ram, and a couple of weeks after the programme I went to Market Drayton cattle market and bought an eighteen-month-old Suffolk tup that I immediately christened Ainsley, in honour of our genial TV host. He was a devil to get into my trailer though. As I tried to haul him out of the auction pen and into the trailer he turned on me and almost knocked me over. On the way home I worried whether I'd have another aggressive animal on my hands like the infamous pig Nancy. My fears went unfounded as Ainsley calmed down hugely and seemed to enjoy being on the farm and having his pick of the ewes.

After the glitz and the glamour were over, it was time to go back to work. I was off the farm a lot at markets and shows, and I was flat out keeping up with the demand for Fordhall meat. The campaign to save the farm had created a big interest in what we did here. Increasingly I came across new customers eager to give our products a try. It was also lovely to be in the position of accepting so many congratulations. During the campaign I often wondered if my customers looked at me as if I was crazy for ever becoming involved in an effort to raise so much money. Now they were taking pleasure in what we had done. The steadily increasing sales seemed to prove that.

One morning in August I took a rare few hours off to welcome some very special visitors to Fordhall. Towards the end of the campaign, Charlotte had tried and tried again to arrange a meeting with the landlord and Mr Godsal, just so she could keep them informed about our progress. We wanted to see them face-to-face and tentatively find out if they would be prepared to extend the deadline should the money not come in on time. Her efforts came to nothing. While they were happy to receive email updates and were obviously reading the papers and watching the coverage on television, they seemed curiously reluctant to meet in person.

However, once the deadline had passed and the money was raised they were more receptive to the idea of meeting, and they agreed to come to the farm on 15 August. We felt we owed it to them to show them what had been achieved. While there had been times over the years that our relationship with them was a difficult one, to say the least, they had given us the opportunity to secure the farm and for that we were grateful. So at 11 a.m., a car containing Mr Godsal, Mr and Mrs Healey parked up in the farmyard and, with that same feeling of trepidation we'd always had in our dealings with the landlord, we walked up to greet them.

At first, they seemed a bit reserved and stony-faced. Curiously, though, their uptightness helped me to relax. What had we got to worry about any more? We had done it. We didn't have to answer to them. I wasn't going to be smug about it, but there was a realisation that we were now equals and no longer tenant and landlord.

We shook hands, and Mr Healey offered his congratulations. We thanked him for it and he smiled a little. Perhaps they'd also been nervous about this meeting, but they didn't need to worry; this was a welcoming committee not a hostile reception. We just wanted them to enjoy looking round the farm and hearing the story of the campaign. We took them on a walk across the fields; past the pigs, through the wood and up to the site of the motte and bailey castle, with its views over Buntingsdale Hall and the Tern Hill Valley. With the cattle strolling gently across the meadow to the spring-fed pool, the air filling with the calls of numerous wild birds, and the meandering River Tern carrying with it the reflections of the late morning sun, Fordhall had never looked so beautiful. I felt immensely proud that, as the farmer, I was able to show all this to our visitors, and especially this particular group, with whom we had been almost inextricably and often emotionally entangled. Now we were free.

All the while we talked them through the history of the farm from Dad's time until the present day. They were genuinely interested and Mr Godsal pointed out to Mr and Mrs Healey various aspects of the farm that had improved dramatically since we'd taken over the tenancy. That was especially pleasing to hear; we had increasingly felt Mr Godsal had been on our side on a personal level, but had had to play everything straight because of his commitments to the landlord. Now he was able to compare the farm before and after the tenancy and give Mr Healey his personal opinion about our achievements which, I have to say, made me feel very proud.

After a lot of talk about our plans for the future, both from the farming and education side of things, they prepared to say goodbye. Their departure in the farmyard was in marked contrast to the solemn way we had greeted each other just two hours previously. Now, there were smiles, kisses and warm handshakes. Mr Healey even bought some shares in Fordhall Farm for some young relatives. We could see that they felt a part of the success of Fordhall. I suppose to an extent, as a trust themselves, their hands had been tied when the temptation of development money had been so strong. Thankfully the bad times were now part of the past. Mr Healey's gesture simply showed just how far this roller-coaster ride had come since we set out on it two-and-a-half years before.

32

Charlotte

The weeks following the end of the fight for the farm saw applications for shares, donations and offers of loans continue to flood in, and we seemed to be working just as hard in the office as we had been during the campaign. There was certainly no time to reflect on the experiences of the last few years.

The emphasis at Fordhall had now changed dramatically. The efforts we had put into saving and securing the farm needed to switch into planning its long-term future. From accumulating money we now had to decide how to spend it and it was a very strange and daunting prospect.

On top of this I was exhausted from the years of fighting and the continual workload on top of my job at the residential home. Now the farm was secure, I also needed job security. The board of trustees met and it was decided that FCLI should employ me full-time as Project Director. The demands of running the initiative would be great, and I needed to focus all my attention on those responsibilities. Once the board had made their decision and had discussed terms, conditions and salary, I handed in my notice and started a new job in the employment of FCLI; my dream job.

That board meeting and the run-up to Ben and me signing the new tenancy agreement with the FCLI was a part of a particularly stressful period for me. The weeks and months of tireless campaigning and the exhausting effort required to keep focused no matter what had taken its toll. Suddenly I felt tired and demotivated and I began to doubt my abilities. Although I had been working through legal matters, complicated contracts, accounts, grant applications and many other aspects of business during the campaign, I began to wonder whether I had the skills required to push the initiative to the next stage.

1 August 2006

The reality of the future began to kick in over the weekend. I was feeling out of my depth and spent a lot of the evening wondering how I was going to lead this project to success. Managing 7500 people across the country, making the most of this amazing resource and learning all the new skills necessary to take the project forward, almost makes me feel sick.

I confided my fears in Sophie and, as ever, she was reassuring and supportive. She reminded me that there had been times during the campaign when I'd hit a low, but had quickly bounced back. It was true, and I realised it was down to tiredness as much as anything else. I had to remind myself that I was in a situation that many would have considered beyond the reach of someone as young as me. After a short while and a concentrated burst of diary-writing, I began to feel much better and I got my old confidence back.

I needed it back as soon as possible. We were now in demand to give talks about the campaign to various conferences and groups, and I wanted to attend as many as I could. The next on the list was the Shropshire Farmers' Club. The talk had been arranged by our most vocal cynic, the man from the Staffordshire County Agricultural Show who had inadvertently given me so much determination in the last few weeks of the campaign. He had met Ben at a farmers' market shortly after our deadline and asked if we would speak.

'Afternoon,' he said to Ben, 'I thought I'd just come over and say hello and say well done on getting the farm. It was quite an achievement.'

'Yes,' replied Ben, trying not to look too smug, 'it certainly was.'

'You know,' said the man, leaning forward and dropping his voice, 'you won't know me, but I met your sister at the Staffordshire Show in the summer. I told her that you wouldn't make that deadline. And you bloody well did. I can't believe it!

Ben accepted the man's apologetic congratulations with good grace. Then he received an intriguing proposal – would we like to speak at the next Shropshire Farmers' group meeting, and tell everyone about the farm, the campaign and the initiative?

In many ways it would be like entering the lions' den, but we would do it. This was a very select group of farmers and wealthy landowners who we knew had always been cynical about Fordhall Farm and its different methods and beliefs. Speaking to them now might not be an easy ride, but it would give us the opportunity to fully explain the project to them. As we arrived and began to mingle with the guests we were joshed by a good handful of people who reminded us that we were 'brave' for coming to talk to them.

After the meal we gave our presentation and, as we spoke, I noticed a good number of guests beginning to tune into what we were saying, especially when Ben mentioned that our 8000 shareholders represented 8000 potential customers at our farm shop. By the end of the evening, every single farmer voiced their support for us.

The progression at Fordhall continued and, as we began to get on top of the enormous backlog of share applications, we were able sometimes to allow ourselves a moment of contemplation about the future. However, quite often these thoughts were forced upon us by activities at the farm. One sunny afternoon, just as Sophie and I had finished a guided walk for a group of council shareholders, several cars drove up the driveway and pulled in by the farm shop. Wondering who the passengers might be, I wandered over to greet them, and was taken aback when the leader of the party, a scholarly- , friendly-looking woman in her mid-thirties, said she had booked an educational day with us.

If she had, I had no knowledge of it, and I felt slightly put out that they'd just turned up, but here they were, a party of teenagers and adults keen to begin their visit to Fordhall Farm. There seemed to be more adults than teenagers, which was explained when one of the adults, a social worker, said they were from a referral unit for young people with challenging behaviour. I didn't want to upset anyone by cancelling their visit so we decided to let them stay. We led the six teenagers and twelve adults into the garden so we could show them what the farm was about. Although Ben was busy, he joined us to talk about the farm, his role as the farmer and the working practices at Fordhall.

Within minutes it was clear why these young people were 'challenging'. They weren't listening at all. They laughed and played among themselves, and took no notice of any of the adults' attempts to quieten them down. It wasn't a situation we were used to, and Ben and I were unsure how to handle it. Luckily, Sophie has youth work skills and she whispered to me that she had a plan to save the situation.

She headed off in the direction of the office and a few minutes later reappeared with the Alphabet Game. This was something we had devised for family days, when there were much younger children around. It was a simple game, which involved the child identifying something on the farm beginning with A, B, C and so on. Surely this wouldn't work with a group of obviously difficult teenagers?

'Come on,' she said gamely, 'let's go into the field. We'll show you round and you can have a go at this competition. And the winner gets free ice-cream!'

Once the teenagers were out in the open, the change that came over them was astonishing. Somehow, the ambience generated by the wide open space, the sound of birdsong and the rustle of the wind through the trees in the wood seemed to have a very calming effect on them. Just as Dad had always done with visitors, I turned over a cowpat and showed them what was living underneath it. They were repulsed, but interested too and they wanted to hear more. They also began the Alphabet Game and were actually taking it seriously. Somehow Sophie seemed to be getting the best out of them.

One girl, who must have been about fourteen, seemed especially keen to learn and she wondered if she could pat a cow on its nose.

'Well,' I said, 'we don't keep any animals as pets, but there is a cow on the farm that's tamer than all the rest. If you approach her slowly and you're gentle she might just let you touch her. But you have to be very calm and respectful around her.'

This cow was Daisy; she was part of a detachment of four cheap heifers that I bought for the farm from my Cheswardine wages in the grim, desperate winter of 2003. When they arrived they were thin, but we fed them up and eventually three of them went to the abattoir and were sold through the farm shop. In August 2005, Ben decided that the time was right for this straggly cow, a Hereford cross who had always had a tame streak in her, to meet the fate of the others. He removed her from the field and kept her in the cowshed overnight, while he sorted out her paperwork for the visit to the slaughterhouse the following morning. When he dug out her 'cow passport', he discovered to his astonishment that she was thirty months and one day old. Since BSE, animals over thirty months cannot be slaughtered for meat. This cow had escaped her death sentence by one day. She obviously had a lucky streak so we decided to keep her and breed from her. We named her Daisy and because she was so tame she often featured in the press pictures of Ben and me.

So the girl walked slowly up to Daisy, who lifted up her head to see who or what was approaching. Daisy has horns and can appear quite intimidating if you don't know her, but the girl seemed to have an inner confidence that propelled her calmly towards the cow. Eventually she got near enough to touch Daisy's nose and she spent several minutes patting our patient cow. When she turned to walk back, her beaming face was a picture.

'That was amazing,' said a social worker standing next to

me. 'I'd never have thought she of all people would be capable of that.'

'Why?' I asked, intrigued. 'Out of all of them she seems to be the most well adjusted.'

'Don't you believe it,' replied the social worker. 'She's the ringleader. If anyone was going to start trouble here today, it would be her.'

I was astonished, but also delighted that the farm had brought out the girl's gentler side. Later on she picked up one of the farmyard chickens and nursed it like she might a kitten. The benefits these children had gained from the farm were inspiring. Sophie had shown me that even the simplest things, united with the natural environment, could really make a difference to people, and I vowed that I would push the concept of an 'outdoor classroom' as hard as I could through the initiative.

As the year wore on we began to look more closely at the structure we had laid down for the initiative, and how we would achieve all that we had set out to do. It would be a long and almost certainly difficult task, but the enthusiasm, love and support that had carried us all through the campaign was still very much in evidence in and around Fordhall, and as winter turned into spring, there was no reason to believe that we could not make all the dreams and schemes we had talked about over the years become reality. It was very pleasing that others thought so too; over the winter we had been nominated for several awards and we felt honoured that the achievements of everyone connected to the Fordhall story were being marked in this way.

The first was the *Shropshire Star* Woman of the Year Award in November, where I was highly commended. We were also entered for the Prince's Trust Awards and we felt very privileged to reach the finals of these 'Young Enterprise' Awards, given that so many worthy businesses and individuals are helped by the Trust each year.

The award we most coveted, however, was the Schumacher Award. This is named after the economist and environmentalist E.F. Schumacher. The award is presented each year to honour people and grassroots organisations whose work 'makes a significant contribution to human scale sustainable development'. We were amazed and delighted to find out that Christiana Schumacher, who lives in Shropshire and is the great-niece of E.F. Schumacher himself, had personally nominated us.

We didn't think we stood much of a chance, so we could hardly believe it when we were told that we'd won. I was very gratified indeed to receive this award, not just because it recognised all the hard work that had taken place at Fordhall but also because E.F. Schumacher's seminal work, *Small Is Beautiful*, happened to be a particular favourite book of Dad's. For that reason, I felt that the work of Arthur Hollins was being honoured just as emphatically as that of his children.

33

Ben

At the end of September – on the day that our tenancy with the landlord expired – Charlotte and I signed a one-hundred-year tenancy with the FCLI. For me, this was a very big moment, and probably more important than the day we secured the farm financially. Right from the very beginning of the fight to save Fordhall Farm and beyond, I had wanted cast-iron assurances about security. Not just those relating to the farm and the special way the land should be looked after, but also for ourselves as tenant farmers.

Security was the one thing Mum and Dad didn't have during their time as tenants at Fordhall, and not knowing what might happen next had been a blight on the lives of the Hollins family. We had enjoyed a happy childhood, but there had been a constant feeling of uncertainty that cast a long shadow over our lives. I had never wanted this for us and, in all honesty, would rather have left the farm than continue to work under a cloud of insecurity, as my parents had done.

The tenancy agreement we signed was the result of many hours making one hundred per cent sure that what we were signing up for would work for us and the Initiative in all the ways we wanted it. The agreement would also be a blueprint for other community land structures to follow and it had to apply equally to the successors at Fordhall as it did to us. In short, every single detail was crucial.

The agreement would incorporate a very clear structure that we had to follow. The actual agreement we were signing was a Farm Business Tenancy (FBT), a more modern agreement than the old Agricultural Holdings Tenancy (AHT) that Mum and Dad had been bound to.

For me, one of the key areas of the new tenancy was the aspect of long-term security, but because of the short-term nature of the FBT, it doesn't usually cover succession. I wouldn't budge on this particular subject. It *had* to look at the long-term future as well as the present, and if it didn't we had to find a way to make it work. Luckily, if both parties agree, the FBT can be made flexible, so we took some of the relevant parts from the old AHT and moulded them into the new FBT.

The deeper I thought about it, the more detail I realised would have to be built in to the new agreement. I would come up with new suggestions on a daily basis, which is perhaps why the new agreement took so long to formulate. But I didn't want to leave anything to chance. The fear of losing control over the farm was too strong and over the months and years of our struggle I developed a confidence I never knew I had. In meetings I was not afraid to speak my mind if I thought it was necessary and there was a lot at stake with the new tenancy.

We made the provision that our children can take over the farm if they wish, as long as they have the experience and ability. We also had to cover as many eventualities as possible. For example, what might happen if Charlotte dies first, or I do, and supposing by some horrible accident we both died together? All the bases had to be covered and we had to read and reread the document many times to make sure we understood and agreed with everything in it. When we came to sign it we were almost speechless. We sat in the big office – once the farm's restaurant and the scene of so much drama over the years – and we couldn't believe that we'd committed ourselves so deeply to the future of Fordhall Farm. I was overjoyed.

For me, it was the best moment of the whole campaign, knowing that our future and that of the farm was finally secure. I could now feed my pigs, manage my sheep and cattle, nurture my grass and run my farm shop for as long as I wanted to. And no sunflowers were invloved.

34

Charlotte

Christmas 2006 was the first festive season we were able to celebrate at Fordhall without the nagging fear of uncertainty over the farm putting a dampener on the celebrations. We had enjoyed the previous Christmas, but we were always aware it could be the last one we ever spent at Fordhall. In contrast, Christmas Day 2006 marked the beginning of a new era for us and the farm. We could finally allow ourselves to relax and make merry.

We planned a feast to die for and we sourced everything locally. Marie-Anne, Ben, Oli and I, as the new couples of Fordhall, toiled in the farmhouse kitchen to create a dinner for all the family, of Fordhall pork, chicken, mashed potatoes, swedes, carrots, leeks, parsnips and roast potatoes. While it was cooking we took our traditional walk across the fields to whet our appetites. Even on this cold and dull midwinter's day, the land seemed to radiate with joy. There were no more clouds hanging over it, or us, and Mum was much more cheerful. As I walked

I couldn't help but wonder how all those people who had helped us to have such a special Christmas were celebrating theirs.

With the start of 2007 came the first full year of the FCLI's operation and a whole new set of challenges for all of us to look forward to. Getting to this point had been a remarkable achievement, but we couldn't afford to be complacent. The real work started here and almost as soon as we'd heralded the New Year we started planning for our first AGM, to be held on 31 March.

But the immense pressures of last year were over and as I came home after attending a conference in February, I had time to jot this entry in my diary:

12 February 2007

I am relaxed, chilled, happy, content, motivated and excited about the future. As I return home on the train from a conference, I can see the world go by outside my window and it is giving me the opportunity to really absorb the last year.

I am on a high as I remember all the good times, the excitement, the adrenalin, the fast pace and the great feeling after each little success and move forward. It's funny how after the event, it's only the good times you remember. All the stress, the worry, the anxiety, the pain, the exhaustion, is quickly forgotten.

Yet, it is the times of stress and worry that made this campaign such an achievement and have thus created an immense feeling of relief and relaxation.

As is usual at Fordhall, we didn't want the AGM to become just another meeting. With 8000 shareholders, all of whom have a say in the future of the farm, it was vital that we made the event as interesting as possible for those who turned up, not only from the area local to Fordhall but from across the country too. We contacted Tom Oliver, from the CPRE, to find out if he was available to chair the AGM itself. We were delighted when he said he was able to take on the task.

One of his most important tasks on the day would be to oversee the election of a new board of directors for the FCLI. The outgoing board had served the initiative fantastically well; they had been supporters right from the beginning and had nurtured and promoted all the ideas here when life seemed far from rosy at Fordhall.

But this election would only play a small part in that Saturday's activities. We built an entire festival weekend around the AGM and, after a great deal of hard work and a return to the long hours of our campaign days, we managed to devise a programme that featured a sustainable farming conference with a host of distinguished guest speakers, plus an open event and food festival to be held at Fordhall the following day. Among the speakers we recruited for the conference were Patrick Holden of the Soil Association and Tom Woolley, an architect specialising in sustainable building.

For Ben and me the AGM was a chance to talk about the future of Fordhall Farm and to meet some of the shareholders who had been in touch with us by letter or email, but whom we'd never met face-to-face. I love this kind of encounter; wherever I go I always seem to meet a shareholder, or at least someone who knows a shareholder, and it's the personal touch that wins every time. It was what had made our campaign so enjoyable, despite the stress and strain. Sometimes I look out at the farm from the bottom of our garden and imagine what 8000 people would look like if they were standing in the fields down towards the River Tern. It's hard to imagine, but one day I'd really love to gather all our supporters in one place just to satisfy my curiosity.

As always we are continually extending the boundaries at Fordhall. What we have achieved is amazing, but there is much more to come in the future – Fordhall has still not reached its full potential. I like to keep moving with a project and Fordhall now has a momentum all of its own, fuelled by the passion and commitment of so many. One of the most immediate challenge for the Initiative is to start up a Forest Schools project in Fordhall's woodlands, using the natural environment as an 'outdoor classroom'.

This demonstrates our future vision for Fordhall perfectly. Throughout the campaign we have seen how farms and farmland can be used for so much more than food production alone. Forest Schools is about teaching children to be innovative and how to take calculated risks. Children are told too often what not to do and how they should behave; they are being stripped of the ability to make their own decisions. A large part of the Forest Schools ethos is to develop children who are not afraid to move things forward and have the confidence to follow their ambitions. Perhaps this is something that Ben and I learned from our childhood at Fordhall and it is an amazing feeling to be able to give that to so many others.

One of the most popular features of the farm has been our nature trail. It takes just forty minutes to walk it, but it's proved such a draw that visitors have been known to disappear for three hours while they enjoy a picnic and the sounds of wild birds across the valley. The trail currently takes in the motte and bailey site, the river Tern and the spring-fed pool. Our aim is to extend it to the water meadows, which for any wildlife enthusiast are a very rare treat. It was these that so captivated John Hughes on his first walk around Fordhall back in 2004, and we'd like others to feel the same way. To do this we have to replace some small bridges over ditches and provide better access across the wetlands.

Access to green space is so important for our health. And visiting farms, not only do we feel better for being outside in the natural world, it also helps the farmer feel less isolated. It has always been a driving passion for me to increase awareness of landscape heritage, biodiversity and agriculture.

We are hoping a quantity of grant funding will assist this project, but we will need to fund some ourselves as well. We are keen for our volunteers and shareholders to be involved with the design as well as the manual labour and this can help contribute to the cost. Traditionally, every county or region had its own style of farm gate that was built by local tradespeople. I would really like to start to bring this lost art back through our farm trail. Some of our volunteers have already designed their own gates at Fordhall, the most admired being the one that enters our picnic area adjacent to the foraging, Gloucester Old Spot pigs. This is a fun yet important project and I can't wait to see visitors walking the full breadth of Fordhall, experiencing its hidden treasures and understanding how our farming system complements nature in every way.

Back at the farm's heart we have big long-term plans for the buildings. The first steps have already begun: late in 2006 we finally moved out of the office in the farmhouse and into two Portakabins opposite the Dutch barn. After some renovation work they are now excellent office spaces and I'm learning not to work for too long at night due to the unlit walk back to the farmhouse! We have also bought two second-hand and locally made yurts, which we use for meetings and volunteer accommodation, but while these are excellent and very eco-friendly, we need something more permanent in the future.

Our long-term plans include a bunkhouse, tearooms and educational space. All these will be built in place of the crumbling farm buildings that were recently dismantled, ensuring that no grassland will be built on. The bunkhouse will serve as a hostel for the groups we expect to stay on the farm in the future, such as inner-city children, families, youth groups or special interest groups like bird-watchers or archaeologists. The tearooms will, of course, sell Fordhall produce as well as local and organic produce and will cater for those who may visit Fordhall for a day out, not necessarily as an educational visitor. After they've walked the trail and eaten in the tearooms they will have followed the complete 'pasture to plate' cycle. Whether they learn something about local food, organics, nature, food miles, or leave with the simple desire to cook more, they will at least have taken something of benefit away from Fordhall.

The existing traditional buildings at the farm we'd like to renovate for educational space and Ben is keen to extend the farm shop in this direction too, eventually with his own on-site butchery.

However, the new sustainable build for the bunkhouse and tearooms will be the most challenging project. Not surprisingly, farming is a world apart from building, which is a trade that we know very little about – but we are keen to learn. We want these buildings to involve our supporters in every possible way. That is through the planning, the design and their eventual construction. I am really looking forward to learning about natural materials, construction, renewable energies and all the related planning issues of building, and we welcome anyone who wants to join us on this journey.

This will take a long time to come to fruition and may cost in the region of £500,000, but the more community involvement there is and the more time skilled people can offer, the cheaper, and more rewarding, it will be.

And, although not an immediate concern, we hope to invest in further research for Dad's CulturSeeder, to see that part of his legacy come to fruition as well.

Of course work on the eighteenth-century farmhouse is another ongoing project and will take many thousands of pounds to complete. It has been there, almost a symbol of what we've fought for, right through this emotional journey. It has had births and deaths in its old rooms, and it has seen the farm around it being built up, deteriorating and being rebuilt again. In a strange way the hole in the kitchen ceiling and the peeling wallpaper next to the shiny new stainless steel toaster are welcome reminders of how far we have come in such a short time.

Dad always told me that one of the most rewarding journeys in life is that of life-long learning. Ben and I are only just at the beginning of ours.

35

Ben

I must be unique among farmers in that once a year I'm required to put on my best jacket and trousers and stand up in front of a room of people to tell them what I've been doing – and what I will be doing – with *their* farm.

The emphasis on 'their' is important. While I lease the farm under the rules of the FCLI, it is still owned by all those people who put their hands so generously into their pockets and purchased a piece of English farmland that would otherwise not have existed in its present form. That's why I'm happy to overcome the dry mouth, shaking hands and watery feeling in the stomach to stand up in front of gatherings like the AGM and talk about Fordhall Farm.

The day after the AGM, Sunday 1 April, was a big day on the farm. We had put together an open event, the first time we'd held a local producers' food fair at Fordhall. The event was also a good excuse to show off all my newly born lambs, piglets and calves. I looked after the barbecue and the car parking, and we set out enough space on our land for around fifty cars. Little did we know how popular the event would be. By 11.30 a.m. those fifty spaces were full and cars were still pouring in. At one point I counted more than 350 cars at Fordhall and the whole farm was alive with an atmosphere of fun and enjoyment. I tried to help out with the barbecue as much as I could but kept getting called away to sort out the parking or round up stray sheep.

Distracted, I wandered across to check on the pigs under the oak tree in the House Field. As I looked across the valley, I could see a large swarm of around forty people heading towards the motte and bailey site. At the front of the troupe was Charlotte, leading her biggest guided walk so far. The most satisfying part of the day, for me, was seeing shareholders and local people just enjoying our farm. As I watched families and couples strolling through the House Field and the Hall Meadow among my flock of ewes and lambs, I could see that this is what community involvement is all about.

When we started in March 2004, with just eleven cattle, six pigs and six sheep, I never could have imagined that by the time of the first AGM I would be in charge of the welfare of more than 200 sheep, 80 cattle and 85 pigs. The situation at Fordhall was so dire that I always assumed I would have to work off the farm in some way. Now, I'm a full-time farmer, and while I draw a wage of just £90 a week from the farm business, I'm able to pay the rent and, because we are selling direct to the public, our business is growing all the time. I only draw a minimal wage so that any profits made can be reinvested into the business to ensure we get up to full stocking rate as soon as possible. Reinvestment is a very important aspect of running a farm, especially one as run-down as Fordhall was. The knowledge that the farm is running successfully and that the new structure is working, after all the hardships our parents suffered, gives me a huge amount of enthusiasm for the work involved.

The publicity we received throughout the campaign, which continues to bring people to the farm, has a big knock-on effect for me as without the farm shop we could not survive. To keep up with the demand for our products, I'm hoping to create a new butchery inside the Dutch barn, which will mean I can butcher my own meat as demand increases further. At the time of writing I butcher meat in the old toolshed, but space is extremely limited and I still need the abattoir to reduce my carcasses for me. That's a big cost for the farm business and if I could do it myself it would represent a considerable saving that could be ploughed back into the farm. If I can get the butchery up and running I may then have the flexibility to expand and start supplying hotels and restaurants with Fordhall meat.

I'm also about to launch an online shop to sell our meat through the Fordhall website. It's a logical step to take, given the dramatic rise in online shopping, and it's a way to get our products to people who can't, for reasons of distance, visit our farm shop in person. Even so, it's an issue that has caused some debate between Charlotte and me. My sister isn't entirely comfortable with online retailing because of the 'food miles' caused by home delivery. She would rather people shopped at their local farm shop than have deliveries brought to them from far away. I understand this, but feel we also have to make a living and keep the farm as a going concern. So now we're looking into ways of achieving online sales while attempting to minimise environmental damage. Whatever solution we reach, we aim to keep shareholders informed of what we're doing through our newsletter and website. Everything we do has to be for the right reasons and we have to be able to explain those reasons properly. In a way, it's a good example of the struggle involved in making a living, building a business and yet not impacting too much on the environment. Not everyone's going to like it, but at least if we're honest about our reasoning, then hopefully people will understand our actions.

One of the most frequent questions I'm asked as a farmer is how I get over my sense of attachment to the animals I rear and then take to the abattoir for slaughter. Farming as we have always farmed at Fordhall means that animal welfare is vitally important to us. We are giving life on the farm, therefore we have a responsibility to ensure it's a good one. And that is why I'm able to take my animals to the abattoir. The whole point of what we're doing here is to prove we're a working farm and to reconnect those people who visit us with a sense of where their food comes from, and why it's important to support good British farming. If today's generation of children believe that milk comes from a plastic bottle and meat from a film-covered polystyrene tray, there's not much hope of farms like ours – a small family farm, selling locally and direct to the consumer – surviving against competition from abroad. Imported meat might be cheaper, but in terms of animal welfare and husbandry standards it's definitely inferior. I like to think that British farms have some of the highest welfare standards in the world so sometimes it can be that little bit more expensive to buy British rather than imported meats. We always ensure our livestock is reared as naturally as possible and I know that all our animals have a happy life while they are at Fordhall.

I'm also keen to help others gain access to food industries such as ours. I already have a young boy from the local school,

Adam, who comes to help on a Monday. He is from a low-income family and all he wants is to be a farmer. Uncontrollable at school, he is a joy to work with on the farm. I really hope that one day Adam will have the same opportunity I have been so lucky to have, allowing his farming dreams to become a reality.

The issue of the twelve-acre Cottage Field continues to be contentious. It still belongs to our old landlord and the tenancy is due to expire in September 2008. What will happen after that no one knows. It's a very important part of the farm because, through our foggage rotation system, it's where our livestock go in winter to escape the worst of the wet and damp down in the lower flood-plain fields. Without this sandy, free-draining field we would have to reduce our stock considerably, and if we do that there's a significant danger the farm will become un-viable. With hope value attached the field is worth £1.2 million. Without it, we're talking less than £50,000. It's a massive differ-ence and of course the FCLI would love to purchase it, but only at the price it is valued at agriculturally. While it's out of the local plan at the moment, there's nothing to stop it being put back in at some stage. Hopefully, however, the groundswell of support we now have will be strong enough to make sure it is kept out of developers' hands for the foreseeable future.

In the meantime, we have agreed to take on an extra thirty acres of land on behalf of the Shropshire Wildlife Trust over in Whitchurch, ten miles away. John Hughes told me about this piece of land and asked would I be interested in taking it over? Of course I was interested. It's a traditional hay meadow with many species of wild flowers and tall hedges, and it hasn't been sprayed with chemicals for many years. We will be registering the land as organic and managing it in the same way we manage Fordhall's fields. After a two-year period it can be officially classed as organic by the Soil Association. I intend to take sheep and weaned calves up there, and they're likely to stay there throughout the summer months. It'll be a case of trial and error, but I'm confident it's a manageable site and if there's the space it's very likely I will buy some more livestock to summer up there.

I want to see the farm grow, but like Charlotte with the initiative, it's vitally important it grows at a sensible, steady pace. The last time rapid growth happened at Fordhall Farm was when Dad's father Alfred grew potatoes intensively during the First World War and almost killed the land with fertilisers. It took Dad many, many years to sort the land out and get it back to what it had been in the nineteenth century. Progress is a good thing, but only at a pace that's healthy for the land and the livestock it holds. Eight thousand people also have a vested interest in Fordhall and the reason they chose to save this farm was precisely because it had been saved from the kind of intensification that has plagued large parts of British agriculture. At a time when everyone is becoming increasingly aware of the effects of pollution and global warming, it is heartening to see so many people understanding the importance of working with the community and supporting local producers and global sustainability.

Fordhall is now a hugely diverse cluster of habitats. From the brook, fed by a series of spring-water pools at the southwest corner of the Long Meadow, which links to the meandering River Tern, to our bluebell woods and wetlands, Fordhall is always alive with birdsong and wildlife sounds – the lapwing, the curlew, the snipe, foxes, woodpeckers, butterflies and the grunts of our pigs as they forage for worms. All our supporters see Fordhall as special and so do we. We intend to keep it that way, hopefully for ever.

36

Ben & Charlotte

The fight for Fordhall Farm almost broke our hearts. Not once, not twice, but many, many times. As children, we watched as our parents suffered and struggled to keep a livelihood going, under the crushing weight of pressure from landlord and developer. We took over the tenancy when we were nineteen and twenty-one, at a time when many thought Fordhall had been abandoned, such was its state of near-dereliction. Apart from a few brave souls who stuck their necks out for us, we had little or no support. We were advised that the best course of action would be to leave the farm, move into a modern council house with a small garden, and get on with our lives. There was no future in our farm.

We couldn't do that. Aside from the weight of history here, a kind of benign power compelled us to stay. We knew there was more to this farm than a collection of abandoned caravans and a dwindling herd of livestock. It had once been a thriving dairy and country club, thousands had passed through its restaurant doors, and there was a richness under the soil – a legacy left to us by our pioneering father who saw the importance of diversity and the link between farming and community at a time when many other farmers were losing such links for ever. We could not abandon such a precious gift, but neither could we stay here without the love, support, help and good advice of all those who came to Fordhall and saw for themselves the innate goodness that lies within its fields.

When we began the campaign and we told people we had to raise the best part of a million pounds to save the farm, we were often told we were crazy. We agreed wholeheartedly, but instead of doing the sensible thing and giving up before we started, we took a gamble. Thanks to the press and the support of everyone who thought we were worth that gamble, we raised the sum required.

We've also relied on a huge amount of luck. We've truly felt that the laws of nature have somehow conspired to bring us into contact with the right people at the right time. If two German tourists hadn't passed that small book to Jean in Market Drayton one sunny summer's afternoon, this might have been a different story altogether. Or, perhaps more accurately, no story at all. We might never have met Mike, nor had the chance to listen to his vision of Fordhall becoming a community attraction and educational resource. If we hadn't met John Hughes, who encouraged us simply to 'tell the story of the farm', with no frills and no clever marketing behind it, we might have been living in a very different place today. If one of our volunteers hadn't lived in the same street as a *Daily Telegraph* journalist, we might never have received such amazing national publicity, which propelled the campaign to its final, successful conclusion. And, if we hadn't had a landlord who was prepared to offer two young people a chance, we would never have been able to begin a life farming at Fordhall Farm.

In short, you never know unless you try. You never know how something might turn out until you pursue it. If it doesn't work out, it was never meant to be anyway. If it does, you've achieved something that it was your destiny to achieve. We have learnt never to underestimate what can be accomplished by harnessing people power. Even the smallest collection of people, fighting for a common cause, can make a difference, because a small group of people soon gathers more supporters and a whole movement then develops. When we took over the tenancy in 2004 of a run-down, once-successful organic farm and started our fund-raising campaign, we had no idea whatsoever that so many people would be interested enough in our story to back us. The response we had and continue to have is both incredible and overwhelming.

Just after we hit our £800,000 target, a lovely lady wrote a letter to us. She said she had seen our story on BBC *Midlands Today* back in the autumn of 2005 and she and her husband agreed that it was great we were having a go. 'My husband was pleased for you,' she wrote, 'but he said "I really don't think they'll do it. Good on them for having a go, but they won't do it." And I said to him, well if everyone thinks like that, they won't. So let's put £50 in, and see if other people do the same. So we did, and look what happened – everyone else *did* do the same, and the farm was saved. We are so happy for you and so completely inspired by what has been achieved.'

That letter proves to us how people can join together for a good cause, even when they have never and probably will never meet. Above all we wanted people to enjoy and feel part of Fordhall Farm and, by throwing open our gates, even to those who might never visit, we have achieved something hugely worthwhile. We asked you for help and you came forward. For that, we are eternally grateful.

Charlotte Hollins and Ben Hollins,
Fordhall Farm, July 2007.

Afterword by Tom Oliver

Welcoming people to the first AGM of the Fordhall Community Land Initiative, I said: 'There is no part of the Fordhall story that does not shine out as an example of good practice, enterprise, generosity, inclusiveness, intelligence, passion and warmth.' I didn't need to search hard for this observation; it was evident all around me. Everyone involved has been responsible in some way for the strikingly powerful message that sings out from this small farm near Market Drayton: that the loss of traditional farms is not inevitable, that communities can resolve to act in the common interest to save them and that the advantages for everyone are considerable.

For Ben, Charlotte and Sophie, and their supporters, their success in securing the farm is just the beginning. An impressive aspect of what has happened at Fordhall Farm is that this commitment is for the long haul. Sometimes it will be tough and, as anyone who understands farming will know, there is no reason why the next day should be any easier than the one just ending. Farming can be a lonely business and, until recently, has been largely ignored or misunderstood by many people not directly involved with it.

But for all that, Ben and Charlotte can say that they have shaped and worked and nurtured a genuinely productive farm, caring for its character, living alongside its abundant wildlife and offering so many others the intensely satisfying opportunity of contributing to this work. Charlotte and Ben have hit on a rare wisdom: settling for what they, their supporters and the farm can yield in perpetuity, and making that as good as it can possibly be.

To build on what they have achieved, and to make Fordhall a viable educational resource for the community, they need your support, and they relish the prospect of you following their example.

Acknowledgements

After reading this book, you will see how difficult it has been to write an acknowledgements section. The fight to save Fordhall Farm has been a long journey and has involved not hundreds, but thousands of amazing people worldwide. However, there are a few people in particular to whom both Ben and I will always be indebted.

First and foremost is our late father, Arthur Hollins. It was his dedication to the land and his optimistic take on life in even the most dire of situations that created such a valuable resource at Fordhall and inspired Ben and me to fight to save it.

Thanks must also go to our mother, Connie, who has been an inspiration through her sheer determination not to give in when everything was against her. A big thank you, too, to our half-sisters, Marianne and Barbara, for their emotional support throughout the whole journey, and a special thanks to Marianne and our brother-in-law Alan for taking the risk to be our guarantors on our first tenancy agreement in 2004. Without that initial faith and backing we would have been evicted that March and never had the opportunity to fight for Fordhall Farm.

Thanks also, of course, to our partners, Oli and Maz, for their emotional support and acceptance of Fordhall as a central part of our lives.

There are more practical thanks due to those who physically helped the campaign to succeed: Philip Meade, of Davis Meade

Acknowledgements

Land Agents, who generously helped Mum and Dad fight through their eviction notices in the early days. Without his help, our family would have been forced to leave Fordhall many years ago.

The German couple that came to Market Drayton in June 2003 with the small German book that started a remarkable chain of events.

Mike Kay and Danny O'Sullivan for their inspiration and drive in the days that followed. Danny in particular pushed us to drive the project forward and gave us the confidence that we could succeed even when success looked to be an impossibility.

Greg Pilley and Martin Large from the Community Farm Land Trust Research Project in Stroud, who funded and helped to create an innovative structure that benefited both the community and the farmer.

Sophie Hopkins, our Community Development Manager until 2007, and who first joined as a volunteer in 2005 and has put in two hundred per cent and many many long hours since. We could not have achieved what we have without her – her dedication has been and above and beyond the call of duty.

Iain Morrison at MFG Solicitors who agreed to carry out all our legal work for the land purchase free of charge. This was an enormous cost that the FCLI could not afford to bear. Iain had the faith and belief in us to step in and help.

Mervyn Davies, our accountant at Howsons, whose help setting up Fordhall Farm Ltd gave us the only opportunity to begin our business.

Tom Henry, for his long hours and vital help with getting our story down on paper. Without him it would have never got to the bookshelves. And, of course, to Sarah Reece and the team at Hodder, for their belief that our story was worth telling. Their encouragement and warmth has made this book a complete joy to pull together.

Cristian Barnett for bringing Fordhall to life with his amazing photography. His images of the farm so perfectly capture the spirit and beauty of the place that we are so fortunate to live in.

To all the members of the press and the volunteers who really helped drive the campaign forward. Without the enthusiasm, support and sheer energy of the latter, Sophie, Ben and I would have died under a mountain of paperwork. We have learnt so much from all those who gave us some of their valuable time and skills, whether accountancy, administration or labour. There is no doubt that without their input we would have lost our way long ago.

To all our farm-shop customers who, by buying local produce, have allowed us to pay the rent and continue farming. We would not be in business without their commitment.

To all our shareholders and donors who believed that their drop in the ocean would make a difference. This belief enabled us to raise £800,000 in less than six months. Thank you to them and our volunteers for showing us what can be achieved when people work together for a common aim.

And last, but my no means least, thank you to all the non-believers who made us more determined than ever to make Fordhall succeed.

JOIN

FORDHALL FARM

Fordhall Community Land Initiative

Reconnecting people to the land

<u>www.fordhallfarm.com</u>

How can I get involved?

1. Buy shares in the Fordhall Community Land Initiative
Shares in the Fordhall Community Land Initiative last
forever and make you a part-owner of Fordhall Farm. They
cost £50 each. You will receive a beautifully presented
share certificate, complimentary copies of the Friends of
Fordhall newsletter for the first year and, of course, the
right to vote within the society. There is no limit to the
number of shares an individual can buy. These shares are
completely non-profit-making – you are investing in the
future of food and farming.

2. Become a Friend of the Fordhall Community Land Initiative
This is an annual subscription that entitles you to quarterly
newsletters, concessions at events and invitations to
social events. The newsletters will keep you updated on
volunteering opportunities, farm life, our education work
and sustainability issues. Individual: £15; family: £30.

3. Give a donation
Any donation, large or small, helps the cause. Please don't
forget to include a Gift Aid declaration so we can increase
every pound you give by 28 pence – it soon adds up!
Alternatively, you could donate materials, such as tools or
office stationery, to help with the running of the Fordhall
Community Land Initiative.

4. Provide an interest-free loan
Each loan is for a period of 5 years, after which time they
are repayable to you in full. They allow us to carry forward
vital educational work and building renovations while the
revenue-creating projects are becoming established.

5. Attend our events and volunteer working weekends
There are a number of events hosted at Fordhall Farm throughout the year, from our annual Family Fun Day in July to the Christmas Food and Gift Fair in December, with various smaller events in between. Keep an eye on our website to see what's coming up. Alternatively, come and join one of our working weekends, held every 6–8 weeks, and meet lots of like-minded people, learn new skills and give something practical back to Fordhall Farm.

For further information, visit our website, www.fordhallfarm.com, phone us on 01630 638696, email us on project@fordhallfarm.com or write to us at Fordhall Community Land Initiative, Fordhall Farm, Tern Hill Road, Market Drayton, Shropshire TF9 3PS.

FURTHER RESOURCES:
www.soilassociation.org.uk/organicfutures – information on the next generation of young organic farmers, the barriers they face and the possibilities of overcoming those barriers

www.communitylandtrust.org.uk – resource-based website focused on affordable housing

www.stroudcommonwealth.org.uk – for the Community Farm Land Trust's free action resource pack for community farm buy-outs and community land trusts by Greg Pilley and Martin Large

www.landforpeople.co.uk – organisation working with communities to make them more sustainable and to create affordable homes